Beyond Checks and Balances

DEMOCRACY, CITIZENSHIP,
AND CONSTITUTIONALISM

Jeffrey Green, *Series Editor*

BEYOND CHECKS AND BALANCES

The Political Purpose of the Separation of Powers

Edited by Connor M. Ewing,
Benjamin A. Kleinerman,
and Charles U. Zug

PENN

UNIVERSITY OF PENNSYLVANIA PRESS

PHILADELPHIA

Published by
University of Pennsylvania Press
Philadelphia, Pennsylvania 19104–4112 USA
www.pennpress.org

EU Authorized Representative: Easy Access System Europe—Mustamäe tee 50, 10621 Tallinn, Estonia, gpsr.requests@easproject.com

Printed in the United States of America on acid-free paper
10 9 8 7 6 5 4 3 2 1

Cataloging-in-Publication record for this book is available from the Library of Congress.

Hardcover ISBN 978-1-5128-2958-7
eBook ISBN 978-1-5128-2959-4

CONTENTS

CHAPTER 1

The Purposes of Constitutional Conflict

Charles U. Zug

Few beliefs about American politics are more firmly entrenched than this one: The Constitution separates power in order to frustrate the operations of government and to make it harder for the state to infringe on the rights of the people. This belief, sometimes called "negative constitutionalism," predominates in both constitutional law and political science, the two major academic disciplines in America that study the Constitution.[1] Beyond academia, it is taught as doctrine in high school civics and history classes. Together with federalism and checks and balances, it is the go-to framework that experts and nonexperts alike use to interpret the American constitutional system.

In this volume, consisting of chapters by authors with diverse scholarly interests and expertise, we take aim at this hegemonic belief. Our goal in so doing is threefold.

First, we wish to *defamiliarize* the separation of powers—to make it into an object of inquiry and curiosity, not something that we simply take for granted as tradition, or as just another "rule of the game."

Second, we wish to rescue the separation of powers from courts and lawyers. Long regarded as a quintessentially legal doctrine that, as such, must be adjudicated by the Supreme Court, the separation of powers is better understood *politically*, as a configuration of powers, incentives, and institutions designed to pursue the architectonic ends of politics.[2]

Finally, we seek to synthesize a distinctive approach to the separation of powers, one that contests and unsettles the old-fashioned negative constitutionalism theory by spotlighting the substantive constitutional goods that the arrangement commonly referred to as the separation of powers is designed to achieve. The separation of powers, on the account advanced in this volume, is about good government, a purpose that includes—but cannot be reduced to—constraints on governmental power.

Constitutional Ambivalence

What warrants a new approach to the separation of powers? Simply put, the fact that neither critics nor defenders of the separation of powers are typically able to maintain their positions coherently.

Consider, for example, how most people who regard themselves as defenders of the Constitution are likely to rationalize the Constitution's division of authority between Congress, the president, and the courts. Most will offer some version of the view with which this chapter began, namely that the Constitution is designed to make it harder for the state to perform its basic tasks, because a frustrated, gridlocked government is less likely to abuse its powers, oppress the public, and deprive individuals of their rights.[3] For their parts, *critics* of the separation of powers are likely to say that it was put in place by eighteenth-century men who failed to appreciate the benefits that an active government has to offer. Classic statements of the former position include writings by Montesquieu and Supreme Court opinions such as *Youngstown v. Sawyer* and *INS v. Chadha*.[4] Statements of the latter include those by Woodrow Wilson and Richard Neustadt.[5]

Though incomplete, both of these rationales point beyond themselves toward a more coherent position vis-à-vis the separation of powers. Beginning with the first, it is simply true that in times of crisis, when rights feel insecure and when state officials look as if they might use their powers to harass or persecute their political adversaries, it can be comforting to know that the structure of the American political system makes it harder for any one official to wield truly final authority. During such crises, we might even be grateful that the US Constitution establishes overlapping and interdependent, as opposed to consolidated and centralized, forms of governmental power. As long as abusive officials are tied up in procedure and red tape—so this argument goes—we can continue to go about our private affairs relatively unmolested by an overweening state.[6]

The argument that power is constitutionally separated in order to frustrate the state's ability to govern has been a constant refrain during both of

Donald Trump's presidencies. Often quite reasonably, legal and political commentators have joined in urging government officials to check and constrain overreaching, even abusive exertions of executive power by a demagogic president. The validity of that concern has been borne out numerous times, perhaps most strikingly by the events leading up to and culminating in the January 6, 2021 riot, when President Trump tried, and ultimately failed, to use his constitutional authority to undermine the results of the 2020 election.

After Joe Biden took office in 2021, it seemed to many that the Constitution's logic had been vindicated and that its founders' warnings had finally been heeded. The difficulty of realizing collective action within a separation of powers framework had stymied the ambitions of a demagogue-turned-tyrant. That just-so story was undermined once again when Donald Trump was reelected president in 2024.

The vicissitudes of twenty-first-century American politics should not distract us from the constitutional crisis that currently has a grip on the polity; in many cases, they are symptomatic of that very crisis. Though the deep causes of America's political turmoil are complex and contestable, one of our aims in this volume is to suggest that defective constitutional understandings, on the part of both officeholders and the broader public, bear some responsibility for our current situation. Consider, for example, that many of the same progressives who have urged a renewed appreciation for the Constitution's separation of powers during Trump's two presidencies have also spent their careers during Democratic administrations advocating for a stronger, more efficient, more centralized American state—a state capable of pursuing progressive goals unconstrained by the antiquated, self-defeating design of the US Constitution. By contrast, in the context of a Trump presidency, many of the same features of the Constitution that had previously served to stifle the ambitions of progressive presidents turned out to serve as useful tools for constraining a presidential demagogue.

Few scholarly about-faces revealed this ambivalence more vividly than the April 2016 publication of Will Howell and Terry Moe's *Relic: How Our Constitution Undermines Effective Government—and Why We Need a More Powerful Presidency*.[7] Written with the Obama presidency's many frustrations in mind—and clearly anticipating a Hillary Clinton presidency in the near future—this book proposed, among other things, revising the constitutional legislative process so that future presidents might more effectively realize their agendas. Needless to say, given the political proclivities of the authors, Trump's surprise election seven months later necessitated a significant revision of their thesis.

The case of Howell and Moe is a familiar one in American politics. Observers lament the Constitution's shackles when their preferred leader or party is in power, only to rediscover the deep wisdom of those same shackles when a new party or leader takes over.[8] Reversals like this signal deeper sources of constitutional confusion, which in turn call for a reckoning with the basic rationale of the American state. Is it tenable, let alone politically feasible, to advocate the Constitution's effacement when it seems to stand in your way, only to reverse course when the Constitution promises to stand in the way of your political adversaries?

Our view is that it is not. As Sotirios Barber shows in his chapter here, a purely negative justification of government—one that emphasizes the need to impede the basic operations of the state—invariably leads to the conclusion that it would be better not to create a government at all. As long as we remain committed to maintaining even a minimally functional state, we need to think about the separation of powers not in terms of the potential harms it might prevent, but in terms of the societal benefits it might help create. To that end, this book draws inspiration from the work of Jeffrey K. Tulis to show what it would look like to reason about the separation of powers, and the Constitution more broadly, as a political architecture designed to incentivize good action through constitutional conflict.[9]

Institutional Design

As Tulis shows in the lead chapter of this volume, one of the chief innovations of the US Constitution was to displace the old-fashioned negative conception of the separation of powers. Debates about the merits of this displacement took center stage during ratification, when critics of the Constitution insisted that the proposed plan of government failed to embrace, among other things, any recognizable scheme of separated powers.[10] After considerable prevarication, sophisticated Constitution advocates responded that this criticism missed the point.[11] The best—though not only—rationale for creating a polity of separated branches is that differently designed institutions are better at performing different, sometimes mutually competing, governmental functions. The point of separating power is to assign these functions in a way that makes the government better at governing, not to make it harder to govern in the first place.

Today it is difficult to recognize this dimension of *The Federalist* because most people think the central, and final, statement on separation of powers in that writing is *Federalist* No. 51. In that essay, Madison develops what he thinks is the best argument for how to preserve the integrity and autonomy of separated branches of government.[12] Responding to Thomas Jefferson's argument (as laid out in Papers No. 49 and No. 50) that constitutional disputes between the branches should be adjudicated through either routine or ad hoc popular conventions, Madison makes the case for a system of *internal* restraints against institutional aggrandizement. In Madison's account, the branches need sources of power, not just legal justifications or "parchment barriers" (in the language of *Federalist* No. 48) in order to maintain their independence. In turn, the inhabitants of these offices must be incentivized actually to use those tools in defense of their institutional turf: "The interest of the man must be connected with the constitutional rights of the place" (*Federalist* No. 51).[13]

Federalist No. 51 helps account for why the Constitution makes the branches interdependent. For opponents of the Constitution, these overlapping powers seemed to constitute an unwarranted departure from familiar notions of separation of powers and to invite consolidation into a single unitary state. For Publius, in contrast, they provided the branches with sources of leverage to be deployed in the case of disputed constitutional authority, sources of leverage that would make the separation of powers work.

Work to what end, though? To answer this question, it helps to recognize that *Federalist* No. 51 is not Publius's final word on the separation of powers, but rather an introduction to the extensive discussion of the particular designs of the core institutions of the Constitution developed in *Federalist Papers* Nos. 52–83. In those essays, the authors make the case for why the particular institutional structures of the Congress, the presidency, and the judiciary make it more likely than not that they will perform distinctive constitutional roles in ways that serve the common good. All of the familiar points developed there to justify the particular shapes of those offices—that a single executive with a fixed term will infuse the state with energy; that longer terms of office in the Senate will incentivize a longer term policy perspective; that expansive electoral districts will incentivize moderation and coalition building in the House; that life terms are needed both to insulate courts from excessive popular pressure and to allow judges to impartially adjudicate disputes about fundamental rights—all of these points and others are arrayed as a broader reflection on the importance of institutional design. Specifically, they suggest that it is possible to create institutions that are structured to incentivize their inhabitants to act in ways that promote the different and sometimes competing ends of constitutional democracy, including consent-based policy, efficient and energetic administration, and the protection of individual rights.

Seen from this vantage point, the branches of the Constitution must be equipped with the resources needed to preserve their independent functions and to prevent subversion or takeover by other branches. In this particular respect, the Constitution might therefore be said to create a separation of functions system, as opposed to a separation of powers system.

What is the basis of this distinction? Understood as a legal doctrine, "separation of powers" implies that every governmental activity belongs to one of the three types of governmental power: legislative, executive, and judicial. Within such a doctrine, resolving interbranch conflict would consist in assigning governmental tasks to specific branches based on the kinds of "powers" those branches are supposed to correspond to. What this approach misses, and what a separation of functions approach captures better, is the idea that the ultimate standard for adjudicating interbranch conflict is not a doctrine of separated powers but rather the government's ability to perform its assigned tasks well. The Constitution assigns particular jobs to particular branches, neither because of some doctrinal requirement, nor because of the need to create a sense of balance or equilibrium ultimately leading to stalemate. Rather, it is because, in the Constitution's estimation, those functions are more likely to be performed competently by those branches. In this picture, competence rather than doctrine is key.

Yet the separation of functions is only part of the broader revisionist story of separation of powers we wish to tell here. That story has two core components.

Instrumentality

The term "separation of functions" can lead one to believe that the ultimate standard for assessing the Constitution at any given moment is whether the Constitution is successfully constraining its different branches to their different preassigned tasks. To be sure, that belief captures an important part of the broader separated powers story, as Flaherty Staab and Siemers show in their chapters. Insofar as different institutions are, in practice, reliably better at performing particular governmental tasks, it is in the public's interest that those institutions be confined to their specific roles. The crucial point, however, is that the Constitution segregates tasks and separates functions not to honor a legal principle but to make the government better at realizing the ends to which the Constitution commits it. Thus, when conceived of as a legal principle as opposed to a pragmatic arrangement, "separation of functions" tends to obscure the instrumental value of separation. Madison states this point forcefully in *Federalist* No. 45, arguing that "the public good, the real welfare of the great body of the people, is the supreme object to be pursued . . . no form of government whatever has any other value than as it may be fitted for the attainment of this object." The ultimate standard for constitutional assessment is a constitution's ability to create and sustain a government that can, in the long run, realize the substantive goods that a constitution sets for itself.

It is worth emphasizing that the precise content of these constitutional goods—what a constitution's imperatives require at any given moment in terms of concrete action and decision making—are contestable, because the causes of disagreement and factionalism are "sown in the nature of man."[14] The point is not that the Constitution presumes to be able to settle disagreements about what its imperatives will demand in particular situations in the future. In Ronald Dworkin's framework, the Constitution does not commit future publics to particular conceptions of broader concepts such as justice, liberty, and the common good.[15] Rather, the point is that the Constitution establishes a polity committed to the long-term pursuit and realization of general goods; the Constitution is aspirational—not retrograde—in orientation.[16] Whether constitutional goods are realized in practice will depend, in turn, on whether the Constitution's structures can reliably incentivize deliberative, publicly desirable decisions from the officials who inhabit those structures. In the American context, constitutional failure takes place when the Constitution can no longer reliably perform this task.[17]

It is therefore conceivable—and not hard to imagine, given the current state of American politics—that the particular ways in which the Constitution *originally* separated governmental functions might fall short of accomplishing the Constitution's broader objectives. To be sure, occasional or sporadic institutional failure is not necessarily sufficient ground for revisiting basic constitutional assumptions and arrangements. Consistent failure, however, will require taking concrete steps to alter the original arrangements made by the Constitution's drafters to separate functions in the ways they believed would most likely enable the government to succeed. In principle, we might say that the Constitution's legitimacy depends on its being open to updated information about its own functionality. If it turns out that the particular arrangement by which the Constitution separates functions is inadequate to the Constitution's own ends, the Constitution must be open to revisiting the norms and practices that define that arrangement.[18]

The Value of Constitutional Conflict

The second shortcoming of a "separation of functions" interpretation is that it can elide the positive value of constitutional conflict between institutions. In the argument developed in *Federalist* No. 51, constitutional conflict is rationalized as a mechanism for preserving the status quo—that is, as a means for preserving the integrity and autonomy of separated branches. The logical conclusion of this position is that, in an ideal world, there would be no interbranch conflict because the branches would recognize and respect one another's separate functions and largely keep to their own affairs. This position is flawed because it elevates institutional separateness to an end, when in fact, as I discussed in the previous section, separateness is a means to an end. That end is the accomplishment of governmental tasks—the creation, implementation, and revision of public policy—in ways that promote the common good.

And yet, as political thinkers have observed since antiquity, the common good is complex. As Tulis argues in his chapter here, members of a community can reasonably disagree about the merits of a given course of action, because the imperatives of good governance do not always cohere or point in the same direction. Rights protections, representation, procedural fairness, consent, the need for security—each of these legitimate concerns demands a distinctive kind of politics, a particular mode of decision-making, and a particular mode of implementation. Yet there is no guarantee that a single state, no matter how rationally designed, will be able to answer all of these concerns at the same time in a given instance, let alone reliably over the course of generations.

For these reasons, a desirable constitutional process must consult a broad range of public concerns. And insofar as it embodies this directive, the US Constitution is therefore best understood not as tolerating interbranch conflict as a last resort, but as *purposefully inducing* conflict in the expectation that, in the aggregate, disagreement, negotiation, and deliberative compromise will result in political outcomes superior to outcomes reached through purely unilateral decision making.

Seen this way, as Bell, Ewing, and Zeisberg emphasize in their chapters, interbranch conflict over constitutional authority can have positive political value, value that is not reducible to the purely material outcomes of those disagreements (e.g., how exactly tax revenue was redistributed, or how much money was saved by eliminating a particular regulation).[19] Constitutional conflict has distinctive value insofar as it can induce a discussion of both the proper institutional venue in which decisions should be made and the best resolution of political, legal, and administrative problems. Who should be doing this job? What is the best outcome? What are the reasons being offered by the institutional partisans who disagree?

How these questions are answered in practice is highly contingent because there is only quite general guidance in the Constitution regarding which branches should handle which problems of public policy. And even those answers must have their content supplied by the branches themselves, who will be the parties to any given constitutional dispute. For example, the Constitution creates different processes for making treaties and regular legislation, but it does not attempt to establish in advance how to distinguish between legislation that would fall under those categories. What happens if the House and the Senate are controlled by factions that disagree whether a particular policy matter should be handled as a treaty or as a piece of domestic legislation—as they were in 1795 when the Jay Treaty was being debated?[20] Or consider the more familiar example of bureaucratic control. As I argue in my chapter on Joe McCarthy and Dwight Eisenhower, the Constitution provides no clear guidance for who should "win," the Congress or the president, in disputes over agency information and personnel. The president fires and, with the consent of the Senate, hires high-ranking administrators and is given powers by the Constitution that presuppose considerable control over the bureaucracy.[21] And yet, it is the Congress that actually creates and funds the agencies that constitute the bureaucracy. Congress can therefore make continued funding, or even agency survival, contingent on access to information the Congress deems relevant—which it does routinely in the form of committee hearings and investigations.[22] Who then should win in an executive-legislative standoff?

Contrary to the predominant view today, sometimes called "judicial supremacy," how these questions are answered in practice should *not* come down to the Supreme Court, which is only one of the three branches of the Constitution and which therefore cannot be presumed to speak for the Constitution as a whole.[23] Indeed, the very idea that the Supreme Court should get to make such decisions is a relatively recent invention and had to be constructed through politics.[24] Rather, as Kathleen Tipler argues in her contribution here, such answers should reflect the priorities of the institutions that share responsibility for making those decisions. It is up to the constitutional players themselves to improvise answers as they encounter these questions "in the wild." The best understanding of the Constitution is that the answers they provide should reflect the relative importance that each branch places on "winning" the constitutional dispute in question. And because each branch embodies a different set of public concerns, each negotiated settlement between the branches approximates how that dispute ought to be resolved on the merits.

Roadmap of the Book

We have organized this volume into two parts. The first, "Foundations," takes up broader themes involving the historical and theoretical roots of the separation of powers. The second part, "Applications," examines the separation of powers in particular institutional contexts.

Part I begins with Jeffrey Tulis's provocative reinterpretation of the US Constitution as creating a new separation of powers system (Chapter 2). In Tulis's account, the Constitution displaces older conceptions of the separation of powers—which had emphasized symmetry and institutional stalemate—with a totally new kind of polity, one that sees institutional conflict as a virtue and as a means for realizing substantive constitutional goods.

In Chapter 3, George Thomas situates the American separation of powers system in comparative perspective. Thomas shows that the US Constitution can be understood as a particular conception of the separation of powers, and that other polities have attempted to secure similar constitutional goals through different institutional designs and arrangements.

In Chapter 4, Sotirios Barber illustrates what it would mean to rescue the separation of powers and the activity of judging from an "originalist" understanding of constitutional authority. Judges following "originalism" fail to uphold their constitutional responsibilities because originalism falsely posits that judging can and should eschew moral judgment. Barber rebuts this view by showing that the Constitution, which is committed to pursuing justice, requires all of its officeholders—including judges—to make decisions with reference to their own best understandings of what justice requires.

In Chapters 5 and 6, Paul Carrese and Brigid Flaherty Staab examine eighteenth-century writings to better understand the perspectives that informed the creation of the American separation of powers system. Carrese uses the thought of Montesquieu to theorize the particular value that courts and judges add to the separation of powers. Flaherty Staab reinterprets John Adams—traditionally regarded as a "mixed regime" thinker—as an early articulator of the separation of functions.

Part II begins with Connor Ewing's extension of the analysis of separated powers to another significant feature of the American polity: federalism. In Ewing's account (Chapter 7), conflict among institutions of the national government can yield important constitutional goods. At the same time, the structure of relationships between levels of government renders intergovernmental conflict incapable of producing either deliberative or authority-generating benefits.

In Chapter 8, Mariah Zeisberg presents a revisionist account of familiar interpretations of conflicts between Congress and the president. Most scholars hold that Congress jealously guarded its warmaking prerogatives until after the Second World War, when the president began to assume a more dominant constitutional position. Zeisberg contests this narrative by showing that late nineteenth- and early twentieth-century Congresses in fact goaded presidents into taking bellicose foreign policy action, and that Congress and the president have existed in a dynamic, as opposed to an institutionally segregated, relationship since long before the Cold War era.

In Chapters 9 and 10, Thomas Bell and I continue with the theme of presidential–congressional relations. Bell examines the arrangement known as the legislative veto, arguing that the persistence of that arrangement, even in the face of judicial invalidation, can be traced to the fact that it performs a useful constitutional function through improvised means. In contrast, I tell a less optimistic constitutional story through the infamous showdown between Joseph McCarthy and Dwight Eisenhower. Ironically, I suggest, Eisenhower helped fortify a norm of congressional abdication by stonewalling the Senate in response to harassing subpoenas from McCarthy's notorious subcommittee.

In Chapters 11 and 12, Keith Whittington and Kathleen Tipler turn to the institutional role of the federal courts. Whittington uses constitutional history and principles to consider when it might be appropriate for the Congress to impeach judges. Noting recent uses of the impeachment power vis-à-vis the president, Whittington considers the role of partisanship in the impeachment process and seeks a principled yet practical standard for evaluating judicial impeachments. Similarly, in Chapter 12, Tipler examines the dispute over which branch, Congress or the judiciary, should be responsible for deciding matters relating to presidential immunity. Tipler shows that such decisions cannot be made legalistically because they implicate deeper constitutional values that are derived from the structures and functions of each of the branches.

In Chapter 13, David Siemers uses the account of separated powers offered in *The Federalist* to assess uses of presidential authority by Bush, Obama, and Trump. According to Siemers, the presidency occupies a particularly fraught position within the constitutional order by virtue of its twin mandates to preserve, protect, and defend the Constitution as a whole and to preserve its own institutional turf.

* * *

The authors of this volume are unified in agreeing that there is a need for a fresh look at the separation of powers and, more specifically, a rethinking of the role of politics in interbranch conflict. At the same time, each of us presents in our respective chapters a particular version of that general intervention; this book is meant to embody intellectual pluralism. Our aim is therefore by no means to "settle" scholarly debates over the separation of powers in a particular direction. Instead, we wish to present a novel perspective that we believe deserves more engagement and that, hopefully, will deepen and complicate the studies of American politics and constitutionalism going forward.

Notes

1. For discussions of positive and negative constitutionalism, see Nick Barber, *The Principles of Constitutionalism* (New York: Oxford University Press, 2018); Sotirios Barber, *Welfare and the Constitution* (Princeton: Princeton University Press, 2003).

2. Louis Fisher was an early advocate of what might be called the political (as opposed to legalistic) interpretation of separation of powers. See Louis Fisher, "The Efficiency Side of Separated Powers," *Journal of American Studies* 5, 2 (1971): 113–131.

3. In *Political Political Theory* (Cambridge: Harvard University Press, 2016), Jeremy Waldron gives a helpful overview of some of these rationales.

4. Montesquieu, *Spirit of the Laws*, Cohler, Miller, and Stone, trans. (New York: Cambridge University Press, 1989).

5. Woodrow Wilson, *Congressional Government* (Baltimore: Johns Hopkins University Press, 1981); Richard Neustadt, *Presidential Power and the Modern Presidents* (New York: Free Press, 1991).

6. For an illuminating discussion of this dynamic during the Trump era, see John Dearborn, Desmond King, and Stephen Skowronek, *Phantoms of a Beleaguered Republic* (New York: Oxford University Press, 2022).

7. Will Howell and Terry Moe, *Relic* (New York: Basic Books, 2016). The authors offered an updated version of their thesis a few years later in *Presidents, Populists, and the Crisis of Democracy* (Chicago: University of Chicago Press, 2022). There they offer the counterfactual claim that had their constitutional reforms been accepted long before, Trump would never have had occasion to appeal to popular frustrations in the first place. While plausible, this argument ultimately takes for granted that a relatively "frictionless" constitutional system will empower good leaders and not bad ones. A similar faith is evinced in Eric Posner and Adrian Vermuele, *The Executive Unbound* (New York: Oxford University Press, 2011).

8. Verlan Lewis goes further with this thesis, showing that partisan contestation in American politics is never, and has never been, about "big government versus small government," because even purportedly "small government" parties invariably revise their philosophies of governance when they regain power. See Verlan Lewis, *Ideas of Power* (New York: Cambridge University Press, 2019).

9. See Jeffrey K. Tulis, *The Rhetorical Presidency* (Princeton: Princeton University Press, 2017); Jeffrey K. Tulis and Nicole Mellow, *Legacies of Losing in American Politics* (Chicago: University of Chicago Press, 2018).

10. For a helpful overview of these core claims, see Saul Cornell, *Other Founders* (Chapel Hill: University of North Carolina Press, 1999); Herbert J. Storing, *What the Anti-Federalists Were For* (Chicago: University of Chicago Press, 1981).

11. On how *The Federalist* strategically responded to such criticisms, see Tulis and Mellow, *Legacies*, chapter 2.

12. For a full discussion of Madison's theory, see George Thomas, *The Madisonian Constitution* (Baltimore: Johns Hopkins University Press, 2009).

13. For a fuller development of the theory behind Madison's statement here, see Jeffrey K. Tulis, "On Congress and Constitutional Responsibility," *Boston University Law Review* 89, 2 (2009): 515–524.

14. *Federalist* No. 10. For a discussion of how the contestable character of politics can be reconciled with the need for an effective government, see Russell Muirhead, *The Promise of Party in a Polarized Age* (Cambridge, MA: Harvard University Press, 2014). I thank John Finn for questioning what it would mean for a constitution to be committed to securing particular as opposed to general goods.

15. Ronald Dworkin, *Taking Rights Seriously* (Cambridge, MA: Harvard University Press, 1978).

16. Gary Jacobsohn, *The Supreme Court and the Decline of Constitutional Aspiration* (Totowa, NJ: Rowman and Littlefield, 1986).

17. See Sotirios Barber, *Constitutional Failure* (Lawrence: University Press of Kansas, 2014).

18. A profound though underappreciated discussion of the legitimate migration of constitutional functions can be found in Herbert J. Storing, "Political Parties and the Bureaucracy," in *Toward a More Perfect Union*, Joseph M. Bessette, ed. (Washington, DC: AEI Press, 1997).

19. Political theorists have shown that the meaning of political events is not self-evident or self-explanatory. Even the most bluntly material changes that are brought about through politics (e.g., physical violence and the distribution of resources) admit of plausible alternative meanings and therefore require interpretation. Scholars of separation of powers and of American politics generally have not been attentive to this dimension of politics. For different versions of this interpretive argument, see Michael Rogin, *Ronald Reagan, the Movie* (Berkeley: University of California Press, 1988); Charles Taylor, "Interpretation and the Sciences of Man," *Review of*

Metaphysics 25, 1 (1971): 3–51; Charles U. Zug, *Demagogues in American Politics* (New York: Oxford University Press, 2022).

20. See Amanda Demmer, "Trick or Constitutional Treaty?" *Journal of the Early Republic* 35, 4 (2015): 579–598.

21. Even the president's power to unilaterally dismiss officials appointed with Senate confirmation had to be constructed politically, however. See John Alvis, Jeremy Bailey, and Flagg Taylor IV, *The Contested Removal Power* (Lawrence: University Press of Kansas, 2010).

22. See Charles U. Zug, "Thank God for the Deep State: Presidential Demagoguery and the 'Unitary Executive,'" *American Political Thought* 12, 1 (Winter 2023): 113–140.

23. See Greg Weiner, *The Political Constitution* (Lawrence: University Press of Kansas, 2019).

24. See Keith Whittington, *Political Foundations of Judicial Supremacy* (Princeton: Princeton University Press, 2006).

PART I

Foundations

CHAPTER 2

Separation of Powers as a New Theory

Jeffrey K. Tulis

Reflecting on the ratification debate, James Madison told his colleagues in the First Congress of the United States that no argument by the Anti-Federalists had been urged with greater success than the charge that the Constitution violated separation of powers.[1] The Anti-Federal charge had rhetorical traction in the political culture at the time because it was true. Many of the state constitutions included the separation of powers principle as an explicit clause. Those clauses announced the proposition that their governments contained several kinds of power, that those powers were defined and distinguished in the constitutions, and that the main branches of the government were prohibited from exercising power not assigned to them by their constitution. There is no separation of powers clause in the Constitution. Why not? In *The Federalist*, Madison shows why the separation of powers idea has to be jettisoned as a fundamental feature of the new design and what should take its place. He does this carefully and subtly, iteratively, urging at first that the Constitution is an improved version of separation of powers rather than something fundamentally new. As Madison's argument unfolds, it becomes clear that the complicated separation of powers system is really a new kind of political design.

It is necessary to make a case today that the Constitution replaces separation of powers with something new because the original case was so subtle, and initially, so cautious that the punch-line conclusion for something new has been lost in American political culture. Versions of the traditional view of separation of power still reign in modern-day political culture, and especially in the judiciary.[2] Three subtleties are noteworthy and were the reasons for a long-term Anti-Federal subversion of the original Constitution. First, Madison made the political and rhetorical choice to retain the term separation of powers while investing it with new meaning rather than to more frankly label the new design with a new term. This new invention can still be glimpsed today (though only glimpsed) when one thinks about the notion of a separation of powers system as the American constitutional order is sometimes described. Not the separation of powers idea, or the separation of powers doctrine—the separation of powers system. The idea and the judicial doctrine to enforce it invoke the way separation of powers is traditionally understood. But when one refers to the separation of powers system, it is usually invoked to distinguish our constitutional system from parliamentary systems, which were exemplars of the traditional separation of powers idea in Locke and Montesquieu. Second, the most insightful Anti-Federalists—many of whom opposed the Constitution because it abandoned separation of powers—exploited Madison's iterative argument after ratification to accomplish through constitutional interpretation what they had lost in constitutional construction. They and their political heirs invoked the early iteration of Madison's defense—the claim that the Constitution improved upon separation of powers—to encourage courts and other political actors to embrace the separation of powers idea as a feature of the very constitution they had earlier rejected for abandoning the idea.[3] A third subtlety helped cement the idea that the traditional separation of powers principle is a constitutive feature of the Constitution. Although the best understanding of the *fundamental* attribute of the constitutional design is not separation of powers, according to Madison, the idea that some distinctions of kinds of power are made in the Constitution is a *subsidiary* feature of the new design. In other words, whatever one labels this new design, the old separation of powers idea is retained as a component, a subsidiary piece, of a new political logic.

Separation of Powers

Looking at the plan of government proposed by the Constitutional Convention that came to be the American Constitution, Anti-Federalists throughout the confederation did not know what to make of it or what to call it. "Again and again, the Anti-Federalists spat out their scorn of this 'spurious brat,' 'this bantling,' this '3 horned monster,' 'this heterogeneous phantom.' 'What kind of government is this?' asked Patrick Henry."[4] The proposed Constitution was not cognizable in familiar categories. If it were a democracy, why were so many elements distant from the people? If it were a republic, why was there no overt concern for the protection of rights? Most crucially, if it were a coherent plan of government, why is there no strict separation of powers, where the functions, duties, and powers were clearly delineated and aligned with the appropriate institutions? The Constitution's complexity seemed to suggest that it rested on no theory at all, because its terms seemed to violate precepts of many of the most important and influential political theorists. The difficult burden of *The Federalist* was to respond to these charges because the challenge was so true on its face. As I said at the outset, the Constitution did not perfect some known theory of governance but instead invented one—new, unprecedented, and hitherto unknown.

Yet by responding to this challenge so prominently and effectively in the text, *The Federalist* unintentionally gave the Anti-Federalists influence upon subsequent interpretation of a Constitution that actually rested on a different perspective and a new theory. Explaining the Constitution, *The Federalist* invents a theory of governance that elevates the significance of structural design and subordinates the issue of separation of powers. The text does not announce this invention as I have just done, but rather *The Federalist* first tries to reassure the reader that the widely accepted principle of separation of powers is not violated. The text begins as a response to the Anti-Federal objections and is framed as an improvement of the familiar rather than the invention of something genuinely new.

It is hard to imagine today, but in late eighteenth-century America the politically attentive public—people who read newspaper columns like those that became *The Federalist*—were familiar with the political theory of Montesquieu, or at least his principle that legislative, executive, and judicial power should be separated and confined to different departments of government. Seemingly at odds with those theories, in the proposed Constitution, the Senate shared appointment and treaty-making power with the executive, the executive held a qualified veto over legislation, and the judiciary had assigned powers sufficient to justify review of the constitutionality of legislation. Legislative, executive, and judicial powers were commingled in the Constitution in these and other ways contrary to Montesquieu's principle of separation.

Seizing on these facts, Anti-Federalists pressed their case to reject the proposed redesign of the governmental order. They argued that the separation of powers principle was an essential protection for liberty—a bulwark against tyranny, that assigning powers cleanly to the appropriate institutions facilitated efficiency in governance, that sharing power would generate too much conflict among the branches, and that the complexity of an arrangement of shared powers made government less understandable to ordinary citizens and therefore less accountable. As Bernard Manin states, "The Anti-Federalists unremittingly advocated precision and certainty in constitutional matters. They complained over and over again that the constitution was 'incomprehensible and indefinite,' 'vague and inexplicit.'"[5]

James Madison, writing as Publius in *The Federalist*, began his rebuttal to these charges by conceding the point that were the Constitution to violate the separation of powers principle as articulated by the "oracle" Montesquieu, that would mark the loss of "an essential precaution in favor of liberty." But the Constitution does not violate Montesquieu's principle, Madison said, because the Anti-Federalists had wrongly interpreted the great oracle himself, whose maxim "has totally been misconceived and misapplied." The real-world model for his understanding was the British regime. "On the slightest view of the British Constitution, we must perceive that the legislative, executive, and judiciary departments are by no means totally separate and distinct from each other."[6] Montesquieu did not mean that branches of government could have "no partial agency in, or control over" another, but rather that no department could exercise the whole power of another.[7]

The experience of the states provided further evidence for Madison that the separation of powers principle was more porous than the hermetically sealed compartments assumed by the opponents to the Constitution. He canvassed every state constitution except Rhode Island and Connecticut whose constitutions were framed "before the principle became an object of political attention."[8] All of the other constitutions mix powers, directly through shared powers and indirectly through devices like modes of appointment. Many of these constitutions contain the separation of powers principle itself as a clause in the text, and Madison shows how some of those clauses legitimate mixing power.

Nevertheless, the state constitutions were closer in form to the model recommended by the Anti-Federalists than was the Constitution. Madison, therefore, profoundly shifted his argument and attacked these forms for insufficiently providing for the effective exercise of the powers assigned. Now it appears that definition and distinction was indeed the essence of separation of powers in the state experience. The state constitutions presumed that clearly designating powers and duties was sufficient to prevent encroachment or usurpation. Madison derided this as just the making of lists, absent any real teeth for enforcement. "[A] mere demarcation on parchment of the constitutional limits of the several departments is not a sufficient guard against those encroachments which lead to a tyrannical concentration of all the powers of government in the same hands."[9] Madison makes clear that in a "representative republic" the danger comes principally from the legislature and some additional resources need to be provided to make the executive a truly coequal branch of government. This worry marks not only a defect in the particular institutional forms of the state constitutions, but also in the separation of powers principle itself. As Manin rightly argues, the principle of separation of powers in Montesquieu subtly endorses legislative supremacy because he drops discretionary powers of "prerogative" found in Locke's version, which had greatly enhanced the executive. Montesquieu's version suggested a hierarchy: lawmaking followed by executive carrying out legislative will or judicial interpretation of legislative intention.

Anti-Federalists argued in general terms about separation of powers, but they were principally concerned about threats from executive and judicial power. They were not really troubled by legislative supremacy, although they conceded the appropriateness of bicameralism to contend with that problem. Federalists pressed the case that times and problems had changed since the Revolution—that dangers were now more likely from the legislature than the executive due to the unequivocal commitment of the regime to representative democracy as the basic constitutional form.[10] Experience under the state constitutions appeared to confirm the Federalists' point, where most executives were very weak. Under the Articles of Confederation there was no separate executive at all. In the Articles, legislative and executive power both were contained in the Congress, yet the Anti-Federalists did not regard the existing arrangement as a violation of the separation of powers principle.

A still deeper problem is revealed as Madison discusses the distinctions between legislative, executive, and judicial power. Assigning the appropriate powers to the appropriate institutions assumes that one can define those powers in the first place. The classic texts of political theory, such as Locke's *Second Treatise* or Montesquieu's *Spirit of the Laws*, for example, refer to power that is "in its nature" legislative, executive, or judicial, but it is exceptionally difficult to define the natures of powers with any precision. Thus, Madison himself describes the task of constitution making as first "discriminating, in theory, the several classes of power, as they may in their nature be legislative, executive, or judiciary" and then providing institutional security for each.[11] He considers the second task as the most difficult, but in fact never seriously attempts to do the first in *The Federalist*. There is scant account of the natures of power in *The Federalist*. Instead, Madison describes the difficulty, perhaps impossibility, of defining power by its natures.

> When we pass from the works of nature, in which all the delineations are perfectly accurate and appear to be otherwise only from the imperfection of the eye which surveys them, to the institutions of man, in which the obscurity arises as well from the object itself as from the organ by which it is contemplated, we must perceive the necessity of moderating still further our expectations and hopes for the efforts of human sagacity. Experience has instructed us that no skill in the science of government has yet been able to discriminate and define with sufficient certainty, its three great provinces—the legislative, executive and judiciary; or even the privileges and powers of the different legislative branches. Questions daily occur in the course of practice which prove the obscurity which reigns in these subjects, and which puzzle the greatest adepts in political science.[12]

What we call legislative, executive, and judicial powers are not functions systematically defined by their natures but instead abstractions derived from the variety of invented practices historically associated with legislatures, executives, and judiciaries. Deriving definitions of power from various institutional practices confounds the problem of deciding whether power is appropriately assigned in the first place and provides still less guidance on the proper scope or reach of power. To repeat, there are accounts of different powers in *The Federalist*—legislative, executive, and judicial—but these are not derived from a theory of *natures* but instead are abstractions from *conventional practices* of the past.

To my knowledge, Bernard Manin is the first scholar to have noted the significance of this problem: "Madison stressed at various points, in the *The Federalist* and elsewhere, that the definition of the three functions, simple as it might at first appear, was in reality characterized by a certain objective indeterminacy."[13] For Manin, the main significance of this fact was that it led Madison to worry that the legislature was "was in a position to extend its power surreptitiously" because it had superior political, legal, and financial resources—and most importantly greater political legitimacy. For me, indeterminacy signals that separation of powers was not workable on its own terms. *A new theory of governmental order was required, one in which indeterminacy would be a virtue to exploit rather than a limitation to overcome.*

After Madison makes his point about the difficulty of cabining power by definition, he raises and rejects the idea that an exogenous process or institution could resolve boundary disputes between the three branches of government. Periodic appeals to the people to form interpretive conventions to settle such disputes—an idea mentioned by Thomas Jefferson—is rejected as corrosive of habits of constitutional veneration necessary for law abidingness and regime stability. He is even more critical of the idea of a council of censors (a body designed to mediate the boundary disputes of regular governmental branches). This device had been tried in Pennsylvania, and Madison details how it replicated the problems of faction and political contestation that it was designed to resolve. "This censorial body, therefore, proves at the same time, by its researches, the existence of the disease, and by its example, the inefficacy of the remedy."[14]

Madison, finally, makes his now well-known argument in No. 51 that the solution to the problem of boundary maintenance can be obtained by departing from strict separation of powers so that the shared powers provide resources for each branch to defend its own constitutional turf. Madison here combines a functional notion of power—that legislative, executive, and judicial power are distinct, different from one another, appropriate to the different tasks of the three branches—with a checks and balances notion of power. In this latter conception, power is a single entity (like electricity or force) that can be divided up, but whose purpose is to defend or counter assertions of power by others. I will return to some of the particulars of this account in the next section. It is important to note here that *Federalist* No. 51 appears to be the conclusion to the discussion of separation of powers. Separation of powers here is still endorsed as a core principle of the American constitutional design, now improved by the melding of two notions of power such that the branches could police their own boundaries. However, one should note that only one major Anti-Federalist objection has been countered—that mixing power would threaten liberty. There is not yet a response to the criticisms that government will not be as efficient, or as accountable, or as free from interbranch conflict as would be a traditional separation of powers arrangement with cleaner demarcations. Madison does address these points, but later, in the discussions of the three major institutions.

Federalist No. 51 is both a conclusion to the argument that the Constitution does not violate the principle of separation of powers and an introduction to an argument that the Constitution will be based on a new theory of governmental organization. The rest of *The Federalist*, Nos. 51 to the end,

No. 85, is an account of this new governmental order. Madison's extended introduction to the account of the governmental design is, of course, a rhetorical/political effort to persuade citizens in stages, beginning with the familiar and leading to the innovative and new. It also serves a theoretical purpose, because separation of powers will not be set aside or abandoned but rather made a subordinate component in a larger theory, as I mentioned at the outset. The story up until No. 51 is about power, with structure playing a supporting role. After No. 51, it becomes clear that the constitutional design is mainly about structure with assignments of power playing a supporting role. I want to stress this point: Traditional separation of powers theory is principally about powers and their distinctions and secondarily about structures to house power. The invention of the Constitution is a design that reverses the emphases of traditional separation of powers. In the Constitution, structures are primary and powers are secondary.

The narrative culminating in *Federalist* No. 51 that I have just sketched and reviewed is not generally regarded as an introduction or preface to the actual constitutional design. It is rather thought to be the whole story. I dwell on this "Preface" because it has become part of America's constitutional consciousness—it is the understanding of the system that most thoughtful participants hold even as the logic of the system rests on a different theory. This is one important way that the Anti-Federalist objections to the Constitution have become absorbed into the constitution of American politics.

Mixed Democracy

As I mentioned at the outset, although separation of powers is nowhere mentioned in the Constitution, as it was in many of the state constitutions, our governmental order is often described as a separation of powers *system*. This use of the idea can be distinguished from a separation of powers theory or *principle* and from a separation of powers *doctrine*. The separation of powers principle refers to design ideas like those described by Montesquieu, Locke, or Carl Schmitt. This is the notion that powers can be distinguished by their natures and assigned to the appropriate institutions. The separation of powers doctrine refers to the practice of courts in attempting to confine the political branches to their constitutionally assigned powers—to enforce, as it were, some version of the separation of powers principle. The idea of a separation of powers *system* is intended to distinguish our governmental order from others, such as parliamentary regimes. This is an unfortunate label because it masks rather than marks the distinctiveness of the American constitutional design. Also, while this familiar label usefully highlights the replacement of legislative supremacy with constitutional supremacy, it does not express the design principle of the Constitution. In this section, I will call this new American invention "mixed democracy" to distinguish it from the old theory of separation of powers to capture this design principle. However, there is no harm in continuing to use the term "separation of powers system" as long as one realizes that it means something new and quite different from the classic idea of separation of powers and something more than constitutional supremacy.

The president, Congress, and the Supreme Court are constituted by congeries of structures and powers, not primarily by powers *per se*. Plurality or unity of officeholders, extent of the terms of office, modes of selection for office as well as specified powers and duties combine to create a set of institutions that behave and "think" quite differently from each other. In older "mixed" regimes these differences could be traced to different social orders and were put in the service of alternative regime principles. A crucial invention of the new American science of politics was to design institutions to represent differing desiderata of democratic governance rather than contending social orders or alternative regimes.[15]

This basic idea—mixed democracy—thus derives from the classical idea of a "mixed regime," but now in the service of improving democracy alone. In the classic notion, basic regime types or claims to rule are given institutional representation in a single polity so as to draw out the strengths of each. Thus, the executive might be a monarch, while one house of the legislature represented the aristocracy and the other the people generally, or democracy. Aristotle makes clear in his famous account that each of these claims to rule by the one, the few, or the many is partial or limited. No one claim offers a fully satisfactory account of justice or the common good. But each claim also has some merit. The ancient mixed regime invention was designed to induce a constitutional struggle between these competing perspectives or claims on the whole polity in order to make the polity better than it would be under the auspices of only one perspective. This idea can be distinguished from a "balanced constitution" or "balanced government." In some of the Roman republics and early modern models based on them, power is divided between institutions to provide checks and balances. In this model, different regimes are not combined but different institutions within a single regime—a republic—are given sufficient power to block the dominance of other institutional centers of power. The function of balance is essentially negative—to block or prevent the excessive use of power by a competing institution.

Because the American constitution also establishes a single regime type, a democratic republic, and because it contains checks and balances, it is often assumed that it is a version of the older "balanced constitution." There is some truth to this observation. Power is divided, in part, to prevent the tyranny of any one institution. Moreover, the American system is not tied to social orders as were mixed regimes and it does not mix multiple regime types. Nevertheless, the mixed regime idea better illuminates the way alternative structures can be designed not just to frustrate one another in order to safeguard liberty, but also to advance positive purposes, to make competing perspectives and powers mutually fructifying. At bottom, the ancient mixed regime was vitally agonistic. Its competing institutions were all assertive, not merely defensive. The mixed regime made a virtue of conflict and of the qualities of the perspectives that were the sources of conflict. The assertions of power in mixed regimes did not aim at stasis or equilibrium but rather at improvement, or transformation, of the claims of each partial view of justice, or of the common good, into something closer to genuine justice or an actual common good. Neither balanced government nor the old version of separation of powers captures this central insight of the mixed regime that was appropriated for the new form of polity invented in America. As Sotirios Barber has shown, the most fundamental feature of the American Constitution is that it is purpose-driven.[16] The Constitution as a whole is designed to advance important purposes, a basic fact that Barber labels positive constitutionalism. The congeries of structures and powers that I have labeled mixed democracy are the engines of this positive constitutionalism. The elements are mixed *primarily* to advance the positive purposes of the constitution and importantly, but only secondarily, to prevent untoward or negative consequences from the uses of power.

The American polity is a mixed democracy because the elements put in productive conflict are attributes or theoretical components of democracy itself rather than alternative regime types. Basic desiderata of all democratic regimes include provision for the expression of popular will in and about public policy; protection of individual rights; and (common to all regimes) provision of security or self-preservation for the regime. Reflecting or expressing popular will, to some degree, is a basic feature of all democratic theories. Most democratic theory is committed, as well, to rights protection as a feature of democracy itself. Self-preservation or security is not particularly democratic—it is a prerequisite of all regimes, including democratic ones. Although not a democratic element itself, a security orientation is indispensable for democracies. Hamilton stressed this point after Anti-Federalists urged that executive energy was inconsistent with the genius of democratic republics. Hamilton replied that the Anti-Federalists had better hope that their supposition was destitute of foundation because if they were correct democracy would be impossible to achieve. Yet, as the Anti-Federalist challenge to Hamilton and his oblique response illustrates, these democratic desiderata exist in tension and sometimes contradiction with each other. Popular will, rights protection, and security promotion often point in differing or contending directions. The American constitutional order can be thought of as an attempt to productively resolve those tensions by representing them in and among competing institutions.[17]

The design challenge is to structure institutions so that, prior to knowing what the policy dispute will be, inducements will make it likely that all the relevant considerations for a democracy are brought to bear on the issue at hand. Consider, for a moment, a controversial issue such as immigration policy. In a democracy, the ideal immigration policy will take account of what the current citizenry wants, what the rights of immigrants are or should be, and what the security needs of the country are. In advance of any debate, not knowing the particulars of the historical moment in which it arises, is there a way to make it likely that arguments about popular will, about rights, and about security will all be brought to bear on the issue? The Constitution structures the three major institutions, president, Congress, and court, to attend to all three democratic desiderata, but for each to be biased in favor of one. Practically speaking, the same person who might hold offices (at different times, of course) in more than one of these branches will see the very same issue differently. Thus, for example, President Obama had different foreign policy views on matters he had previously spoken to as Senator Obama. As long as officeholders seek to advance the perspective of their branch, and as long as the same issue presents itself to multiple branches, the full array of democratic considerations will be brought to bear on the policy at hand.

Each of the major branches is designed to advance desiderata of democracy through a distinctive dispositional state. *The Federalist* devotes much of its text, following No. 51, to describing and defending these dispositional states as products of the distinctive structures and powers assigned by the Constitution to each branch. For example, the long description and defense of unity, along with a four-year term, re-eligibility, and a more open-ended vesting of power in the executive is shown to be conducive to decisiveness and dispatch. Conjoined with enormous discretionary power, unity is also shown requisite to a forward-looking virtue, an ability to see and attend to nascent problems before they are visible to the people at large. One can call this the prospective advantage.

The legislature is described and defended as a plural branch, representative of the many. Its distinctive dispositional quality, if it is working at its best, is deliberation through representation. Although deliberation is useful for long-term planning and can be vital for legitimacy and effectiveness, crises usually call for quick action, for which the deliberative institution is at a disadvantage. However, retrospectively, looking back, the legislature has the dispositional advantage and a political upper hand. Looking back, the representative character of the institution enables its deliberations to reflect the actual felt experiences of the nation at large.

In traditional separation of powers theory, the Constitution's major branches are equal and coordinate all the time. In fact, and in the theory of mixed democracy, the major branches are not equal and coordinate all the time. Rather, they are equal and coordinate over time. The president has distinct advantages for action at the outset of a war or crisis or even the beginning of a policy initiative. As rational choice theorists remind us, and as *The Federalist* urged, the president is the first mover of American politics. That advantage is counterbalanced by the fact that Congress has the last say, the last word, as evident in its power to impeach and convict. If the power of impeachment were more viable than it is presently, all the other powers of Congress (hearings, investigation, funding, consent to appointments, censure, and so forth) would have real teeth and would enhance the Congress's retrospective advantage whether or not impeachment was exercised. Impeachment needs to be viable, although it need not, and should not, be routine.

The judiciary stands between the president and Congress structurally, but not politically. The Supreme Court is composed of a few—not one, and not many. Its distinctive dispositional aspect is judgment. In traditional separation of powers theory, the court is seen as an arbiter of disputes between the president and Congress over their respective powers. But in the theory of *The Federalist* and in the practice of the court for most of its history it does not play this role—precisely because the disputed powers of president and Congress are not well suited to definition and distinction for reasons Madison mentioned in the long quotation I cited earlier.[18] The court does concern itself with the actions of the president and the Congress, but as a by-product of its fundamental orientation to rights vindication. Since the 1950s the court has increasingly interceded in so-called separation of powers cases. For most of American history, consistent with the mixed democracy idea, political contestation rather than legal arbitration was the mode of resolving conflicts and tensions between the political branches. The reason for this stems from the difficulties of defining the boundaries of power discussed above. Properly structured political contestation serves to define the boundaries of power.

Consider disputes about executive privilege. As an abstract matter, the Constitution does authorize the president to keep advice secret for a variety of reasons (security, law enforcement, and the integrity and efficiency of advice giving itself). But the same Constitution authorizes Congress to gather information from the president to further its own institutional duties, including legislation and oversight. As a simply legal matter each branch has a defensible claim. How are they to be balanced? It is hard to fashion a legal response to that question. Courts might attempt a balance but to do so they would need to make political assessments regarding the weights that should be assigned the competing institutional claims. Properly structured, constitutional contestation itself is a better measure of these relative weights.[19]

"Executive privilege" is not mentioned in the Constitution. It is an inference from the vesting of executive power legitimately asserted by officeholders since the early history of the republic. It can only legitimately be asserted, or waived, by *sitting* presidents because it is an attribute of the office—not a right of an individual. Even today, presidents routinely assert executive privilege to shield confidential communications of their predecessors, whose policy and partisan positions might be at odds with those of the current officeholder. Former presidents, however, are no longer officeholders and are no longer positioned to assess and advance the interests of the office. For reasons sketched below, only actual officeholders are well positioned to assess the long-term interests of "their" branch of government. Such assessments are inherently political questions—involving both the long-term assessment of institutional interests and the competing weight of other political considerations such as the legitimate claims by Congress. It is a distortion of the judicial function for courts to instruct presidents, or the Congress, on their own institutional interests—as would be necessary under a traditional "separation of powers" arrangement where courts might "balance" the competing claims of president and Congress.

One measure of constitutional pathology in our time is the recent turn by the Supreme Court to wrongly interpreting the American system as one of traditional separation of powers, in which the meaning, assignment, and balancing of those powers is a judicial function. This problem is evident in the recent "immunity" decision by the Supreme Court. Misunderstanding the nature of the constitutional order—previously well understood by courts—Chief Justice Roberts makes two major mistakes. First, he assumes that former officeholders have standing to make claims on behalf of the presidency. Only sitting officeholders do. Second, he repudiates the current president's understanding and assessment of the long-term interests of the presidency today. The judicial arrogance of the immunity decision is breathtaking and a direct by-product of the legalization of a system designed to be politically agonistic.

There are occasions when the relative weight at issue is the court's own institutional duties. *United States v. Nixon*, which ruled that the president's executive privilege could not shield him from disclosing the tapes implicating him in the Watergate cover-up, is a good example. In that case, the tapes were needed for judicial proceedings. The constitutionally legitimate claim of privilege (which the court acknowledged and indeed endorsed as a matter of abstract legal principle) was balanced against the judiciary's constitutionally authorized powers and responsibilities. The court, in effect, ruled for itself and it succeeded because it gained the assent of the public. The immunity decision did not pose this issue for the court because the officeholder did not assert immunity in the ongoing judicial proceedings.

Advancing the institutional perspective of each branch requires the translation of the motives of the officeholders into public-regarding reasons for their institutional positions.[20] This is the main significance of the insight that ambition will counteract ambition. Political scientists read that insight from *Federalist* No. 51 as evidence of checks and balances. But the whole insight includes the idea that the interests of the officeholder will be connected to "the constitutional rights of the place."[21] How so? In the very first number of *The Federalist* the distinction between motives and reasons is drawn to urge the proposition that the merits of reasons stand independent of the motives for uttering them. If politicians can be induced to make arguments that are public regarding, hypocrisy becomes a virtue of institutional design even if a defect of individual character. Famously, according to *The Federalist*, the Constitution is a design for a system that does not require virtue inculcation but can rely on self-interest instead. This does not mean that no virtue at all is required—a modicum of it is necessary and can be found in most, according to *The Federalist*. This modest expectation depends on the possibility that officeholders' self-interest can be elevated and their mistakes disciplined by a sense of shame. Until Donald Trump, we did not have a clear example of a president who fell below that minimum expectation and assessment of human nature.

Returning to the logic of institutional hypocrisy, the Constitution induces a series of translations. Through constitutionally designed incentives, individual self-interest is translated into ambition, ambition into policy position, policy position into policy argument, and in some important instances, policy argument into constitutional argument. The genius of this induced train of actions is that at no moment need the actor be motivated by his or her argument, even though he or she feels compelled to respond to the arguments of others. As long as politics is induced to trade on the plane of reasons, no matter what the motivations, constitutional democracy succeeds. From this vantage point, conflict—constitutional conflict—is a good thing. It puts in productive argument the multiple desiderata of democracy. This kind of conflict was commonplace in the nineteenth century. As Josh Chafetz details in his important book, *Congress's Constitution*, the legislature has all sorts of tools at its disposal to use in its arguments with the president that have fallen into disuse in the twentieth century.[22] Not only have the tools themselves fallen into disuse (and this is my point, not Chafetz's argument), there used to be a kind of common law of legislative and presidential behavior. Legislators and presidents made their own constitutional arguments without reference to court doctrine and with reference to their own prior arguments and practices. Precisely because those institutions did not resolve their disputes through the judiciary, they needed to know and remember their own traditions of constitutional argumentation.

At this point, let me review several of the key features that distinguish the new architecture of the Constitution from traditional separation of powers. Mixed democracy privileges structure over power. It does contain within it assigned powers, but it is the institutional arrangement of structure and power that is designed to craft distinctive dispositions. Constitutionally induced conflict is a virtue that is exploited rather than a vice to be avoided in order to bring multiple dispositions to bear on the polity's most important problems. These various constitutional attributes are in the service of a purpose-driven Constitution. Understood this way, one can think of all these complicated pieces of structures and powers as hierarchically arranged. That is, most of the design elements and most clauses of the Constitution can be thought of as means to advance something more important. For example, plurality and specific legislative powers are means to deliberation. Unity, duration, and more open-ended power as in the Article II vesting clause are means to energy and dispatch. Life terms in the judiciary and the review of cases (rather than abstract issues on their own) are means to judgment. One could detail and refine lists like these. I mention them briefly here to close with another feature that marks the new mixed regime as very different from traditional separation of powers.

In the traditional view, still captured in court doctrine today, it is important to enforce the distinctions between powers whether or not enforcing those distinctions makes the government as a whole more effective, responsible, or just. Under a mixed democracy view, power can sometimes migrate. If the demands of a complex economy require the legislature to delegate power to the executive, the legislature might take on what was previously thought to be an executive power (as in the legislative veto). The Congress does this because it determines that for matters of regulation delegation to congressionally designed institutions can perform Congress's functions better than the Congress itself. If Congress abandons its deliberative role, as it did in the Gingrich revolution, and simply votes campaign promises into law, absent any hearings, debate, deliberation, or response to presidential objections, a president might invent a new kind of veto in which he promises to sign a law if a simple majority vote is achieved after it can be credibly claimed that deliberation occurred (even if he disagrees with the law). Such a president—call him a neo-Whig president—would concede that elections matter, that majorities should rule (against the president's own preferences), but that presidential duty requires that an irresponsible Congress be induced to deliberation. In this instance, energy migrated to the legislative, so a concern for deliberation must migrate to the executive. If the Senate is controlled by a faction that refuses to vote on a presidential nominee, or refuses to vote to eliminate the office, a president may induce deliberation by threatening to appoint if Congress abdicates. If a president refuses to respond to the security threat of a foreign nation, a Congress may find that it needs to energize the government, if the president abdicates.[23] Traditional separation of powers theory fetishizes assignments of powers. The American Constitution elevates the multiple purposes those powers are supposed to serve. These hypotheticals are all *examples* of what the Constitution's new theory of governance might imply once one understands the Constitution as a hierarchically arranged set of means toward ends. They illustrate the underlying notion that separation of powers-as-mixed-democracy is *mainly* a political design to be enacted by politicians rather than a set of legal terms to be parsed by jurists. Because of the hold that the archaic idea of separation of powers still has on our political culture, these examples will seem an anathema to many Americans.

Notes

1. *Annals of Congress* 380 (1789).

2. Even the most sophisticated and insightful academics tend to elaborate the Anti-Federal legalistic view. See, for example, Jeremy Waldron, *Political Political Theory: Essays on Institutions* (Cambridge: Harvard University Press, 2016), Chapter 3: "Separation of Powers and the Rule of Law."

3. Nicole Mellow and I discuss this issue in our book, *Legacies of Losing in American Politics* (Chicago: University of Chicago Press, 2018), 54–59, as well as the rhetoric and politics of Anti-Federal appropriation of the iterative form of *The Federalist* more generally.

4. Hebert J. Storing, *What the Anti-Federalists Were For* (Chicago: University of Chicago Press, 1981), 54.

5. Bernard Manin, "Checks, Balances and Boundaries: The Separation of Powers in the Constitutional Debate of 1787," in *The Invention of the Modern Republic*, ed. Biancamaria Fontana (New York: Cambridge University Press, 1994). See also, Herbert J. Storing, *Anti-Federalists*, 54–59.

6. Publius [James Madison, Alexander Hamilton, and John Jay], *The Federalist Papers* [1788], ed. Clinton Rossiter (New York: New American Library, 1961). All subsequent references in the text to *The Federalist* are to the Rossiter edition, which is titled *The Federalist Papers*, according to a twentieth-century convention. I designate each reference by the number of the paper, the page number, and the now known author. *Federalist* No. 47. 302. (James Madison).

7. *Federalist* No. 47. 302. (James Madison).

8. *Federalist* No. 47. 305. (James Madison).

9. *Federalist* No. 48. 313. (James Madison).

10. Eric Nelson has shown that this concern for bolstering weak executives, even monarchs, against strong legislatures predates the American Revolution. Nelson, *The Royalist Revolution: Monarchy and the American Founding* (Cambridge: Harvard University Press, 2014).

11. *Federalist* No. 48. 308. (James Madison).

12. *Federalist* No. 37. 226. (James Madison).

13. Manin, p. 49.

14. *Federalist* No. 50. 320. (James Madison).

15. Storing, *Anti-Federalists*, 54–56.

16. Sotirios A. Barber and James E. Fleming, *Constitutional Interpretation: The Basic Questions* (New York: Oxford, 2007), chapter 3, "The Principal Features of the American Constitutional Order: The Positive Constitutionalism of *The Federalist*." See also, Sotirios Barber, *On What the Constitution Means* (Baltimore: Johns Hopkins University Press, 1984); Sotirios Barber, *Welfare and the Constitution* (Princeton, NJ: Princeton University Press, 2003).

17. I give a visual depiction of mixed democracy in a figure on page 43 of *The Rhetorical Presidency*, Princeton Classics edition (Princeton: Princeton University Press, 2017).

18. See especially, Jesse H. Choper, *Judicial Review and the National Political Process: A Functional Reconsideration of the Role of the Supreme Court* (Chicago: University of Chicago Press, 1980).

19. Gary J. Schmitt, "Executive Privilege: Presidential Power to Withhold Information From Congress," in Joseph M. Bessette and Jeffrey Tulis, *The Presidency in the Constitutional Order* (Baton Rouge: Louisiana State University Press, 1981, and Routledge, 2017); David A. Crockett, "Executive Privilege," in Joseph M. Bessette and Jeffrey K. Tulis, *The Constitutional Presidency* (Baltimore: Johns Hopkins University Press, 2009); Gary J. Schmitt and Jeffrey K. Tulis, "Long Read: Trump v Thompson Shows That When the Court Weighs In on Executive Privilege It Is Bad for Congress, for a Sitting President, and for the Court," *USApp: American Politics and Policy Blog*, February 10, 2022. https://eprints.lse.ac.uk/114081/1/usappblog_2022_02_10_long_read_trump_v_thompson_shows_that_when_the.pdf

20. For the logic of translation of partisan policy to constitutional argument, see Jeffrey K. Tulis, "On Congress and Constitutional Responsibility," *Boston University Law Review* 89 (April 2009) 2, pp. 515–524.

21. *Federalist* No. 51. 322. (James Madison).

22. Josh Chafetz, *Congress's Constitution: Legislative Authority and the Separation of Powers* (New Haven, CT: Yale University Press, 2017).

23. Mariah Zeisberg, *War Powers: The Politics of Constitutional Authority* (Princeton: Princeton University Press, 2013).

CHAPTER 3

The Madisonian Separation of Powers in Comparative Constitutional Perspective

George Thomas

In *Federalist* No. 47, James Madison famously insisted: "The accumulation of all powers, legislative, executive, and judiciary, in the same hands, whether of one, a few, or many, and whether hereditary, self-appointed, or elective, may justly be pronounced the very definition of tyranny."[1] The Madisonian separation of powers is commonly thought to prevent an abuse of power because it disperses power among different branches of government and gives each branch checks on the other branches. We see this sentiment in Montesquieu's often cited platitude, quoted by Madison in *Federalist* No. 47: "'There can be no liberty where the legislative and executive powers are united in the same person, or body of magistrates,' or, 'if the power of judging be not separated from the legislative and executive powers.'"[2] Yet it is certainly true, as Bruce Ackerman notes, that scholars and jurists give pietistic references to Madison's and Montesquieu's separation of powers as essential to preserving liberty without offering much in the way of empirical analysis.[3]

Comparative constitutional analysis suggests that a Madisonian separation of powers is not the only way to secure liberty and prevent tyranny. In comparative terms, separation-of-powers systems are usually contrasted with parliamentary systems. But even the classic Westminster parliamentary system embraces some form of separation of powers. When we turn to constitutional structure in modified parliamentary systems, we see a formal separation of powers that is quite distinct from the Madisonian version. Placing the Madisonian separation of powers in comparative constitutional context can help us better understand the different versions of separation of powers that actually exist, pushing us to think more clearly about how and why power is separated. As Jeremy Waldron notes, a primary argument for the separation of powers is to separate government into its essential functions. The logic here is largely one of functionality and effectiveness given the nature of different types of power. But there is, following Waldron, a second point here that is conceptually distinct from this first point; that is, the dispersal of power among different institutions to prevent a concentration of power. This has the effect of diffusing power but is much less attentive to the *functional* logic of the separation.[4] Similarly, the idea of checks and balances, which gives different institutions a check on one another, shares much in common with the idea of dispersing power. But rather than simply dividing power among different branches, checks and balances gives each branch some say over what other branches can do.[5]

This chapter contrast the Madisonian understanding of the separation of powers with the European understanding of the separation of powers. These different conceptions of the separation of powers both try to solve questions at the heart of constitutional government—including creating an effective but limited government—but they do so in remarkably different ways. They also offer an important contrast in how best to enforce the limits of a written constitution by making it binding on the departments of government. In the Madisonian vision, the separation of powers is understood as part of a political dynamic, and constitutional enforcement is understood in largely political terms. In the European case, the separation of powers is understood in legalistic terms, and constitutional enforcement is understood as a political-legal process that exists outside of politics. And yet for all of the important differences between the Madisonian and European understandings of the separation of powers, there are some convergences: Each system wrestles with the enduring question of how to balance politics and law in perpetuating and securing constitutional democracy.

The first section of this chapter articulates a Madisonian understanding of the separation of powers, partly contrasting it with the understanding of originalist jurists like Antonin Scalia, who insists on a formalist and legalistic view of the separation of powers. A crucial point in the Madisonian view is a refusal to trust any one department of government with the task of acting as the guardian of the Constitution. Rather, constitutional conflict within the separation of powers is a central way to enforce constitutional limits. This more informal and political understanding of the separation of powers is in distinct contrast to the more formal and legalistic understanding of the separation of powers that we see in Europe where a constitutional court is established as the guardian of the constitution. Yet before turning to the contrasting vision of the separation of powers as exemplified by both the German and French models, I pause to briefly examine the classic Westminster parliamentary system. The usual contrast between the separation of powers and parliamentary government misses how parliamentary systems embrace elements of the separation of powers.[6]

The second section of this chapter focuses on the more formal understanding of separation of powers that exists in Europe and how it yields a more legalistic understanding of constitutional enforcement. From the European perspective, precisely because the legislative branch is understood to represent national sovereignty, there has long been skepticism of the judiciary exercising judicial review in an American form. The European understanding of the unique functions of government leads to a more formal separation of powers between the branches, a view that is particularly powerful in civil law systems.[7] Yet in the second half of the twentieth century, both parliamentary and semi-presidential systems in Europe developed constitutional courts with the powers of constitutional review. This section turns to what Ackerman has dubbed "the new" separation of powers in the German model of constrained parliamentarianism and what Cindy Skach calls "the newest" separation of powers in the French semi-presidential model. Like the traditional Westminster model, a modified parliamentary system as seen in Germany and a semi-presidential system as seen in France both embrace the idea of diffusing power that is an essential characteristic of constitutional democracy. At the same time, in sharp contrast to both the American separation of powers and the Westminster model, both the German and French models embrace a formalist understanding of the separation of powers when it comes to constitutional review. As articulated by Hans Kelsen, institutions charged with upholding the constitution by way of constitutional review are understood to function as a "negative legislator."[8] From this perspective, the American system violates the formal separation of powers by giving the judiciary a place in the lawmaking process by way of judicial review.[9] In contrast, constitutional courts are held to be outside the separation of powers. In fact, as Louis Favoreu argues, the difference between the American and European understanding of constitutional review reflects "different conceptions of the separation of powers."[10] A central task of constitutional courts and constitutional review is to monitor the separation of powers as part of guarding the Constitution, which necessarily placed such institutions outside "the traditional categories of state power."[11]

The third section of this chapter turns to the tension between law and politics inherent in both understandings of the separation of powers. Although the striking differences between the American and European conceptions of the separation of powers remain most notable, there has been a trend to understand modern constitutionalism as a legal enterprise that situates the American Supreme Court and European constitutional courts as the very essence of constitutionalism. Beginning from the idea of separated governmental powers, the judicial and legal functions are conflated with constitutionalism as a whole. Yet we should be skeptical that constitutionalism can be reduced to law or that we can avoid constitutional conflict. Situating the Madisonian separation of powers in comparative constitutional perspective highlights important divergences between the American and European understandings of separation of powers—particularly as it applies to constitutional law—while at the same time revealing that all of the institutional arrangements in contemporary constitutional democracies embrace some notion of diffused power and functional distinctions between types of power. In general terms, rather than attempting to situate one model as preferable, as if institutions can easily be rearranged within different countries, it may be that these different perspectives on the separation of powers are both capable of solving similar problems, even if they each come with advantages and drawbacks that we should better understand.

The Madisonian Separation of Powers

The Madisonian separation of powers is too often understood to deliberately create a "vetocracy" because it seeks to prevent tyranny rather than create an effective government.[12] Justice Brett Kavanaugh captures this sentiment: "The separation of powers primarily protects freedom from government action" and that is because the framers wanted it "to be hard to pass legislation."[13] Yet the idea that the separation of powers would enable a "vetocracy" to preserve liberty misconstrues Madison's institutional thinking. It places checks and balances at the center of his constitutional system when, in fact, it was only one part of it. Madison's constitutional design was, first and foremost, meant to provide the basis of an energetic government capable of meeting the demands placed on it. Dividing power into different branches was a means of preventing concentrated power that could be easily abused (and thus preserving liberty), but this fact should not obscure the notion that separation was just as surely meant to secure an effective government.[14] It did so, in part, by allowing for conflict between the branches within the separation of powers. This was also a central way the Madisonian separation of powers would secure the Constitution.[15] The Madisonian separation of powers, as detailed in Charles Zug's introduction and Thomas Bell's chapter, is more political than legal.

In *Federalist* No. 47, where Madison insists that the accumulation of all powers in a single department may be deemed the very definition of tyranny, he just as importantly notes that in a functional system of government there must be some "partial mixture of powers." While this paper is relied on by Justice Scalia to argue for a formalistic separation of powers, the thrust of Madison's argument in *Federalist* No. 47 is to reject just such an understanding.[16] Anti-Federalist critics of the proposed constitution were arguing that it violated the idea of separation of powers because the "departments are by no means totally separate and distinct from each other."[17] Madison insisted that this was a virtue. He also insisted that some mixture of powers was embraced by the British Constitution, by Montesquieu, and by the Massachusetts Constitution of 1780 (even while textual provisions impossibly insisted on a formal separation where the different departments were entirely separate). In *Federalist* No. 37, Madison similarly argued that we could not always draw clear lines between the *types of power* to be exercised by the different departments. Madison insisted that "experience has instructed us that no skill in the science of government has yet been able to discriminate and define, with sufficient certainty, its three great provinces the legislative, executive, and judiciary." Indeed, contrary to formalists like Justice Scalia, Madison noted that the conceptual distinction between the different types of power and the different functions of government had puzzled the "greatest adepts in political science."[18] Rejecting an overly formalistic understanding of the separation of powers, Madison argued that the real threat of liberty came when "the *whole* power of one department is exercised by the same hands which possess the *whole* power of another department." It is this scenario, and not a mixing of powers within the different departments, where "fundamental principles of a free constitution are subverted."[19] A powerful way of preventing this concentration of power was to provide for a mixing of power within the branches, thereby fostering conflict between them where "ambition must be made to counteract ambition" as Madison argued in *Federalist* No. 51.[20]

From the perspective of constitutional design, power is diffused among different branches of government, but the branches of government are also institutionally structured in a manner that facilitates the exercise of a particular kind of constitutional virtue. As Jeffrey Tulis's chapter argues, the American Constitution actually rejected the formal separation of powers we see advocated by Anti-Federalists and embraced by putative originalists like Justice Scalia.[21] Rather than formally separate power based on the "nature" of the power—something Madison doubts can be done—the Constitution focused on institutional structure as a way to advance the purposes of the Constitution, which also allowed for a mixing of departments by way of checks and balances. Whether or not one agrees with the whole of Tulis's argument, he points to the fact that the Madisonian separation of powers system is primarily about advancing the positive purposes of government and only secondarily about limiting abuses of power. And the separation of powers system brings out the essential features of democratic governance by way of institutional design. Rather than reposing trust in any one branch, or creating "a power independent of society," the political dynamic between the branches is the essential means of policing constitutional boundaries.[22]

Beyond the Madisonian Separation of Powers

Critics of the Madisonian separation of powers have long bemoaned the tautological assertion that a lack of separated power is the very definition of tyranny. As Ackerman puts it: "Given the British success in avoiding the inexorable slide into tyranny predicted by Madison and Montesquieu, perhaps we should give up on the very idea of the separation of powers?"[23] Ackerman thinks that separation remains valuable, but he offers "Constrained Parliamentarianism" based on the German model as the "new" separation of powers. This arrangement brings together the executive and legislative as in a parliamentary system but stands apart from the Westminster model in providing for a constitutional court to keep the parliament in check by way of a written constitution (including protecting fundamental rights). Unlike the Westminster model (which has now been altered in the UK), the legislature can only vote to dissolve the sitting government (akin to the executive branch) if it does so by voting in a replacement government (a positive vote of no confidence). Building on Ackerman, Cindy Skach offers the French semi-presidential model as the "newest" separation of powers, which has taken hold in several constitutional democracies post 1989.[24] Ackerman and Skach reveal how the separation of powers exists in important ways beyond the

American model and with important conceptual differences. Before turning to the German and French models, I want to highlight that even the Westminster model embraces elements of the separation of powers.

Popular Sovereignty in Parliamentary and Separation of Powers Systems

Just how the people underlie the institutional scheme is among the most important differences between a parliamentary system and the American presidential or separation of powers system. In *The English Constitution*, Walter Bagehot insisted the crucial difference between these models is that the legislature and executive are chosen by the same process in the parliamentary model while being chosen by a different electoral process in a separation of powers model.[25] A single election fused the executive and legislative functions. Bagehot thus rejected Montesquieu's idea that the English Constitution embraced the separation of powers or was a mixed polity. As Jean-Jacques Rousseau argued, efforts to divide sovereignty "into legislative and executive power" turned the "the sovereign into a fantastic being, formed of disparate parts; it is as if they created a man from several bodies, one with eyes, another with arms, another with feet, and nothing else."[26] Bagehot plays up this contrast: Parliamentary systems embrace a simple version of popular sovereignty "in which the ultimate power upon all questions is in the hands of the same persons." The American system, even if wholly republican, is a "composite government, in which the supreme power is divided between many bodies and functionaries." For Bagehot, the Westminster model "is framed on the principle of choosing a single sovereign authority, and making it good: The American, upon the principle of having many sovereign authorities, and hoping that their multitude may atone for their inferiority."[27] The crucial point is how easily elections—and popular sovereignty—may be translated into governing authority.

Bagehot's view continues to frame the conceptual delineations between the Madisonian separation of powers and parliamentary systems. Following Bagehot, Ackerman argues that the essential difference between a separation of powers model and a parliamentary model is the question: "How many elections should a political movement win before gaining how much law-making authority?"[28] Under a parliamentary model, one election is enough to gain plenary authority. And this is precisely because in a parliamentary system one election bestows sovereign authority on the legislature, which then chooses the executive. Combining these functions by way of a single election makes the government much more responsive to popular will and much more effective in carrying it out. In democratic terms, parliamentary democracy is preferable to presidential democracy (the separation of powers) precisely because it does not give us separate elections that necessarily divide popular authority among different and potentially competing branches of government. Moreover, as Bagehot puts it, a parliamentary model remains responsive to popular will because the government can be dissolved by a vote of no confidence (though this is now more complex even in the UK). The government can be switched without an election, or a new election can be called in the event of stalemate between the executive and legislative branches. A presidential system, with fixed elections and competing versions of the people in the different branches of government, allows for no such thing: "The American government calls itself a government of the supreme people; but at a quick crisis, the time when a sovereign power is most needed, you cannot find the supreme people."[29]

The American separation of powers embraces a more complex view of democracy and sovereignty. Tulis captures this by labeling the Madisonian separation of powers a "mixed democracy," and Paul Carrese's chapter suggests a balanced and complex view of democracy underlying Montesquieu's separation of powers. The Madisonian model requires numerous and sustained electoral victories across a range of institutions before a political movement may exercise full sovereign authority. Given this, sustained gridlock, or "vetocracy," may be a feature of the American separation of powers. Such an institutional dynamic, with different and competing elections across different political institutions, does have a negative function. The idea is to prevent a concentration of power in any one person or body that can be immediately responsive to popular will. But this underlying feature of separated powers also entails a positive function that would lead to better governance. Consider that the institutions of the national government represent different versions of the people. The people are not represented as a single entity, but are broken into different parts, each represented in American national institutions. Even the terms of national offices, staggered as they are, were designed both to give voice to the people in different capacities, as well as to shape and educate that voice. Still, scholars are right to ask whether the Madisonian separation of powers is the best way to prevent tyranny. Are there better ways to foster effective government while preventing it from taking a tyrannical turn?

Before turning to the logic of newer separation of powers systems to explore these questions, I venture that even the Westminster model has features of the separation of powers that are too often overlooked.

Separation of Powers Within the Parliamentary System

While the Westminster model is usually placed in opposition to the Madisonian separation of powers, we should recall that Montesquieu offered the British Constitution as his ideal model of government and held the separation of powers as a central feature of the British polity. The division of power between legislative, executive, and judicial entities also mixed power by combining elements of monarchy, aristocracy, and democracy. The British Constitution developed in significant ways between Montesquieu's time and Bagehot's time. But even prior to the development of the Westminster model, Madison noted that in the British Constitution "the executive magistrate forms an integral part of the legislative authority."[30] Using this as an example, Madison rejected a formal separation of powers and argued that some mixing of the different departments was beneficial. As I averred above, problems arise for a free constitution only when the *whole* "power of one department is exercised by the same hands which possess the *whole* power of another department."[31] When the same body both creates the law and applies it to particular cases, exercising the whole of each power, then the chances for an abuse of power are high.

Even if Montesquieu's analysis of the British Constitution is outdated, the Westminster model nevertheless embraces elements of the separation of powers. Highlighting this point, Cheryl Saunders argues, "even in the United Kingdom there are distinct legislative and executive institutions, which operate in distinct ways, even if their membership overlaps."[32] There is a formal separation between the executive and the legislature within the Parliament, even if there is also a "mutual dependence" in that the chief executive must be supported by a majority of the legislature.[33] There is informal overlap in that members of the executive branch are also usually members of the legislative branch. Yet mutual dependence still provides for separation: The legislative vote of no confidence marks a distinction between the legislature and executive and can act as a check on the executive, just as the executive power to call for new elections can be a check on the legislature. Such checks occur primarily by way of an institutionalized party system, but even with the idea of parties as the central institutional check we can see a latent form of the separation of powers in Parliament as a whole: The legislature provides for deliberation and the jarring of parties, while the executive administers the laws and can act decisively. To be sure, the executive can be tamed more quickly in a parliamentary system as the government can effectively change without a change in the majority party or without new elections. But even here, this is precisely because the executive is understood to be formally separate from the legislature—even if it is also directly accountable to it. The French Constitution, for example, even recognizes this formal separation between the executive (the government) and the legislature (the parliament), devoting Title III to "The Government" and Title IV to "Parliament," though under Article 23 of Title III, members of the government cannot hold parliamentary office, unlike in the British scheme.

Within the Westminster model conceptual and formal distinctions also persist with regard to the rule of law and the judiciary. While much has been made of parliamentary sovereignty, the judicial function in interpreting and enforcing ordinary law places courts as distinct from legislative and executive bodies. Judicial authority to hold acts of parliament unconstitutional has long been rejected, but judicial independence in interpreting law has been a central feature of parliamentary government.[34] Independence and distinction of function in the application of law echoes Montesquieu's insistence "that the power of judging" must be separate from other governmental functions, which is about the integrity of the judicial function and the rule of law. It is tempting to say this is the essence of Montesquieu's separation of powers, which persists in parliamentary systems. Montesquieu's arguments for separating the judicial function, after all, did not speak to *constitutional adjudication*. Yet the power of constitutional courts to enforce a written constitution is a central feature of the "new" separation of powers and the "new constitutionalism" that developed in the second half of the twentieth century.

The European Separation of Powers and Constitutional Courts

On the European continent, the separation of powers developed in a formalistic manner that was skeptical of Madison's intermixing of power among different departments. The understanding in Europe may look much more like the separation of powers advocated by some Anti-Federalists and embraced in early American state constitutions (or as embraced by originalists like Justice

Scalia). If Tulis's understanding of the American separation of powers system is right, the European understanding represents the road America did not take, which is partly evident in that the European understanding precluded (at least in theory) anything like American judicial review. While there are important differences between the European model and the Westminster model, the idea of sovereignty vesting in the lawmaking body found powerful expression in continental Europe and was reinforced by the civil law tradition.[35] Precisely because it represented national sovereignty, parliament was seen to be supreme over the executive and judiciary in its lawmaking function. In contrast to the American version of separation of powers that included judicial view, "a strict separation of powers rule prevailed and the judiciary was not given the right to interfere with the activities of the legislature."[36] Judges were to follow the law as articulated and codified by the sovereign body—acting as "mere passive beings" subservient to the law in Montesquieu's words—and were denied "jurisdiction over higher law."[37] While the constitution was accepted as an act of the sovereign will, the prevailing tradition, especially in France, understood the sovereign as a continuing presence usually represented by the lawmaking body—parliament. The laws passed by parliament were held to embrace Rousseau's "general will." To allow the judiciary to second-guess such laws by exercising constitutional review would undermine the very notion of law as articulated by the sovereign.[38]

Lucien Jaume captures this understanding: "The sovereignty exercised by Parliament was completely identified with the sovereignty possessed by the people. The general will could therefore only be expressed through its representatives and, from the moment of their election, the law enacted by representatives amounted to the 'expression of the general will.'"[39] This understanding represents a vital strand of the French constitutional tradition. Like Jaume, John Bell traces this understanding to the Revolution and describes the *loi* as the highest authority in France because it is "an expression of the general will."[40] Similarly, Alec Stone Sweet argues that "from the first moments of the Revolution, the Rousseauian identification of legislation with the general will, and legislators with popular sovereignty, were constitutionally enshrined."[41] Thus parliamentary supremacy reigned in France as the embodiment of the active sovereign. The statutes Parliament passed were not subject to constitutional limitation in the American sense: The formal separation of powers precluded the empowerment of the judiciary to hold Parliament to the Constitution. To do so would grant the judiciary the power to engage in *lawmaking*, violating both the separation of powers and national sovereignty.

Constitutional Review and the Separation of Powers

This formal understanding of the separation of powers prevailed on the Continent. Yet much like in the Westminster model, a refusal to grant the judiciary jurisdiction over the constitution, rejecting judicial review, did not mean rejecting independent courts when it came to ordinary law. The judiciary was seen as essential to the rule of law; it was in the business of adjudicating legal disputes, which required applying legal rules created by another branch to particular cases. To fairly and faithfully do so required the judiciary to stand apart from the politics of creating law. It was against this backdrop that Kelsen developed unique constitutional courts empowered to exercise constitutional review. As supreme law, Kelsen thought, a constitution must bind ordinary law. Yet accepting the continental understanding of separated powers, he did not think the judiciary was in a position to enforce the constitution against acts of parliament. As Kelsen articulated it, declaring a law unconstitutional was more akin to a legislative act—the "decision of the Constitutional Court [is] a negative act of legislation"[42]—than a judicial act. Kelsen thus sought to create specialized constitutional courts, separate from ordinary judicial institutions, that were vested with the central authority to enforce the written constitution by way of constitutional review. While there is variation, the general European model embraced a centralized and specialized institution responsible for constitutional adjudication. And while this was understood as a formal law-like process with constitutional courts as the mouthpiece of the constitution in very much the way that the judiciary was understood to formally and rationally apply legal rules, it was entirely separate from ordinary courts and law. It was, for Kelsen, a legal-political way of enforcing the constitution, but one that was situated outside the ordinary institutions of government. In profound contrast to the Madisonian understanding, Kelsen insisted that the power to act as "guardian of the constitution" could not be conferred "upon one of the organs whose acts are to be subjected to control."[43] For Kelsen, constitutional courts fit with the European separation of powers because the parliament remained the key lawmaking body and the judiciary remained the interpreter of the laws it passed.[44] Constitutional courts sit in a unique constitutional space. They are tasked with enforcing the separation of powers and the constitution, but in theory exist outside of both.[45] Favoreu, a leading French advocate of this model, positions constitutional courts as a power "above the others that is charged with monitoring the three essential functions of the state (executive, legislative, and judicial) to ensure that they are exercised within the limits set by the Constitution."[46] Kelsen's model of a constitutional court first found expression in the Austrian Constitution of 1920–34, which the jurist had a hand in drafting, but would more fully develop as the "European Model" after World War II. Specialized constitutional courts situated as the supreme guardian of a written constitution that usually included a charter of fundamental rights were a distinct feature of what Martin Shapiro and Alec Stone Sweet call "the new constitutionalism" that emerged in Western Europe after World War II.

In Germany, the Federal Constitutional Court (FCC) is tasked as the guardian of the Basic Law. As the guardian of the Basic Law, the FCC plays a key role in overseeing the integrity of the three branches and maintaining the proper balance among them. In fact, the Basic Law confers on the FCC express authority to settle disputes among the highest institutions of the Federal Republic and textually specifies the separation of powers as an *unamendable* principle of Germany's constitutional order. Article 20 (2) proclaims that "all public authority emanates from the people," but then declares that "it shall be exercised . . . by specific legislative, executive, and judicial bodies." Article 79 (3) establishes the separation of these branches in perpetuity by "[prohibiting] any amendment to this Basic Law affecting the . . . principles laid down in [this] Article."[47]

Burt Neuborne situates the French Constitutional Council (CC) in similar terms—as a neutral arbiter of the separation of powers and guardian of the Constitution.[48] The Constitution of 1958, which brought the Fifth Republic into being, created a Constitutional Council that was textually marked off from judicial authority.[49] Like the German FCC, the Constitutional Council is tasked with enforcing the Constitution and its decisions are binding on all public authorities. But the Council operates in a unique way. When statutes are challenged on constitutional grounds (and initially they could only be challenged by various government officers) they go to the Council prior to being promulgated as law. Should the Council find a statute unconstitutional, the Constitution commands that it not be promulgated or implemented—so, in fact, it would never become law. Constitutional review as exercised by the Council in these cases is both abstract and *a priori*. Neuborne characterizes the Council based on Montesquieu's division of the operations of government: the enunciation of rules, the implementation of rules, and the particularization of rules.[50] The legislative body announces rules, the executive implements the rules, and the judiciary applies rules to particular cases. While Neuborne concedes this model is simplistic, it is nevertheless helpful.

The crucial feature of the European separation of powers is that specified functions belong to particular branches and those branches are confined to their respective sphere. This is about the integrity and functionality of each institution wielding a distinct kind of power assigned to the appropriate institutional body. It is inappropriate, for example, for the executive to engage in lawmaking functions. If the executive intrudes into the lawmaking realm or acts without legislative authorization, the executive is seeking "both the power to enunciate rules and the power to implement them."[51] The Council then enforces the negative and functional aspects of the separation of powers by forging "judicially defined limits on legislative, executive, and judicial behavior."[52] The French separation of powers follows Montesquieu's insistence that an independent body is necessary to apply the "particularization" function—that is, to apply a general rule to a concrete case. Even in protecting fundamental rights, Neuborne argues that the Council follows the logic of separated power by ensuring that each institution exercises its powers within the confines of its function.

Constitutional Law over Constitutional Politics?

Constitutional courts were developed in the postwar period precisely because jurists like Kelsen argued that enforcing a constitution was not part of the ordinary legal and judicial duties bestowed on courts within the separation of powers. Such a power was, in short, a political power to act as guardian of the constitution. Unlike ordinary courts of law, constitutional courts would sit outside of the normal political process, exercising a legal-political power to enforce the constitution in a very legalistic manner. This development casts a constitution itself in profoundly legalistic terms and relies on law-like enforcement in an attempt to avoid—or perhaps transcend—politics in enforcing the constitution. Notice that this understanding of the separation of powers, while embracing the notion of diffuse power, does not include the complementary principle of checks and balances. Indeed, as a matter of theory, the idea of checks and balances does not apply to an institution like the Constitutional Council or a constitutional court that is tasked with enforcing the rules of the game.[53] The body that enforces the rules is a unique and specialized organ that acts as a neutral arbiter of rules, standing apart from ordinary politics as the umpire of constitutional processes. Dominque Rousseau, a skeptic, nevertheless captures this understanding: "The Council adds nothing, creates nothing; it merely applies to Parlement a norm whose meaning constrains Parlement and subjects the legislator to a norm that the Council itself must obey and for which it is only a spokesperson."[54]

Given recent developments in the French Constitution that provide for constitutional review of legislation after the fact, Federico Fabbrini argues that the Council has truly become a constitutional court in Kelsen's terms—an independent tribunal tasked with safeguarding the Constitution: "The constitutional judge is the guardian of the fundamental values enshrined in the Constitution."[55] Whatever the particulars of this debate, the crucial point for my purposes is that the European tradition of the separation of powers does not embrace the American corollary of checks and balances: "Functions are separated, following Montesquieu, but the imperative is to enable the institutions of the state to exercise public power for the public good."[56] Madisonian checks and balances are largely precluded from this conceptualization.

Critics like Dominique Rousseau are skeptical of the idea that constitutional courts exist outside the separation of powers to enforce it and act as the guardian of the constitution in an apolitical and juridic fashion. Can a political body tasked with protecting the constitution truly operate in an essentially legalistic fashion? The appointment of judges to constitutional courts might be seen as a check on them and an indication that they are not truly outside the separation of powers. In Germany, judges on the FCC are elected by the legislature and must get a two-thirds vote. They serve for a twelve-year term but must retire at sixty-eight and are not eligible for reelection. The French CC has nine members, who serve a single nine-year term with a three-year rotation. Three new judges are appointed every three years, one each by the president of France, the president of the National Assembly, and the president of the Senate. In the UK, with a much more limited Supreme Court, which only recently was enabled to decide a narrow range of constitutional questions, twelve judges are appointed as members of the House of Lords. New justices are selected by a commission on judicial appointments, which includes two sitting judges (the president and vice president of the Supreme Court). The commission's selection is then referred by the prime minister to the monarch. And while jurisdiction is often conferred by the constitution—as in Germany and France—this can be altered by legislation.

Far more controversial, however, is the argument that constitutional courts exist outside of politics in their own peculiar constitutional space. How best to characterize constitutional courts (including France's CC), particularly in relation to the separation of powers, is the subject of much debate.

And much of this debate turns on the formal distinction between law and politics. Kelsen and those following him have a formalistic view of law. Law is the application of norms (rules) to cases in a clear and logical manner. In the application of rules, judges are understood to be neutral and faithful arbitrators but not judicial "automatons." This is in contrast to creating law, where there is complete discretion and creativity; bargaining, compromise, and pushing a particular agenda are all ordinary features of the law-making process. This is the world of politics. A constitution limits this world of discretion. It leaves plenty of play for politics within the legislature in creating law, but it also limits that discretion with constitutional rules that constrain the power of lawmaking. The application of these constitutional rules (norms in Kelsen's terms) falls to constitutional courts because they are, theoretically, concerned only with following the constitution. "According to classical separation-of-powers theory," judges are slaves to the constitution.[57] They do not exercise a will of their own. In Kelsen's pure world of law, constitutional courts are beyond politics because their decisions are "absolutely determined by the constitution."[58] To be fair, Kelsen was not naïve about politics. In fact, he sought to create constitutional courts to act as guardians of the constitution precisely because he recognized that enforcing the constitution was a political-legal act that could not be conferred on ordinary courts of law or any of the ordinary institutions of government. Yet his solution to this dilemma relies on a deeply legalistic understanding of the constitution and constitutional enforcement.

Stone Sweet raise doubts about the distinction between law and politics at the heart of Kelsen's idealized version of constitutional courts: A pure legal realm beyond politics is an impossible fiction. It is not simply that the application of a constitution will always allow for some discretion (a point Kelsen himself insisted on).[59] Yet when we situate a constitutional court within a set of institutions responsible for maintaining and enforcing a constitution, even if it is theoretically the umpire of the system, it inexorably becomes part of the political and lawmaking process.[60] This is particularly true of the French Constitutional Council's abstract and *a priori* constitutional review, which essentially extends the lawmaking process—bringing the Council in to decide the constitutionality of a statute in what otherwise would be the end of the lawmaking process.[61] Political debate over lawmaking turns into constitutional debate as bills inevitably get referred to the Council for political/constitutional reasons and not just as a matter of law. Dominque Rousseau, from inside the French academy, sees France's CC as part of the balance of power among three competing institutions—the government, parliament, and the Council—in articulating constitutional norms.[62] Skeptics of such a formal distinction between law and politics think this is true whether constitutional courts exercise abstract review, as they do in France and Germany, whether it is *a priori* or *a posteriori*, or whether it is concrete review where the constitutional court decides a concrete case as it does in the American scheme of judicial review. Inevitably, constitutional courts shape how politics is conducted by the other branches of government and cannot sit in an independent constitutional space.

Even if we think of constitutional courts as faithfully applying the rules of the constitution to questions before them, the court has discretion in exercising its judgment. Applying a written constitution is not simply a mechanical process; it allows for discretion in reaching constitutional judgments. In theory, judges can be treated as absolutely bound by the constitution, but in practice they must exercise judgment that determines how to understand the constitution. That does not mean all such judgments are political, but, just as surely, it is difficult to adhere to the simple fiction that judges are merely the mouthpiece of the constitution—constitutions do not speak for themselves. The important question may be the mindset that members of constitutional courts adhere to—do they strive to apply constitutional rules in a neutral manner? I take it this is a central contention of Carrese's chapter—that judges who stop believing in the formality of the law begin to act more politically. We can accept that judges have discretion—and must exercise judgment—while still thinking that this activity, at its best, is different from ordinary politics. Such discretion has almost certainly increased as constitutional courts have taken up the protection of abstract rights, which Kelsen's original defense precluded. Indeed, Kelsen's ideal constitutional court focused only on enforcing basic constitutional rules precisely because protecting constitutional rights would draw these courts into the political process. Yet as developed in the second half of the twentieth century, European constitutional courts have become protectors of rights. For Stone Sweet, this has meant that constitutional courts have become "'positive legislators.'"[63] Even so, we might appreciate how constitutions try to shape politics in important ways that limit ordinary political discretion, narrowing the terrain of politics by way of constitutional law even while recognizing that constitutional law requires some discretion in order to render constitutional judgments.

Conclusion

The prevailing conception of the separation of powers in Europe diverges from the American Madisonian understanding in important ways, yet the foundational questions raised about law and politics within the separation of powers should strike American readers as deeply familiar. Indeed, even the idea of a constitutional court that stands apart from other institutions as the defender of the constitution finds powerful expression in America. In analyzing modern constitutionalism, Charles McIlwain insisted, "the doctrine of the separation of powers has no true application to judicial matters." McIlwain went on to argue that, historically speaking, the whole idea of checks and balances as a political feature had "no institutional background whatever except in the imaginations of closet philosophers like Montesquieu."[64] McIlwain insisted that limits on government by way of law, the defining feature of modern constitutionalism for him, should be altogether distanced from the separation of powers. The crucial point is that the body trusted with enforcing the law—and treating the constitution as higher law—does not exist within the ordinary give and take of the separation of powers and is not subject to checks and balances. It stands, rather, as an umpire of the constitutional system; it is uniquely situated to enforce the constitution as law precisely because it stands outside of politics.

Obviously, McIlwain's contentions are remarkably similar to the arguments for constitutional courts developed by Kelsen. Yet they have deep roots in American constitutionalism that point to tensions in the separation of powers. I have argued that the Madisonian separation of powers should be seen first and foremost in functional terms—assigning the functions of government to uniquely crafted political institutions. One feature of this specialized function is to separate institutions tasked with legal decision-making from those engaged in more ordinary politics, which creates a division between law and politics at the heart of the separation of powers; it also gives voice to the most famous statement in separation of powers—that the judiciary must be independent of the executive and legislature. This is so even in parliamentary systems (like the Westminster model) that resist the separation of powers more generally. But this raises questions of whether it is proper to think of checks on institutions tasked with adjudicating the law. Concerns along these lines are only heightened when we treat constitutions as law. Such concerns paved the way for unique constitutional courts that sit outside the traditional categories of state power. While America has a quite different legal tradition than continental Europe, there are nevertheless efforts to situate courts as neutral umpires outside the separation of powers even while building on it.

In *Federalist* No. 78, Hamilton argued the "interpretation of the laws is the proper and peculiar province of the courts. A constitution is, in fact, and must be regarded by the judges as, a fundamental law. It therefore belongs to them to ascertain its meaning as well as the meaning of any particular act proceeding from the legislative body."[65] Hamilton went on to call the judiciary the "faithful guardian of the Constitution." And this was due to the judiciary's unique independence from politics as well as the appointment of justices "who unite the requisite integrity with the requisite knowledge" to adjudicate constitutional law. (In France, members of the Council are referred to as *les sages*, the knowledgeable ones.) Yet we should not be alarmed at the judiciary's unique position, because, unlike the other branches, it is bound by law and must stay outside of politics. Hamilton even followed Montesquieu's insistence that judicial power was negligible because it was simply the pronunciation of rules. Marshall's famous *Marbury* opinion similarly plays up the judiciary's unique position in interpreting the law: "It is emphatically the province and duty of the judicial department to say what the law is." Even more, it is the very "essence of judicial duty" to sort out a conflict of laws.[66] Like Hamilton, Marshall insisted that courts could not have a will of their own because they are bound by the law (the Constitution in this case). In *Marbury*, Marshall insisted he could decide the case before him only because it was a *legal* question before the court. The corollary is that political questions could never properly be decided by the judicial branch: The law binds and limits judges who in articulating its principles just happen to bind the other branches to its commands.

The distinction between law and politics is at the heart of Hamilton's and Marshall's justification of judicial review much in the same way that it is central to the development of Kelsen's constitutional courts. These arguments are rooted in the unique nature of the judiciary and the place of law within the separation of powers. At the same time, as Kelsen recognized, when the constitution is considered higher law, it removes the institution legally enforcing the law of the constitution from the scheme of separated powers. But can this be done? Or does it, as Stone Sweet suggests, "subvert separation of powers schemes"?[67] These are long-standing concerns in both America and Europe. Indeed, Edouard Lambert, a French academic, wrote *Le Gouvernement des judges et la lutte contre la legislation sociale aux Etats-Unis* criticizing "government by judiciary" in America as a violation of the separation of powers in the early years of the twentieth century. A century later, these concerns continue apace in both Europe and America.[68]

Situating the Madisonian separation of powers in comparative constitutional perspective illuminates the functional logic of the separation and helps distinguish it from related political principles like the diffusion of power and the idea of checks and balances. And while the American and European separation of powers diverge in important ways, there are important areas of convergence. If the "new constitutionalism" in Europe with its "new" separation of powers attempted to overcome the tension between constitutional law and politics, it is not clear it has. This may be, as I think Madison recognized, an impossible task. Here, in fact, critics of Europe's constitutional courts as existing outside of politics in their own constitutional space find common cause with American critics of judicial supremacy and the idea that the Supreme Court is simply the legal umpire of the constitutional system. Both reject this veneer of formalism, insisting that courts must be situated as part of constitutional politics within a constitutional order of diffuse and separated power. What is essential here—and revealing of modern constitutionalism as a complex form of democracy—is the balance between different institutions that represent an insoluble tension between law and politics within a constitutional scheme that cannot be reduced to a single constitutional value, nor can it be captured by a single constitutional institution. Conflict between constitutional values and institutions is inherent to the constitutional enterprise.

Notes

1. Alexander Hamilton, James Madison, and John Jay, *The Federalist Papers*, ed. Ian Shapiro (New Haven: Yale University Press, 2009), 245.

2. Hamilton et al., *Federalist* No. 47, 246.

3. Bruce Ackerman, "The New Separation of Powers," *Harvard Law Review* 113 (3) 2000: 638.

4. Jeremy Waldron, *Political Political Theory* (Cambridge: Harvard University Press, 2016), 49.

5. Walter Bagehot, *The English Constitution* (New York: Oxford University Press, 2001), 160–61.

6. Michel Rosenfeld, "Constitutional Adjudication in Europe and the United States: Paradoxes and Contrasts," *I Con*, vol. 2, no. 4 (2004): 637.

7. Burt Neuborne, "Judicial Review and Separation of Powers in France and the United States," *New York University Law Review* 57 (3) 1982: 375–76; Alec Stone, *The Birth of Judicial Politics in France: The Constitutional Council in Comparative Perspective* (New York: Oxford University Press, 1992).

8. Hans Kelsen, "Judicial Review of Legislation: A Comparative Study of the Austrian and the American Constitution" *Journal of Politics*, vol. 4, no. 2 (1942): 183–200.

9. Alec Stone Sweet, *Governing with Judges: Constitutional Politics in Europe* (New York: Oxford University Press, 2000), 33.

10. Louis Favoreu, "Constitutional Review in Europe," in *Constitutionalism and Rights: The Influence of the United States Constitution Abroad*, ed. Louis Henkin and Albert Rosenthal (New York: Columbia University Press, 1990), 55.

11. Favoreu, "Constitutional Review in Europe," 56.

12. Francis Fukuyama, *Political Order and Political Decay* (New York: Profile Books, 2019), 488; Ackerman, "The New Separation of Powers," 640.

13. George Thomas, *The (Un)Written Constitution* (New York: Oxford University Press, 2021), 144.

14. Hamilton et al., *The Federalist* No. 47, 246.

15. George Thomas, *The Madisonian Constitution* (Baltimore: Johns Hopkins University Press, 2008), 21–24.

16. Thomas, *The (Un)Written Constitution*, 88. See *Morrison v. Olson* 487 U.S. 645 (1988), Scalia dissenting at 697–699.

17. Hamilton et al., *The Federalist* No. 47, 246.

18. Hamilton et al., *The Federalist* No. 37, 182.

19. Hamilton et al., *The Federalist* No. 47, 247.

20. Hamilton et al., *The Federalist* No. 51, 264.

21. Thomas, *The (Un)Written Constitution*, 86–89.

22. Thomas, *The Madisonian Constitution*, 16–17; Hamilton et al., *Federalist* No. 51, 266.

23. Ackerman, "The New Separation of Powers," 640. Given that both Montesquieu and Madison draw on the British experience in advocating their understandings of the separation of powers, it is not clear this critique applies to them nearly as powerfully as latter-day advocates of presidentialism who do not as carefully attend to the details of their arguments. See Steven G. Calabresi, "The Virtues of Presidential Government," *Constitutional Commentary* 18, 51 (2001).

24. Cindy Skach, "The 'Newest' Separation of Powers: Semi-Presidentialism," *I Con*, vol. 5, no. 1 (2007): 93–121.

25. Walter Bagehot, *The English Constitution* (New York: Oxford University Press, 2001), 14.

26. Jean-Jacques Rousseau, *The Social Contract and the First and Second Discourses*, ed. Susan Dunn (New Haven: Yale University Press, 2002), 171.

27. Bagehot, *The English Constitution*, 160.

28. Ackerman, "The New Separation of Powers," 643.

29. Bagehot, *The English Constitution*, 23.

30. Hamilton et al., *Federalist* No. 47, 246.

31. Hamilton et al., *Federalist* No. 47, 247.

32. Cheryl Saunders, "Theoretical Underpinnings of Separation of Powers," in *Comparative Constitutional Theory*, ed. Gary Jacobsohn and Miguel Schor (Elgar Publishing, 2016), 71.

33. Alfred Stepan and Cindy Skach, "Constitutional Frameworks and Democratic Consolidation: Parliamentarianism versus Presidentialism," *World Politics* 46 (October 1993): 3.

34. Martin Loughlin, *The British Constitution* (New York: Oxford University Press, 2013).

35. Rosenfeld, "Constitutional Adjudication in Europe and the United States," 633.

36. Federico Fabbrini, "Kelsen in Paris: France's Constitutional Reform and the Introduction of A Posteriori Constitutional Review of Legislation" *German Law Journal*, vol. 9, no. 10 (2008): 1300.

37. Stone, *The Birth of Judicial Politics in France*, 227. Fabbrini, "Kelsen in Paris," 1301. We should recall that jurists in America, such as John Bannister Gibson, denied that the Constitution could "come before the Court" for strikingly similar reasons. Thomas, *The Madisonian Constitution*, 29.

38. Stone, *The Birth of Judicial Politics in France*, 24. Rousseau, *The Social Contract*, 179.

39. Lucien Jaume, "The Constituent Power in France: The Revolution and Its Consequences," in Martin Loughlin and Neil Walker, eds., *The Paradox of Constitutionalism: Constituent Power and Constitutional Form* (New York: Oxford University Press, 2007), 79–80.

40. John Bell, *French Constitutional Law* (New York: Oxford University Press, 1992), 80, 84.

41. Stone, *The Birth of Judicial Politics in France*, 24.

42. Kelsen, "Judicial Review of Legislation," 187.

43. Hans Kelsen, "Who Ought to Be the Guardian of the Constitution?" in Lars Vinx, ed., *The Guardian of the Constitution: Hans Kelsen and Carl Schmitt on the Limits of Constitutional Law* (New York: Cambridge University Press, 2015), 175.

44. Kelsen did not view the judge as a "legal automaton," but as exercising a distinct function within the separation of powers that is different from lawmaking. Kelsen, "Who Ought to Be the Guardian of the Constitution?", 189.

45. Alec Stone Sweet, "Constitutional Courts," in Michel Rosenfeld and Andras Sajo, eds., *The Oxford Handbook of Comparative Constitutional Law* (New York: Oxford University Press, 2012), 818.

46. Favoreu, "Constitutional Review in Europe," 56.

47. Donald Kommers, John Finn, Gary Jacobsohn, George Thomas, and Justin Dyer, *American Constitutional Law: Governmental Powers and Democracy* (St. Paul, MN: West Academic Publishing, 2018), 198–99.

48. Neuborne, "Judicial Review and Separation of Powers in France and the United States."

49. Stone, *The Birth of Judicial Politics in France*, 11.

50. Neuborne, "Judicial Review and Separation of Powers in France and the United States," 370.

51. Neuborne, "Judicial Review and Separation of Powers in France and the United States," 387.

52. Neuborne, "Judicial Review and Separation of Powers in France and the United States," 382.

53. Yes, constitutional courts are subject to membership and jurisdiction, which might be understood as checks on their power; yet the language does not recognize these as checks.

54. Dominque Rousseau, "The Constitutional Judge: Master or Slave of the Constitution," *Cardozo Law Review*, 14, 775 (1992): 775. See also Rousseau, "The Conseil Constitutionnel Confronted with Comparative Law and the Theory of Constitutional Jurisprudence (or Louis Favoreu's Untenable Paradoxes)," *I Con*, vol. 5, no. 1 (2007): 28–43.

55. Fabbrini, "Kelsen in Paris," 1311.

56. Saunders, "Theoretical Underpinnings of Separation of Powers," 83.

57. Stone Sweet, "The Politics of Constitutional Review in France and Europe," *I Con*, vol. 5, no. 1 (2007): 77.

58. Stone, *The Birth of Judicial Politics in France*, 229.

59. Stone Sweet, "Constitutional Courts and Parliamentary Democracy," *West European Politics*, vol. 25, no. 1 (January 2002): 816.

60. Stone, *The Birth of Judicial Politics in France*, 234.

61. Stone, *The Birth of Judicial Politics in France*, 231.

62. Rousseau, "The Conseil Constitutionnel Confronted with Comparative Law and the Theory of Constitutional Justice," 39–40.

63. Stone Sweet, "Constitutional Courts," 827.

64. Charles Howard McIlwain, *Constitutionalism: Ancient and Modern* (Indianapolis, IN: Liberty Fund, 1947), 132.

65. Thomas, *The Madisonian Constitution*, 34.

66. Thomas, *The Madisonian Constitution*, 30.

67. Stone Sweet, "Constitutional Courts," 817.

68. Such critiques include Boudin, *Government by Judiciary* (Ann Arbor, MI: W. Godwyn, 1932); Raoul Berger, *Government by Judiciary: The Transformation of the Fourteenth Amendment* (Cambridge, MA: Harvard University Press, 1977); Stone Sweet, *Governing with Judges* (2000); Ran Hirschl, *Towards Juristocracy: The Origins and Consequences of the New Constitutionalism* (Cambridge, MA: Harvard University Press, 2007).

CHAPTER 4

Originalism, Moral Objectivity, and the Lost Constitutionalism

Sotirios A. Barber

At the end of his first presidential term in 2021, Donald Trump had appointed more than 25 percent of the federal judiciary, including a third of both the federal appeals courts and the US Supreme Court. Many of these judges profess an originalist approach to constitutional meaning. Though the precise meaning of originalism has never been clear, prominent self-styled originalists (Clarence Thomas, Richard Epstein, Randy Barnett) regard the present national state as an unconstitutional development.[1] They profess fidelity to what Barnett calls the "lost constitution" of the American founding.[2] I argue here that while America's true constitution has indeed been lost, the lost constitution is a positive or ends-oriented, pro-government constitution, not the negative constitution of libertarians like Barnett. This lost constitution reflects a positive constitutionalism, and this positive constitutionalism makes better historical and textual sense than negative constitutionalism. Positive constitutionalism also makes better sense practically, for it alone supports what hope there may be for a government that meets the nation's challenges in morally defensible ways.

The Lost Constitutionalism

The lost element of Barnett's lost constitution is what he calls "the presumption of liberty." He believes that judges ought to entertain this presumption in cases involving the scope of governmental power vis-à-vis private power or liberty. Barnett's presumption is against government. It requires governments to satisfy libertarian judges that laws are both necessary and proper to pursue constitutionally authorized ends, like national security and prosperity. This presumption of liberty contrasts with the presumption of constitutionality—the presumption that laws are constitutional unless shown to violate structural principles and liberties that, says Barnett, are "somehow 'fundamental.'"[3] Barnett's actual presumption is not of liberty simply, however; it is a presumption of a kind of liberty, namely liberty *from government*—in America's case, not private governments, like neighborhood gangs, large corporations, and the market, but electorally accountable, constitutional governments of the nation and the states. Liberty-from-government is not liberty simply, for it can mean a loss of liberty when no government addresses threats to liberty from third parties like Randy DeShaney.[4] Randy beat his four-year-old son Joshua into a permanently retarded state. Joshua's mother, divorced from Randy, sued county officials under the Fourteenth Amendment for failing to protect Joshua. In an opinion emblematic of negative constitutionalism, William Rehnquist opined for the Supreme Court that even after repeated reports of child abuse from ER personnel, a county welfare agency had no federal constitutional duty to protect Joshua. Justices Roberts and Thomas cited *DeShaney* with approval in their dissents in *Obergefell v. Hodges*.[5] Though Barnett holds with Locke that government emerged to answer threats to liberty from private power,[6] he seems to assume that once government is established, private power (liberty in private hands) is less a threat to liberty than public power. More than this, Barnett assumes that once government is established to address private power's threat to liberty, protecting private power from government somehow becomes an end of government—indeed, the end of government. Accordingly, he would require America's state and national governments to show that their actions comport with a broader constitutional commitment to private power (abstract liberty) over public power. To restore this lost presumption of liberty against the national government, Barnett would return to a states' rights reading of the enumeration of powers in Article I, sec 8, the necessary and proper clause, and the Ninth and Tenth Amendments.[7] To restore the presumption of liberty against the state governments, Barnett would reverse the Supreme Court's states' rights reading of the privileges and immunities clause of the Fourteenth Amendment.[8]

In *Legacies of Losing in American Politics*, Jeffrey Tulis and Nicole Mellow show that the lost constitution is not the constitution that seeks primarily to limit government, but the constitution that seeks primarily to enable government.[9] This is the pro-government, ends-oriented constitution of the Federalist Party, the party whose leading voice declares in *Federalist* No. 1 that "the vigor of government is essential to the security of liberty" and that "a dangerous ambition more often lurks behind the specious mask of zeal for the rights of the people than under the forbidding appearance of zeal for the firmness and efficiency of government."[10] Tulis and Mellow show that the administrative state is at home in this constitution of the Federalist Party, and that the positive constitution is now a lost constitution because both the American Right and the mainstream American Left see the Constitution as designed chiefly to limit government, not to empower it.

Tulis and Mellow show that negative constitutionalism is a legacy of the Anti-Federalists. Though they lost their campaign against the Constitution, the Anti-Federalists won the battle over how to interpret the Constitution; hence our anti-government interpretation of a pro-government constitution.[11] The findings of Tulis and Mellow would leave right-wing constitutionalism adrift because they force rightists to make an argument of the kind that their originalism forbids. If the history of the American founding fails to support their opposition to a strong state, or if that history speaks equivocally, rightists must defend negative constitutionalism with a moral argument, and this would mean abandoning their originalism.

Though the findings of Tulis and Mellow are unassailable, I need not treat them as authoritative here, for this essay is an exercise in normative theory and (*pace* originalism) normative conclusions cannot follow from historical facts. The constitutional document in fact does read as an instrumental norm—a set of means to preambular ends, public purposes all. The winners of the ratification debate—namely, the Federalists—in fact did plan for a strong national government, "adequate to the exigencies of government."[12] But nothing normative follows from these facts. How judges or anyone else ought to read the US Constitution is a moral question; answering it demands a moral argument.

If we treat the question of the Constitution's basic normative character as the moral question that it is, Tulis and Mellow will win the contest for how to describe the American founding. This conclusion is a matter of simple practical reasonableness: Negative constitutionalists cannot make sense of the American founding as a rational act. The founding *established* a government *de novo*; it did not restrain a government that was already established. If by liberty one means liberty from government, or if government threatens liberty more than private power, establishing a government to secure liberty makes no sense. Liberty from government cannot be the end of government for liberty from government is secured best where there is no government; liberty from government is perfectly secure in a state of nature. Nor does establishing government make sense if harm from government is seen as more likely than benefits from government. Establishing a government for the *chief* purpose of limiting it is as pointless as inventing a machine to impede its functioning.

How, then, did America's pro-government party lose the debate over how to read a pro-government constitution? Tulis and Mellow submit an answer that affirms the Anti-Federalists' leading argument against the Constitution: A big country with diverse political and economic cultures is unsuited for peaceful rule by one national government. In 1789 (even today?), democratic union was, at best, a remote aspiration. Tulis and Mellow emphasize how the nation's divisions made the framers' proposal a radical proposal—"a plan for a new way of life, not just a new arrangement of power."[13] This situation compelled supporters of the proposed government to mollify the Anti-Federalist opposition. This the Federalists tried to do by denying what the Anti-Federalists correctly saw as the Constitution's consolidationist or big-government logic.

Thus, in answer to Anti-Federalist charges that a consolidation of government was afoot, Hamilton predicted in *Federalist* No. 17 that "the mere domestic police of a State" or "the supervision of agriculture" "can never be desirable cares of a general jurisdiction."[14] Yet in *Federalist* No. 23 Hamilton conceived limited government as limited only by its ends, not in the means for pursuing those ends, and later in the same paper he conceived those ends as "the most essential national concerns," namely the nation's external defense and internal commerce.[15] This confusion about the Constitution's logic combined with other factors to create an opening for what Tulis and Mellow call the "Anti-Federalist appropriation" of the American founding: an anti-government construction of a pro-government constitution.

Factors other than the Anti-Federalist appropriation include the social conditions for its success over the years. Among these we can number the nation's cultural divisions, ignorance of the founding among political progressives spawned by memories of racial injustice, Marxist historiography, and a general depreciation of tradition in societies committed to growth through technological innovation. I dwell here on an additional reason for the loss of the Federalist constitution: declining belief in the possibility that propositions of political morality can be true or false. Just as an Anti-Federalist construction of the Federalist constitution is common to the mainstream American

Right and Left, so is the belief that propositions about good and bad, right and wrong are matters of individual preference or social convention, matters for reporting in scare quotes. Mainstream liberals argue for a living Constitution largely from an openly historicist or conventionalist rejection of trans-historical values and the additional claim (a contradiction, not an entailment) that each generation has a right to live by its own standards.

So, the Left's denial of an objective morality is no surprise. But the case is otherwise with the American Right. Some of its leading figures claim that its originalist approach to constitutional interpretation reflects its commitment to the natural law philosophy of the American founding.[16] This claim is false.

The Interpretive Debate and the Constitution as a Whole

The American debate over how to find what the Constitution means is several questions lumped together. Participants in the debate are not always aware of what question they are answering or how their answers are being received. Whether, in a concrete case, a command of equal protection permits a state law banning interracial marriage involves many questions, including: what the equal protection clause permits or proscribes; the meaning and weight of precedent cases; how to dispose of the instant case under present social circumstances; how to divide governmental functions among different institutions; and the normative character of the basic law as a whole—whether, in particular, it is designed chiefly to enable power or to limit it. *Naim v. Naim* (1956)[17] has long illustrated the difference between what the law means and what a court should do on a given occasion. Though Virginia's ban on interracial marriage clashed with *Brown v. Bd. of Ed.* (1954), that fact alone could not compel the Supreme Court to say so in 1956. Prudence, not precedent, determined what to do in a time of what southern politicians called "massive resistance" to the *Brown* decision. Indeed, prudence was more than a counsel of prudence; for judges who take the Constitution at its word, prudence was a constitutional command.[18] The preamble of the Constitution indicates that the articles that follow the Preamble are ordained and established to pursue the ends listed in the Preamble. This makes the Constitution as a whole an instrumental norm. Instrumental norms counsel actions that advance their ends, and what advances an end in particular circumstances depends on those circumstances.

Courts should therefore construe the equal protection clause to further the end for which it was established. Like the Constitution as a whole, the equal protection clause makes sense only as means to a desirable state of affairs, like a color-blind government or, what's different, an equal opportunity society (more on this later). But judicial decisions occur in concrete historical circumstances, and constitutional decisions apply to material conditions that change with time. Applying the law in a doctrinaire fashion at the wrong time can defeat the purposes of the law's establishment. This was the situation in *Naim*, and the court did the constitutional thing in that case by punting to the future. Prudence is integral to the application of an instrumental norm and treating the Constitution as an instrumental norm is simply a matter of fidelity to what the Constitution actually says.

On the other hand, prudence itself may reject a policy of strict fidelity to what the Constitution says, for openly prudential adjudication may expose a truth of constitutional democracy that a democratic culture cannot abide: its dependence on what amounts to an aristocracy—for those societies lucky enough to generate an aristocracy. The Constitution is an instrumental norm. Period. But this truth determines no act, including the act of disclosing this truth to the public and the further act of deciding concrete cases consistently with this truth. An argument against disclosing this truth to the public flows from the declaration in Article VI that the Constitution is law. Conventionally, law suggests not an instrumental norm but a regulatory norm, a norm regulating the government. Viewed from the supremacy clause of Article VI, the Constitution envisions a certain quality of *government*, not a certain quality of society. From this view, the equal protection clause guarantees that government *will not deny* equal protection, *not* that the government will actively pursue an equal-opportunity society, for the pursuit of the latter may demand violation of the former (think of racial quotas).

Furthermore, an instrumental constitution would suppose one version or a range of mutually compatible versions of the good life, while renowned dictum has it that the Constitution is "made for people of fundamentally differing views."[19] People who identify with ways of life that fall outside the permissible range would see the Constitution as reducing them to second-class citizens, in violation of the equal protection command. Finally, an instrumental constitution risks elite rule, for instrumentalism implies prudence, and only public-spirited and competent individuals can be trusted with prudential authority. This is still a democracy, is it not?

A response to this argument could begin with a concession arguendo. Suppose the equal protection clause promised no more than a color-blind government. Though this concession seems modest, it would suffice to sink a negative view of the equal protection clause. A government empowered to redeem this promise would soon see that a racist population will not support a color-blind government. But if the Constitution guaranteed an equal protection government, then it would also provide the means to address conditions that defeat the possibility of such a government. If the government is a democracy, where public opinion eventually rules, a constitutional promise of equal protection would have to grant the government power to combat racist attitudes among its people. Put differently, a democratic constitution that promised a color-blind government would grant power to cultivate a color-blind society, as the US Constitution does in the enforcement provisions of the Civil War amendments. Our color-blind constitution therefore could not be made for people with *fundamentally* different views.

This does not mean that the American Constitution denies persons who happen to be racists equal protection, for the Constitution can protect them as persons, if not as racists. Racism is not integral to personhood; racism is a set of attitudes and beliefs that persons acquire and that persons can shed, attitudes and beliefs that must be combated if the constitutional government is to keep a promise of equal protection, however defined. Delivery on the promise of a color-blind government thus entails a power to cultivate people's attitudes—constitutionally correct attitudes, if you will. To the national security and general national prosperity sought by (and for) the voting population of 1789,[20] one can therefore add the equal-opportunity society promised implicitly by the Civil War amendments.[21]

Many will resist this conclusion, for constitutionally correct sounds a lot like politically correct, and these days politically correct is politically incorrect. No problem: Nothing in the Constitution says anyone must approve of the equal protection clause or, for that matter, constitutional government itself. The Constitution leaves people free to think the Constitution is a mistake and even to counsel replacing it. Elitist judges in America have protected these rights against folks who profess to believe the Constitution sacred. And as the nation sinks from elitism toward a thuggish populism, critics of the Constitution can hope that their judges will continue to protect the right to criticize the Constitution.[22] In any case, the Constitution as written is an instrumental constitution, and an instrumental constitution that provides for judicial review requires judges virtuous enough to be trusted with prudential power. This can be an undemocratic result only on a view that holds democracy unable to institutionalize a concern for justice and other values—the real things.

Originalism and Moral Objectivity

The debate over how to find what the Constitution means should have ended if not with Ronald Dworkin's analysis of Richard Nixon's constitutionalism in 1972,[23] then certainly with Michael Moore's 1985 essay, "A Natural Law Theory of Interpretation."[24] Dworkin and Moore showed that judges can find constitutional meaning in hard cases only through moral judgments and that honest judges will admit the fact. Honest and good-faith judges will not hide behind the Framers' skirts. Judges worthy of their appointments will seek constitutional meaning through open, self-critical reflection and deliberation, and they will accept personal responsibility for their choices. Moral choice is unavoidable in hard cases; the only real question is whether these choices are responsibly made and openly defended. Originalism is either delusional or fraudulent.

Two broad considerations compel this conclusion. First, in hard cases, neither constitutional text nor constitutional history speaks unequivocally. Second, the meaning of a constitutional term cannot be reduced to anyone's concrete conception of that term—that is, someone's definition or example of an idea like equal protection, or liberty, or commerce, and so on. If equal protection means anything it means equal protection itself, a species of justice, and it is to justice that any conception of equal protection (any historical definition or example) is responsible. The same holds for constitutional ideas other than individual and minority rights, like ideas involving institutional functions and boundaries. I will show this momentarily with regard to the separation of powers.

Moore has argued at considerable length that, in the end, responsible and competent constitutional interpretation will include an all-things-considered judgment of what advances the good and just society.[25] Moore is an analytic philosopher. He applies technical teachings drawn from contemporary metaethics and the philosophies of language, action, mind, and law. But a common-sense reading of the Constitution's preamble will get you to the same place. The Preamble's list of public goods ("Justice," "the common Defence," the "Blessings of Liberty," etc.), along with its conspicuous omission of historically attractive goods like empire and salvation, amount to a bourgeois version of the good and just society.[26] The Preamble indicates that the articles in the body of the Constitution constitute a set of means to the ends that the Preamble enumerates. This is what the Constitution says, and if it means what it says, the Constitution is an instrumental norm and is to be construed as an instrumental norm (where harm does not come of it—remember the *Naim*). Background principles of practical reason give the rules for construing instrumental norms. Madison stated those rules in *Federalist* No. 40: First, if possible, every part of a legal command should be allowed some meaning and made to conspire to some common end. Second, where the parts cannot be made to coincide, sacrifice the less important to the more important, the means to the end.[27] Thus, the powers granted government are means to the public goods for which they were established and should be construed accordingly.

Moore defended his theory of interpretation through a thought experiment involving a hypothetical statute authorizing organ removal for transplant from patients who had died. The issue facing surgeons under this statute was whether prospective organ donors were actually dead. Just as we must concede a difference between "he's really dead" and "I/we think/say he's dead," we must and do distinguish between death, a natural state, and definitions of death, which definitions and examples of death are mere social/professional conventions. As an empirical generalization of everyday communication, people act as if the word death refers to the natural state and the natural state is normative for historical applications of the term and for conventional definitions and examples of the natural state. Thus, Moore observes that as the medical community discovered that patients whose heart and lungs had stopped could be revived, brain death replaced heart-lung stoppage as the definition of death, heart/lung stoppage ceased to be the point at which organs were removed, and though the definition of death changed, the referent of the word death remained the same. That is, "death" continued to refer to a natural state, not the definition of death. (Had "death" referred to a definition of death, we would end with an infinite regress. Nor could "death" refer to a definition of death consistently with the social practice of defining things, for definitions are not self-referential; they relate to things other than themselves.[28]) Moore's point is that as we changed our practice, we would feel no need to change the law that permitted organ removal only upon the donor's death. "Death" would have referred and would continue to refer to death, a natural state, not to our definitions of this natural state or to our old examples of this natural state or to our past applications of the word death. Moore thus characterizes not only our conventions regarding the word death, but also our presuppositions regarding reality, namely, the natural state of death itself *and* the responsibility of our linguistic practices (referring, defining, exemplifying) to that natural state. Whether there actually is a natural state to which the word death refers and to which our conventions are responsible, we cannot avoid thinking that there is.

Parallel reasoning holds for legal-moral ideas like equal protection, due process, and, more broadly, justice (equal protection and due process being forms of justice). Thus, we do and must think that there is a normative gap between justice and any conception of justice. If Hitler had achieved his Thousand-Year Reich, the difference between justice and the Reich's conception of justice would remain throughout that millennium, as before and after—or so those of us who use the term justice in everyday life do and must believe, no matter what we say for academic reasons. Claim that "justice" can refer only to some definition of justice, and we would have a choice between two results, both absurd: a word defining itself, or a word defining nothing at all.

If, following Moore, we exhaust the logical possibilities regarding the referents of legal-moral ideas like due process, we are left with one approach to constitutional interpretation in hard cases. Moore calls it the natural law approach, Dworkin calls it the moral reading, and James Fleming and I call it the philosophic approach. Resisting any such conclusion, originalists have reformulated their position several times in recent years. The effort has failed. Fleming has shown that all versions of originalism can be reduced to one of two forms: abstract originalism and concrete originalism. Because abstract originalism holds that "due process" refers to due process, the abstract idea, not to any historical definition, example, or application of the general idea, abstract originalism is equivalent to Dworkin's moral reading.[29] That leaves concrete originalism, no iteration of which can escape the incoherence of reducing a general idea either to some concrete definition or to some example of the idea

In any case, no one really rejects Dworkin's approach even though many claim they do. Right-wing jurists often say they reject it because they see little difference between it and the living Constitution approach that they associate with the old progressives and the old value-skeptical social scientists writing in constitutional law pre-Dworkin. But, however packaged, originalism is all pretext. Self-styled originalists are moral readers like everyone else; they just won't admit it—or, rather, to date they have chosen not to admit it. This may change now that they have firmed their hold on the federal judiciary.

To see the pretextual nature of originalism, consider the debate in *Obergefell v. Hodges* (2015).[30] Justice Kennedy appealed from traditional conceptions of sexual morality to a morality affirmed by "reasoned judgment." For himself and Justices Scalia and Thomas, Chief Justice Roberts replied with what amounted to his own moral reading. He appealed from tradition to an extratextual good with moral weight—from a tradition of judicially enforced constitutional principle to a majoritarian conception of democracy which he just assumed was closer to democracy itself, the real thing. Roberts also assumed that this real thing (i.e., democracy) had moral weight, for he made it part of an argument that ended in a rule of conduct: Let the several states decide the issue of same-sex marriage.

Roberts went further. His dissent separated democracy from fairness and the common good and accorded democracy more weight than fairness and the common good. Roberts conceded at the outset of his dissenting opinion that "petitioners make strong arguments rooted in social policy [i.e., the common good] and considerations of fairness." But, he added, "judges have power to say what the law is, not what it should be," and since "our Constitution does not enact any one theory of marriage" and same-sex marriage is not deeply rooted in American tradition, the Constitution leaves same-sex marriage to each state, and judicial preemption of the decision amounts to "stealing this issue" from the "democratic process." This was the gist of Roberts's response to Kennedy's arguments regarding what fairness and the common good should have meant for the same-sex petitioners, and this response left Kennedy's elaboration of fairness, and equal protection, uncontested. Roberts thus implied that the Constitution privileged two expressions of democratic opinion—the expressed law and traditional morality—over what reason revealed about fairness and the common good. No one can square the implications of Roberts's dissent with the Constitution that Publius defended, for the whole point of Publius's constitution was to reconcile popular government to objective standards of political morality, including fairness and the common good.[31] So Roberts's conclusion was his own, and the world knows what that conclusion is: no federal constitutional right to same-sex marriage. What the world does not know is the reasons for Roberts's conclusion; they hide in an originalist closet. And this may explain originalism's survival so many years after its demolition at the hands of Dworkin and Moore: It's a closet for reasons that cannot step proudly out of the closet.

Roberts claimed to speak as a judge—one vested with power to say what the law is, not what it should be. To square himself with constitutional principles,

Roberts cited Publius's remark in *Federalist* No. 78 that lacking force and will and possessing only judgment, the judiciary is the least dangerous threat to the people's liberty.[32] But this failed to answer Kennedy. Kennedy claimed to exercise neither force nor will; he claimed to exercise judgment—"reasoned judgment." Kennedy also reasoned about the law—the actual language of the positive law—language that reads "liberty" and "equal protection of the laws." Moreover, Kennedy acted within a tradition that had embraced many unenumerated rights within the liberty in question. This tradition had established the federal judiciary's duty to determine whether state policies in family law and other areas (education, criminal justice, race relations, business regulation, etc.) satisfy the demands of liberty and equal protection. As for Publius, before the Bill of Rights and the Civil War amendments, he said in *Federalist* No. 78 that beyond "infractions of the Constitution," a politically independent judiciary should serve as a "safeguard" against injuries to the "private rights of particular classes of citizens, by unjust and partial laws."[33] This claim of judicial power in the service of justice beyond the positive law would certainly sanction justice-seeking interpretations of the positive law. Why, then, would it deny a reasoned interpretation of liberty and equal protection to ensure fairness for same-sex couples? You cannot say it's because same-sex sex is sinful unless you are prepared to ignore the establishment clause and punish all other transgressions of biblical sexual morality. Kennedy's reliance on reasoned judgment will lack legitimacy only among writers who either do not understand the American founding or deny its legitimacy. For the American founding sought more than majoritarian democracy; it sought to reconcile popular opinion and public policy to objective standards of private rights and the public interest.

The Separation of Powers

The system of separated powers defended in *The Federalist* has two broad functions: preventing tyranny and enhancing prospects for good government. Publius argues that to maintain the Constitution's separation of powers after the founding, the nation can rely neither on the politicians' devotion nor on the electorate's devotion to the Constitution.[34] True, says Publius, both the politicians and the public can be relied on to establish a constitution, but only so long as the pressures of the Revolution suppress the partisan and self-serving tendencies of human nature and stimulate patriotism, popular trust in patriotic leaders, and the patriotic desire to look good in the eyes of the world.[35] But since the spirit of the Revolution will pass, says Publius, and though we should cultivate devotion to the Constitution to the extent that we can, we should rely chiefly not on devotion to the Constitution but on a system that connects personal ambition to the duties of political office, artfully arranges political offices, and checks one personal ambition against another.[36]

Doubts that checks and balances would work have existed since the founding.[37] The system can work only when circumstances align with private ambitions to preserve the Constitution, not when private ambitions align against the Constitution. If self-aggrandizement is the end sought by each actor in the system, and if each actor sees constitutional duty as the means to self-aggrandizement, practical reason counsels sacrificing means to ends when the means fail and when one can get away with it—that is, when constitutional duty demands personal costs that the actors can avoid and want to avoid.

To maintain the system when the costs are high, therefore, more is needed than checks and balances. The first need is patriotic leadership—more than the chance appearance of patriotic leaders, patriotic leadership institutionalized and therefore a leadership stratum of the community. This segment of the community will have sound reason to believe the constitutional system an effective means to the common good, and it will be devoted to the Constitution for that reason. Second, the public must trust this leadership community even when the constitutional system seems lagging in progress toward broadly shareable public ends, like national security and prosperity. Finally, the self-seeking individuals who make up the larger population will not trust a leadership stratum unless they expect progress or a return to progress toward broadly shareable goods. These three conditions call for cultivating a leadership community that earns the public trust by governing well.

Shortly after ratification, leading members of the founding generation appreciated the need for such a policy. This group included George Washington, Thomas Jefferson, Benjamin Franklin, and Benjamin Rush. It also included James Madison, notwithstanding his reliance on checks and balances as the primary method of constitutional maintenance. Thus, Washington, Madison, and the rest called for a national university to draw talented youth from different parts of the country, educate them in the nation's capital to the arts and attitudes of liberal democracy, and send them out to promote those same skills and attitudes in their local communities.[38] Though the Constitution's Article I, sec. 8 specifies no education power, the Constitution grants several powers under which Congress could have established the national university. If authority for the military academies at West Point and Annapolis could derive from Congress's powers to raise and maintain an army and a navy (I.8.12–13), authority for an additional educational institution could have derived from Congress's powers to establish lower federal courts (I.8.9), establish executive departments (II.2.2), and govern the District of Columbia (I.8.17).[39] Publius fully appreciated the need for political, judicial, and administrative leadership that was competent, committed to constitutional ends, and independent of immediate popular pressure. He tried to structure his institutions to recruit such leadership,[40] and he submitted a general theory of responsible government that justified it and described its most basic functions: educating the public to the difference between its objective interests and the demands of justice on the one hand, and its unreflective inclinations on the other—and pursuing the former in defiance of the latter if need be.[41]

Publius's theory of responsible government reflects his positive constitutionalism. By responsible government, he meant a government responsible *to* the people *for* certain substantive results, like national security, national prosperity, and justice. Because coercive government is the agent in this fiduciary model, a responsible government may have to act—will have to act—against the public's inclinations from time to time in pursuit of the public's true interests. Such is the meaning of responsibility *for*, and such is the government's fiduciary duty.[42] But ultimately the electorate shall judge; such is the meaning of responsibility *to*. Responsible government therefore must be a government that improves the people, turns them around, from unreflective inclinations to their true interests—it must "suspend the blow meditated by the people against themselves, until reason, justice and truth can regain their authority over the public mind."[43] Responsible government therefore must be educative government.

This is a hands-on government, an "energetic" government in Publius's terms. It does not just sit back and avoid tyranny. It is strong enough to enforce the law[44] and prescient enough to pass good laws in the first place.[45] This need to pass and enforce good laws requires "energy in government," and energy in this government is supplied chiefly by the president. Publius's constitution is a constitution of presidential power—presidential power as educative power, power that acts "when the interests of the people are at variance with their inclinations" to make them sensible of the former.[46]

Publius's constitution is also a constitution of judicial power, for error comes in varieties that include moral error as well as causal error. Recall the much-neglected passage of *Federalist* No. 78, cited above, regarding judicial power in cases of injustice not covered by specified constitutional provision: A constitutional judiciary will work against "unjust and partial laws" with or without a constitutional hook.[47] Such was Publius's view even before the Bill of Rights and the Civil War Amendments provided the hooks.[48] Why? Because the Constitution as a whole is ordained to reconcile popular government to objective standards of justice, security, and the general welfare.

Many of today's observers believe that the assertive and independent judiciary of *The Federalist* conflicts with democracy. Yet writers who hold this view compromise their commitment to democracy. For these writers (1) either deny that there are objectively better conceptions of values like justice and the public interest, or (2) they depreciate democracy by implying that a democratic culture cannot aspire to those better conceptions and arrange its institutions accordingly. A moral skeptic might deny that there is anything like a real justice for which democracy can strive. But no reflective skeptic could say this while arguing for democracy or any version of democracy. If justice does not exist as a real relationship in view of which to distinguish better or worse conceptions, the same applies to democracy and other normative notions: There can be no better or worse conceptions of democracy and democracy can be no better than tyranny. No reflective friend of democracy could hold any of these skeptical beliefs, and no intellectually responsible observer can associate these beliefs with the American Constitution and its founding.

A full account of what Publius's theory of responsible government means for judicial power in America is a large subject whose parts involve issues that cannot be covered here. These issues include the nature of judicial decision in a common law system, the possibility of trans-historical values and a trans-generational political identity, and whether a rational mind must assume that words like "liberty" refer to real things (about which we, individually and/or collectively, can be wrong). I have touched on some of these issues here, and I have discussed them at length in other writings.[49] Whatever one's position on these issues, Publius's position is clear. Just as he sees no contradiction between democracy and strong executive power, he sees no conflict between democratic principles and independent judicial power.[50] Publius argues for representative and constitutional democracy, not pure democracy. He sees the task of constitutional government as one of leading public opinion, not following it—a task of improving public opinion by reconciling it to objective standards of right and wrong, true and false. Publius feels that if democracy proves incapable of doing the right thing (pursuing the public interest as a real good in morally defensible ways), democracy is rationally indefensible.[51] Publius's theory of judicial power is part of his theory of responsible government. He sees the federal judiciary as one of the instruments for educating the public to its true interests.[52] Though he may well have disapproved of specific decisions of the court over the years—for he recognizes that judges often disagree among themselves and that they might sometimes err about justice and the general welfare[53]—he argues for a strong judiciary with the power to declare legislative enactments unconstitutional.[54] And in *Federalist* No. 9, Publius lists a strong judiciary as one of the institutions that would save popular government from its historical swings between anarchy and tyranny.[55]

As for the source of judicial criteria—that is, where the courts should look for guidance when deciding cases—note again what Publius says in *Federalist* No. 78: "It is not with a view to the infractions of the Constitution only, that the independence of the judges may be an essential safeguard against the effects of occasional ill humors in the society." A strong judiciary is also "of vast importance in mitigating the severity and confining the operation" of "unjust and partial laws" that "injur[e] the private rights of particular classes of citizens." Publius thus looks beyond the specifics of written law to the principles of justice and reason themselves. This comes as no surprise given his general view of the Constitution as a means for reconciling public opinion to objective standards of political morality. As he says in a famous passage of *Federalist* No. 51: "Justice is the end of government. It is the end of civil society. It ever has been and ever will be pursued until it be obtained, or until liberty be lost in the pursuit. In a society under the forms of which [like majority rule] the stronger faction can readily unite and oppress the weaker, anarchy may as truly be said to reign as in a state of nature."[56]

Publius might well have dissented from several of the Supreme Court's landmark decisions over the years. But there is no reason to think he would have complained that judicial review is an undemocratic institution. He saw judicial review as one of the ways democracy redeems the image it projects to the world. In one of his most important arguments, Publius rejected a practice of appealing to the people to settle constitutional disagreements between the branches of the national government. Though this practice was proposed by Thomas Jefferson, Publius opposed it because he distrusted that the general public could rise above partisan passions when deciding among contending constitutional interpretations. Appeals to the voters, he said, amounts to appeals to the "passions . . . not the reason, of the public. . . . But it is the reason, alone, of the public, that ought to control and regulate the government."[57] Since Publius relied on courts, not plebiscites, to settle constitutional controversies, he implied that on occasions of constitutional conflict, the federal courts can be expected to come closer to representing the reason of the public than either public opinion polls or the elected legislatures of Congress and the states. Strong courts are therefore right at home among a people seriously concerned with proving to mankind the possibility of reason in public affairs.

As for the place of strong courts and presidents in the separation of powers, Publius defended a version of the separation of powers that deliberately weakens Congress and provides for a large degree of executive and judicial independence from Congress.[58] He did this despite his acknowledgment that distinguishing administrative power and judicial power from lawmaking power can be difficult.[59] As it turns out, separating powers, and the separation of powers, were not as important to him as progress toward the ends of government. As he says in *Federalist* No. 45, "The public good, the real welfare of the great body of the people, is the supreme object to be pursued, and . . . no form of government whatever has any other value than as it may be fitted for the attainment of this object."[60]

Real welfare of the great body of the people? True interests as distinguished from mere inclination? Educative government? Justice as the end of government, pursued if need be to the loss of liberty? This is hardly the constitutionalism of those who limit the meaning of equal protection to some historical definition or example of the idea, whether that definition or example is morally defensible or not. This constitutionalism of *The Federalist* is the lost constitutionalism.

Why Was the Old Constitutionalism Lost?

The Federalists who argued for ratification are as responsible as the Anti-Federalists for the loss of the positive constitution. The reasons extend beyond the Anti-Federalist appropriation enabled by Federalist rhetoric in the ratification campaign. In his reliance on checks and balances as the chief method of constitutional maintenance, Publius supposed that the Enlightenment's new science of politics could link private incentives with the duties of office to produce results dictated by what he called "better motives."[61] Faith in this scheme deflected a concern to cultivate civic virtue; it also enhanced a constitutionalism of private rights over public purposes.[62]

Publius's large commercial republic—that is, capitalism—contributed in numerous ways to the loss of the positive constitution. It made self-aggrandizement socially respectable, and it removed shame from self-indulgence. It produced the culture from which early twentieth-century moral philosophy distilled various antirealist teachings (emotivism, conventionalism, subjectivism, etc.) that persuaded progressives as well as conservatives like Robert Bork and William Rehnquist.[63] And richly funded right-wing academic programs and legal movements (including the Federalist Society) have promoted small-government ideology and kept originalism alive a half-century after its defeat in the fora of evidence and logic.[64]

Global warming, rolling pandemics, growing inequality, advancing oligarchy leagued with deepening cultural division—these developments are beyond amelioration by unregulated markets. One would think that these challenges would revive a pro-government constitutionalism, and to some extent they have. The most salient of these developments at this writing is led by Adrian Vermeule, a Harvard law professor, and Patrick Deneen, a Notre Dame political scientist. These writers propose a "regime change" in which Roman Catholicism's official understanding of the common good would determine organic public policy in all areas of American life, including foreign policy, domestic economic policy, technological development, education, family law (e.g., ending no-fault divorce and same-sex marriage), reproductive care (banning abortion nationwide), and sexual morality.[65] Constitutional theorists should take this development seriously not only in view of the failure of rights-oriented constitutionalism to meet the nation's problems but also in view of Catholic integralism's growing strength in the Republican Party, as manifest in Donald Trump's selection of J. D. Vance as his running mate in the presidential election of 2024.[66] That Catholic integralists can achieve their aims within America's existing constitutional framework is debatable at best, but before putting that framework at risk, constitutional theorists who acknowledge the need for a system that works might remind themselves of what I've described here as America's forgotten constitutionalism: the ends-oriented constitutionalism of the American founding.

Publius saw humanity's governing aspiration and the aspiration of the founding generation as "establishing good government from reflection and choice." The US Constitution's amendability manifests this aspiration, and this aspiration subordinates any conventional institution, like the Constitution itself, to the end or ends that justify its establishment. The American founding generation acted on this principle when it ignored Article XIII of the Articles of Confederation to establish the Constitution of 1789. An ends-oriented constitutionalism thus makes reason the supreme law of the land.[67] We can say, therefore, that what may be unconstitutional under the Constitution of 1789 may yet be consistent with the founding's governing aspiration. This aspiration need not exclude support for religious institutions, practices, and beliefs, for some of the latter can enhance means and serve ends that worldly logic and experience can affirm. Worldly reason might even concur in Deneen's call for the state's promotion of a culture of prayer. Deneen justifies this call by citing correlations between the decline of religious observances and "rising levels of 'deaths of despair'" (deaths from suicide, drug overdose, and alcoholism) among America's "less-educated, less-upwardly mobile working class people."[68] To support this claim Deneen cites neither scripture, clerical declaration, or miraculous visions; he cites the social-scientific findings of two Princeton economists.[69] Deneen's justification for promoting prayer is thus a secular justification. As such, it affirms the value only of those religions and religious observances that serve secular values. Such a policy would imply the subordination of church to state; it would also involve discrimination among religious faiths. Though America's present constitution, as interpreted, could not admit governmental discrimination among different faiths, the more basic constitutional commitment to government by reflection and choice could justify discriminating among different faiths. This is a point worth noting should a contest develop between the common-good constitutionalism of the American founding and the common-good constitutionalism of the American Religious Right. In any event, both of the latter have good worldly reasons for rejecting the negative constitutionalism that prevails in America today.

Notes

1. See Richard A. Epstein, *How Progressives Rewrote the Constitution* (Washington, DC: Cato Institute, 2006), esp. viii–xi, chaps. 2, 4; Ralph A. Rossum, *Understanding Clarence Thomas* (Lawrence, KS: University Press of Kansas, 2014), esp. 34–49, 78–94, 123–32.

2. Randy Barnett, *Restoring the Lost Constitution: The Presumption of Liberty* (Princeton, NJ: Princeton University Press, 2004), 4–5, 33–38.

3. Id., 4–5.

4. See *DeShaney v. Winnebago*, 489 U.S. 189 (1989).

5. 576 U.S. 644 (2015).

6. Id., 63–64, 75.

7. Id., 153–66, 239–42.

8. Id., 195–203, 328.

9. Jeffrey K. Tulis and Nicole Mellow, *Legacies of Losing in American Politics* (Chicago: University of Chicago Press, 2018), 24–25, 29–41.

10. Jacob E. Cooke, ed., *The Federalist* (Middletown, CN: Wesleyan University Press, 1961), 5–6.

11. Id., 59–67.

12. *The Federalist*, 259 (No. 40).

13. Id., 34.

14. *The Federalist*, 106.

15. Id., 146–48.

16. See, e.g., Barnett, *Lost Constitution*, 54–60, 80–82.

17. 87 S.E. 2nd 749 (Va.1955); 350 U.S. 891 (1956). In this case the Virginia Supreme Court upheld the state's antimiscegenation law against a claim that it violated *Brown v. Board of Education*, 347 U.S. 483 (1954). The Virginia court declared that *Brown* did not prevent a state from preserving the "racial integrity" of her people. The US Supreme Court remanded with a pretextual instruction to complete the record. The Virginia court reaffirmed its decision, which the US Supreme Court then declined to review. The litigation occurred during the period of "massive resistance" to *Brown* by the southern states.

18. Judges worthy of prudential power is an implicit constitutional imperative for which an imperfect constitution has failed to provide. The same holds for political leadership generally. More on this below.

19. *Lochner v. NY*, 198 U.S. 45, 76 (1905), Holmes, dissenting.

20. See Stephen Holmes, *Passions and Constraint: On the Theory of Liberal Democracy* (Chicago: University of Chicago Press, 1995), chap. 8.

21. See Abraham Lincoln, "Message to Congress in Special Session, July 4, 1861" ("This is essentially a people's contest. On the side of the Union it is a struggle for maintaining in the world that form and substance of government whose leading object is to elevate the condition of men; to lift artificial weight from all shoulders; to clear the paths of laudable pursuits for all; to afford all an unfettered start and a fair chance in the race of life.").

22. For a conception of First Amendment and other rights as elements of power to pursue real goods, see Sotirios Barber, *Welfare and the Constitution* (Princeton, NJ: Princeton University Press, 2003), 146–47.

23. "The Jurisprudence of Richard Nixon," *New York Review of Books*, May 4, 1972, reprinted under the title "Constitutional Cases" in *Taking Rights Seriously* (Cambridge, MA: Harvard University Press, 1977), 131–49.

24. *Southern California Law Review*, 58:2 (1985): 277–398.

25. Michael Moore, "Natural Law Theory of Interpretation," *Law and Legal Interpretation* (Taylor and Francis, 2017), 386–88, 389–90, 396–97.

26. See generally, Martin Diamond, "Ethics and Politics: The American Way," in Robert Horwitz, ed., *The Moral Foundations of the American Republic* (Charlottesville, VA: University Press of Virginia, 1986), 75–108.

27. *The Federalist* No. 40, 259–60.

28. See Sotirios Barber and James Fleming, *Constitutional Interpretation: The Basic Questions* (New York: Oxford University Press, 2007), 84–91.

29. James Fleming, *Fidelity to Our Imperfect Constitution* (New York: Oxford University Press, 2015), 30–42, 91–97, 129–31.

30. 576 U.S. 644 (2015).

31. Barber and Fleming, *Constitutional Interpretation*, 45–55.

32. *The Federalist*, 522.

33. Id., 528.

34. Id., 332–33, 348 (No. 48); 342–43 (No. 49); 344 (No. 50).

35. Id., 340–41 (No. 49).

36. Id., 340 (No. 49); 349 (No. 51).

37. Herbert Storing, *What the Anti-Federalists Were For* (Chicago: University of Chicago Press, 1981), 56–57.

38. George Thomas, *The Founders and the Idea of a National University* (New York: Cambridge University Press, 2015), chap. 1, esp. 2–6, 30–33, 48–52.

39. Jefferson overcame initial constitutional doubts and led the move to establish West Point in 1802. Part of his motive was to create an officer class imbued with a republican culture of technical merit as distinguished from a putative European militarism of individual pomp and heroic display. See Samuel Watson, "West Point and the Struggle to Render the Officer Corps Safe for America, 1802–1833," in Robert McDonald, ed., *Thomas Jefferson's Military Academy: Founding West Point* (Charlottesville, VA: University Press of Virginia, 2004), 155–58.

40. *The Federalist*, 62–62 (No. 10: greater chance of fit representatives in a large republic); 384–7 (No. 57: factors favoring House members' fidelity to their constituents); 415, 422–25 (Nos. 62, 63: senators willing to vindicate the public interest against transient public opinion); 460–61 (No. 68: an electoral college to afford "a moral certainty" that the presidency will seldom fall to an unfit character); 521–24 (No. 78: mode of appointing and life tenure for federal judges will insure their competence and independence).

41. Id., 424–25 (No. 63); 482–83 (No. 71).

42. Id.

43. Id., 424–25 (No. 63).

44. Id., 95–96 (No. 15).

45. Id., 135–41 (No. 23); 146–150 (No. 23).

46. Id., 482–83 (No. 71). See also Barber and Fleming, *Constitutional Interpretation*, 50–53; Herbert Storing, "The Problem of Big Government," in Robert Goldwin, ed., *A Nation of States* (Chicago: Rand McNally, 1968), 80–81.

47. *The Federalist*, 528 (No. 78).

48. Herbert Storing, "The Constitution and the Bill of Rights," in Robert Goldwin and William Schambra, eds., *How Does the Constitution Secure Rights?* (Washington: American Enterprise Institute, 1985), 25–26.

49. See esp. *The Constitution of Judicial Power* (Baltimore: Johns Hopkins University Press, 1993), chaps. 2, 7.

50. Id., 38–48.

51. *The Federalist*, 51 (No. 9); 57 (No. 10); 471 (No. 70).

52. Compare id., 527 (No. 78) with 425 (No. 63) and 482 (No. 71).

53. Id., 139–40 (No. 22); 523, 526 (No. 78).

54. Id., 143–44 (No. 22); 524–29 (No. 78).

55. Id., 51.

56. Id., 352.

57. Id., 342–43 (No. 49).

58. Id., 350 (No. 51); 482–83 (No. 71); 492–94 (No. 73); 524 (No. 78).

59. Id., 235–36 (No. 37).

60. Id., 309.

61. Id., 349 (No. 51).

62. Benjamin Barber, "The Compromised Republic: Public Purposelessness in America," in Horwitz, ed., *Moral Foundations of the American Republic*, 45–48, 53–58.

63. S. Barber, *Constitution of Judicial Power*, chaps. 4, 5.

64. Jane Mayer, "How Right-Wing Billionaires Infiltrated Higher Education," *The Chronicle of Higher Education*, Feb. 12, 2016.

65. See generally, Adrian Vermeule, *Common Good Constitutionalism* (New York: Polity, 2022), esp. 37–42, 228, 109 n.103; Adrian Vermeule, "Beyond Originalism," *The Atlantic*, March 31, 2020; Adrian Vermeule, "A Principle of Immigration Priority," July 20, 2019 at https://mirrorofjustice.blogs.com/mirrorofjustice/2019/07/a-principle-of-immigration-priority-.html; Adrian Vermeule, "A Christian Strategy," *First Things* (Nov. 2017). See also, Patrick Deneen, *Regime Change: Toward a Post-Liberal Future* (New York: Random House, 2023), esp. 92–94, 164–65, 182–85, 232–35. For an argument that Vermeule and other Integralists ignore Church teachings about the autonomy and independence from each other of church and state, see Jason Blakely, "The Integralism of Adrian Vermeule: Not Catholic Enough," *Commonweal Magazine*, Oct. 5, 2020.

66. See Matthew Schmitz, "Catholic Converts Are Reshaping Republican Politics," *New York Times*, Aug. 18, 2024; Jack Jenkins and Aleja Hertzler-McCain, "Five Faith Facts about Trump's VP Pick, J.D. Vance," *The Christian Century*, July 18, 2024. View PDF (christiancentury.org) accessed 8/17/2024; Laura K. Field, "J.D. Vance Has a Bunch of Weird Views on Gender," *Politico*, July 24, 2024, https://www.politico.com/news/magazine/2024/07/24/jd-vance-gender-views-00170673 accessed 8/17/2024.

67. Sotirios Barber, *Constitutional Failure* (Lawrence, KS: University Press of Kansas, 2014), 71–78, on the implications of *The Federalist* 1:3–5 and 40:265–67.

68. Deneen, *Regime Change*, 231–32, 236.

69. Ibid., 246 n.47, citing Anne Case and Angus Deaton, *Deaths of Despair and the Future of Capitalism* (Princeton, NJ: Princeton University Press, 2020).

CHAPTER 5

The Principle of Moderation in Montesquieu and America: Constitutional Equilibrium and Judicial Tempering

Paul Carrese

After more than a century of academic and elite criticism by Woodrow Wilson and his progeny of the constitutionalist principle of separation of powers as an anachronism impeding efficient, progressive, and democratic governance, it is striking that Americans still hear fervent invocations of this principle by critics of every presidency—including by progressive and Democratic critics of Republican party presidents. We might wonder at this admission against interest by academics who generally accept the progressive critique of the Constitution's cumbersomeness, lack of democratic representation, and inability to respond to democratic demands for change, and who generally favor the Wilsonian plan to consolidate power in the federal government, the presidency, and the new administrative state—contrary to the letter and spirit of separation of powers.[1] The long hostility toward this principle by our academic and political elites has included neglect, for the most part, of sources such as Montesquieu and his protégé Blackstone most relied upon by the American founders for understanding the why and the how of distributing government powers into distinct if somewhat overlapping institutions. It is telling, therefore, that parties (and their advocates) known to advocate overreach from one governmental power into others, or a blurring of boundaries in the name of progress or popular will, so regularly cry foul once electoral fortunes turn and they are on the receiving end of such constitutional mischief.

If such hypocrisy is the tribute vice pays to virtue, it affirms Montesquieu's insights into human nature and a free constitutional order; for he invokes just such hypocrisy to justify his complex version of distributed and balanced powers. Decent people, seeking a moderate rather than violent order, should not rely upon the virtue of the rulers but instead should construct a balanced array of powers to prevent the political extremes that concentrations of power always produce. Thus, it could be a sign of underlying constitutional resilience today that parties and intellectuals long complicit in negating the separation of powers can become its fervent advocates. That said, little else in America's intellectual and political climate today bespeaks health. Repeated surveys and studies register low popular confidence in the major governing institutions and professions of American life, with only the military excepted; not even the Supreme Court induces majority confidence. Surveys also register low levels of civic understanding about basic constitutional and political principles. The latter is as true of graduates of elite universities and colleges as of high school graduates.[2]

Academics who occasionally rediscover separation of powers as a shield of liberty against presidents or more recently Supreme Court majorities they disfavor, and especially as protection against more populist and demagogic presidents (as each party now claims about presidents of the opposing party), might consider a more genuine regard for the principle ultimately at issue. A century of elite neglect or derision of a constitutionalism of distributed powers has produced a massive concentration in the presidency and a new administrative state of legislative, executive, and adjudicative power. This trend also has produced, to a lesser but still significant degree, a concentration of legislative and judicial power in a federal judiciary that long has operated under new, progressive ideas of broad constitutional development-via-interpretation. A significant part of America's descent in recent decades into polarization and civic dysfunction stems from passionate electoral contests over the winner-takes-all prize of this new presidency, including control of the philosopher-guardian seats on the top federal courts largely controlled by presidential nomination. Even small progress in restoring a genuinely balanced constitutionalism of separation of powers, therefore, will take considerable intellectual recovery and political rededication.

Such progress will require turning away from fixation on the reappearance of Jacksonian populism and illiberalism in the form of the Trump presidency and continuing populist insurgency, given that Trump and his fervent supporters are symptoms, not causes, of a broader constitutional degeneracy. A more constructive path to recovering constitutional balance and civic health is to restore the intellectual and civic duty to study—rather than dismiss, or appropriate only when tactically convenient—the great constitutionalist debates of America's founding era. A necessary corollary is study of the jurists and philosophers who most influenced Hamilton, Madison, Jay, Adams, Jefferson, and leading Anti-Federalist authors. These are the debates and ideas that shaped Washington's thinking—the vital center and single most important shaper of America's complex, separated system of differing powers and levels of government. Academic critics of extremism today should rediscover and debate anew this intellectual and political lineage, lest they contribute to the political imbalance and immoderation they decry.

A crucial dimension of that founding debate is the argument, novel in all of known history, for an independent judicial branch in the newly constituted government. Especially telling is the argument that a separate judicial power would have a distinctively moderating effect across the constitutional order, ensuring balance or equilibrium and avoiding extremes of power. Montesquieu is invoked by both Federalists and Anti-Federalists as the chief authority on separation of powers. So we should wonder: Why did he invent the independent judiciary as part of his distinctive version of separated powers? Further, why would a too-powerful judiciary of the sort Americans have invented in the past century defeat rather than serve the larger constitutionalism of moderation Montesquieu and the American framers advocated?[3]

The Montesquieuan Path to Recovery: A Constitutionalism of Moderation

Americans have been trying for a century to operate but also transform a complex constitutional order of separation of powers and federalism without adequate understanding of the reasons for its complex structures, or of the likely costs of abandoning that basic spirit. This deficit-spending of our civic knowledge has produced political dysfunction and crisis, a kind of civic bankruptcy. A metaphor from the digital age might illuminate our predicament: Bold reformers left in place a particular computer hardware (our difficult-to-amend constitutional structures) but thought we could evade its limits by running completely new operating-system software through it. What could go wrong with Woodrow Wilson's plan (tolerating the anachronism) to run Apple software through a PC frame?[4] If many progressive intellectuals today seem to grasp the ultimate price of such distortions and degeneracy of our constitutional order, especially disregard of separation of powers, then we should restore an understanding of America's original hardware-software package. Such understanding also would improve our capacity to assess what inevitably needed adjustments might genuinely improve system functioning versus those that would undermine it.

The single indispensable European source to study in such a recovery of our constitutional principles, and of the spirit or software informing the institutions, is the French jurist and philosopher Montesquieu. He was the epitome of the moderate Enlightenment as distinct from its rationalist and radical strain.[5] He also was the foremost influence on the constitutional debates that produced the 1787 Constitution, the Bill of Rights, and the first decades of implementing these basic laws.[6] Montesquieu's great influence on American political and constitutional thought, from the 1760s to the 1790s, stems most directly from the two chapters of his *The Spirit of Laws* (1748, English translation 1750) that were most widely read and reprinted in America: his studies of the English constitution (Book 11), then of the political culture of liberty it spawned (Book 19). The American reliance on this fundamental constitutional principle also stems from Blackstone's *Commentaries* on the English constitution and laws (1765–69); we mostly overlook that the great English jurist cites Montesquieu as the first modern philosopher to whom he is indebted for his orientation toward English constitutionalism.[7]

Montesquieu develops in *The Spirit of Laws* the full modern conception of separation of powers, as the first philosopher to argue for three such distributed powers. His constitutionalism also gives America the novel concept of federalism, and within separation of powers theory the novel concept of bicameralism in the legislative power. Nonetheless his most distinctive contribution to separation of powers is an independent judiciary. His insight is that the least political and powerful player in Europe's civic life, the judges and lawyers, should be the crucial tempering or moderating agent in politics—and this function requires a separate constitutional branch. For Montesquieu a legal-judicial emphasis on reason more than passion or party, and on individual security of subjects or citizens more than projects of ideology or power, is the less-political way of removing some extremes of politics, whether in monarchies or republics.

The relatively greater civility of modern liberal politics in the liberal democracies and across the globe that slowly has been achieved over the past 275 years owes much to this constitutionalist innovation to separate the judicial power and fortify the rule of law. We can understand Montesquieuan civility as, minimally, less sanguinary penal codes; but more robustly as a political culture of the rule of law and protection for political dissent, diverse thought, religious liberty, criminal due process, and other civil liberties.[8] Montesquieu thus adapts Aristotle's prudent search for a mixed or balanced regime, the polity dominated by a middling class and its middling virtues, as one basis for a moderated modern philosophy of individual rights and a humane politics.[9]

Today's progeny of Woodrow Wilson's transformative political science tend not to understand that they are Wilsonian, given Wilson's repudiation of Montesquieu and America's founding political science in *The Federalist* as part of an emphasis on change and democratic progress in a new science; that is, given that they probably have not studied Montesquieu, most don't understand how Wilson embodies the spirit of single-minded dogmatism Montesquieu's constitutionalism seeks to preempt. For it is a larger spirit of moderation, balance, and avoidance of single extremes of power or ideology that informs America's founding version of separation of powers. This software-hardware combination, of separated institutions and a political culture of moderation to flow through and operate them, is adapted from Montesquieu and Blackstone. This constitutionalism of moderation is, on the one hand, a positive argument for three distinct powers and the equilibrium among them; both because a division of labor produces better rule in each area and because a plurality of voices in debate produces better laws. On the other, it is a negative argument, that dispersing power prevents the concentration that produces extremes by providing the check of mutual obstruction to blunt expected attempts toward excesses.[10] The positive dimension or argument should not be reduced to the latter and lost (as often is done). But the reverse also holds: We should grasp Montesquieu's prudent argument for the benefits of friction and checking. As a lawyer and senior judge, he celebrates the distinctive reasonableness of an independent judiciary. Nonetheless, he blends the positive and negative rationales given the judgment that completely virtuous rule is impossible in human affairs, thus there needs to be a distribution if only to provide for checks on rulers.

Publius, Montesquieu, and True Constitutionalism: The Quiet Centrality of the Judiciary

Publius, both as Hamilton and Madison, cites Montesquieu in *The Federalist* as "the oracle" who is "always consulted and cited" on separation of powers

(No. 47)—but more fundamentally Publius draws upon him for the larger approach to a complex constitutionalism that seeks a decent, middling politics to avoid extremes.[11] If educators today have heard of only *Federalist* Nos. 10 and 51 (if that), then they are missing the real story, which begins with Hamilton's invocation of Montesquieu in No. 9. He is the one authority cited for the constitutionalism Publius is expounding, the "great improvement" in "the science of politics" the 1787 Constitution offers. The five modern "principles" of republican government listed, either unknown by the ancients or only "imperfectly," come from Montesquieu.[12] We might add that three (the second, third, and fifth) are absent from Locke's theory of separation of powers. Distribution or separation of powers is the first; then bicameralism in the legislative power; an independent judicial branch is the central principle; fourth is representation of the people by elected deputies in the legislature; finally federalism, the "enlargement of the orbit" of republicanism in a federal republic composed of several republics. This last is the particular subject of essays 9 and 10; but No. 9 has presented the political science of Publius more completely than any prior essay.

Indeed, all the emphasis on America's founding as essentially Lockean stumbles on the fact that his political science offers only one of the five principles (elected representation) in the full American form. Further, the Montesquieuan package of principles aims toward complexity and balancing of powers as the safest path to moderation and decency in a free politics, the latter hardly being central to Lockean constitutionalism. Thus Publius in No. 9 invokes Montesquieu on federalism but more fundamentally claims that the entire authority of the master supports ratification, not Anti-Federalist criticisms. The further exposition of federalism and separation of powers in No. 10 or in No. 51, indeed in most of the remaining essays, is an explication of these five principles. Madison next invokes "the celebrated Montesquieu" in No. 43 on the meaning of republicanism, then in No. 47 on separation of powers. Others in this volume expound upon this dialogue between Publius and Montesquieu, and upon the Madisonian conception of separation of powers in the middle essays of *The Federalist*, giving all the more reason here to note the mostly overlooked significance of *Federalist* No. 9 including an independent judiciary as the central item of the great improvements brought by Montesquieu's constitutionalism.

Indeed, the recent scholarly emphasis on the Madisonianism of Publius obscures the reliance on Montesquieu in this early statement by Hamilton of Publius's political science. We also underplay how Montesquieu deeply animates Hamilton's extraordinary defense of an independent judicial power in No. 78, Publius's final invocation of the philosopher. The argument therein for a power of constitutional review implicit in such a judicial power, and necessary for its independence, is widely studied; less so is Publius's subtle reliance upon Montesquieu for this bold effort. Hamilton's challenge is to persuade republicans that a completely novel conception of judicial power—at least in its overt independence and potency—poses no threat to republican liberty and indeed is indispensable for it. He cites *The Spirit of Laws* for reassurance that of the three powers in such a system, "the judiciary is next to nothing."[13] Because a branch of professional judges is not politically powerful or prominent, it both is the "least dangerous branch" phrased negatively, but phrased positively this quality is precisely what makes it indispensable for moderating all political power. It teaches everyone to be governed by law, or lawfulness.

A crucial component of Publius's argument thus is the claim that the American federal judiciary will be defined by "integrity and moderation," giving it the stature to inculcate the principle of rule by law.[14] Anti-Federalists had argued that this innovation of not just a separate but quite capable judiciary is controversial, needing substantial republican justification. Hamilton responds that an independent judiciary of learned, self-disciplined professionals acts as umpires of the separation of powers, simultaneously one power within the system and the one that must be trusted—as the legally expert power—to adjudge in contested cases whether other powers are abiding by the Constitution's command to exercise only their own duly granted authority, or, overreaching.

Of course, it is a paradox of the present day, almost 240 years after *Federalist* No. 78 and 275 years after Montesquieu's innovation, that this conception of a trustworthy and nonthreatening power proved so successful that a substantial portion of the legal-judicial caste eventually persuaded itself to push further and acquire still greater power. Innovators like Oliver Wendell Holmes Jr., starting in the late nineteenth century, basically argued that all this stored-up trustworthiness was going to waste: There was new thinking needed in the constitutional order, system updating to be implemented, and only the judicial caste had the knowledge and latitude (insufficiently exploited thus far) to do so scientifically and efficiently.[15] Woodrow Wilson explicitly repudiated Montesquieu to give us an enormous presidency, master of all it could get away with in updating an ever-evolving "democracy." Holmes was subtler in his transformational effort; Montesquieu and *The Federalist* did not rate much of a mention; and through such subtlety his vice of destroying the very foundations of the judiciary's trustworthiness as umpires hypocritically paid tribute to the unique virtue of the Montesquieuan judiciary. His legal realism deployed legalistic or sophistic moves to repudiate the old model of a law-bound, constitutionally governed judiciary; henceforth the only rational, legally sound way to think of common-law judges was as wielders of power and makers of new law, not voices and interpreters of law that bound them yet also needed application to new cases. A century hence, after US Supreme Court rulings that more or less openly have sought to transform and update both the constitutional order and its original conception of rights, we see every appointment to the court becoming a political battle, occasionally to a depraved degree of ferocity. We see the presidential and senatorial powers to nominate and confirm judges being crudely weaponized in electoral campaigns, with judicial nominees evaluated mostly for the policy results they might achieve or thwart rather than for a legal-judicial quality distinct from politics. These maladies indicate the deficit-spending or even self-destruction of the carefully calibrated constitutional order of separated powers Montesquieu and Publius offered. Having repudiated or ignored the software meant to operate our constitutional hardware, confident we had invented new and improved plans, we find ourselves beset by the power-drenched, irrational politics Montesquieu sought to moderate or preempt in the first place.

Securing Liberty Through the Constitutionalism of Tripartite Powers

The history of American constitutional thought from the 1780s to the adoption of the Bill of Rights, including the achievement of several elected governments under the new federal Constitution, is largely a story of adapting the broad principles offered in the *Spirit of Laws*, especially but not exclusively in Part Two of the work, Books 9 to 13. They achieved an American form of a constitutionalism of liberty comprising federalism, separation of powers, and checks and balances, including an independent judiciary to protect individual rights and tranquility.

Montesquieu presents his novel institutional theory of a tripartite separation of powers, with its novel judiciary, as arising from a concern for liberty, understood as both political and individual liberty. Book 11 addresses political liberty in a constitution while distinguishing political liberty regarding the individual citizen, treated separately in Book 12—with a focus on the judiciary. He notes that liberty has meant many things in Western thought, in different governments, but it does not simply mean popular government, nor loose or ineffectual laws; it truly means, under a government of laws, "only having the power to do what one ought to want, and in no way being constrained to do what one ought not to want."[16] He then specifies liberty as "the right to do everything the laws permit."[17] This discussion sets up an initial statement on separation of powers, one presupposing the political science of the preceding ten books. He implies we must replace the classical constitutionalism of virtue (as in Sparta), as well as classical political philosophy or aristocratic republicanism (of Plato, Aristotle, or Cicero), with a constitutionalism of liberty, moderation, and separation of powers. Further, neither democracy nor aristocracy inherently secure freedom; rather, "political liberty is found only in moderate governments."[18]

The crucial point is that such moderation occurs "only when power is not abused; but it has eternally been observed that any man who has power is led to abuse it." The classical quest for fully virtuous citizens or philosopher kings is mistaken: "Who would say it! even virtue has need of limits." These premises yield Montesquieu's classic argument for a distribution of powers: "So that one cannot abuse power, power must check power by the disposition of things. A constitution can be such that no one will be constrained to do things the law does not oblige him to do, or be kept from doing things the law permits him to do."[19]

Montesquieu then moves to an extended case study of England. Various governments have had various purposes (for Rome, expansion; for ancient Marseilles, commerce), but there "is alone one nation in the world whose constitution has political liberty for its direct purpose."[20] The work's most widely read chapter then examines "the constitution of England." That said, he begins with statements about not England but the structure of any government or constitution, and what must be done to secure political liberty. In every state there are "three sorts of powers"—legislative, executive (mostly directed to external affairs), and judicial (executive power directed to judging crimes or disputes between individuals in criminal or civil law). He then refines his definition of liberty: "Political liberty in a citizen is that tranquility of spirit which comes from the opinion each one has of his security; and in order for him to have this liberty, the government must be such that one citizen cannot fear another citizen."[21] He posits further facts: What most governments fail to do, and what only moderate governments achieve, is to distribute or separate these three powers so as to secure individual tranquility, for "there is no liberty" unless legislative is separated from executive power, and each also is separated from judicial power. "All would be lost if the same man or the same body of principal men, either of the nobles or the people, exercised these three powers" or even any two of them.[22]

He then turns to a detailed examination of each power, but curiously, not in his initial order—legislative, executive, judicial; he instead examines judicial power first. This move reinforces his view throughout the work that the spirit of moderation is best secured through an elevated prominence for the judicial power that preeminently focuses on the security and tranquility of individuals. This prominent status for judging early in this chapter on England is reinforced when he turns from the level of general principles to a discussion of specific regimes—"the kingdoms of Europe," "the Turks," and "the Italian republics." He marks the independence of the judging power as the key to separation of powers and moderate government, with the latter two in turn identified as the indispensable means to securing individual liberty or tranquility:

> In most kingdoms in Europe, the government is moderate, because the prince, who has the first two powers, leaves the exercise of the third to his subjects. Among the Turks, where the three powers are united in the person of the sultan, an atrocious despotism reigns. In the Italian republics, where the three powers are united, there is less liberty than in our monarchies.[23]

In this initial study of England in *The Spirit of Laws*, Montesquieu emphasizes the judicial power in a peculiar way by focusing upon its citizen-jury component, in contrast to earlier discussions of professional judges, particularly in monarchies (especially in Book 6); only later in the chapter does he discuss the appellate function of the Law Lords in the upper house of the legislative power. The judicial role is significant, and he will further emphasize this in Book 12 analyzing individual liberty per se, but for now he declares that as a political presence the citizen-jury mode is "so to speak, invisible and null."[24] This is a crucial principle of a moderate judicial power that Publius will cite in *Federalist* No. 78, but that later advocates of judicial power in American constitutionalism overlook. He then turns to a bicameral legislature and the executive, declaring these three political branches to be the effectively important "three powers." The negative dimension of the distribution is that, both within the bifurcated legislative and between legislative and executive, the checking each performs against the other prevents an accumulation of despotic power. This requires some blurring of the distribution lines, or sharing of powers, which now is described as checks and balances. The positive function to the distribution, its principle of division of labor and thus of expertise, often is neglected today: Montesquieu emphasizes that legislatures are best at deliberating, a single executive is best at acting, and a judicial branch is best at judging cases with a legal prudence attuned to individual security. Within the legislature, the lower house is best at reflecting the people's views and the upper branch is best at protecting the views of the few and performing functions requiring more expertise, such as appellate judging. This positive, functional distribution usually is described as separation of powers.

Moreover, Montesquieu anticipates the criticism about gridlock or inefficiency often made by those like Wilson more concerned with democratic consent and government efficacy, thus advocating a parliamentary system with an executive chosen from the majority party in a lower legislative house to fuse the legislative and executive powers with a popular mandate. He notes in the chapter's closing section that "the fundamental constitution" of this government finds each branch of the legislative "chained to the other" and in turn "the two will be bound by the executive power, which will itself be bound by the legislative power." The three might therefore "form a repose or an inertness," but "as, by the necessary motion of things, they are constrained to move, they will be forced to move in concert."[25]

The chapter's closing thoughts then prepare for the remainder of Book 11 on political liberty in other constitutions by noting that a separation and balancing of powers in a constitutional equilibrium is, given the right conditions, the most natural or historically prevalent form of government for certain peoples—and especially in Europe. Indeed, he does not want to "disparage other governments" or say that "this extreme political liberty should mortify those who have only a moderate one."[26] He amplifies this fundamental principle of his philosophy: "How could I say" that governments with a moderate liberty should be sheepish, "I who believe that the excess even of reason is not always desirable; and that men almost always accommodate themselves better to middles than to extremities?" The next chapter thus addresses anew the topic of moderate liberty, arguing that the "monarchies we know" each have a "distribution" of the three powers, which, while not identical to England's, nonetheless "more or less approach political liberty"—for "if these did not approach it, the monarchy would degenerate into despotism."[27] The question of moderate government is of greatest concern, not the traditional form of republic or monarchy—nor any copying of England's government. The bulk of the remainder of Book 11 on constitutionalism and political liberty therefore develops his conceptions of separation of powers and judicial power by examining the medieval Germans, the ancient Greeks, and the Romans. Amid examining the Greek republics he amplifies the crucial moderating role of judicial power by directly addressing all future makers or reformers of constitutions: "Among a free people who have legislative power . . . the masterwork of legislation is to know how to place well the power of judging."[28]

"The Integrity and Moderation of the Judiciary"—and How America Is Depleting It

After his focused study of liberty in relation to "political right," thus a constitution, Montesquieu turns in Book 12 to "civil right," defined in Book 1 as the civil and criminal laws affecting the daily lives of citizens or subjects. Here, he defines political liberty yet again: it "consists in security, or at least in the opinion one has of one's security." Thus the greatest threat to, but also greatest support for, liberty lies within the judicial power: "This security is never more attacked than by public and private prosecutions. It is therefore on the goodness of the criminal laws that the liberty of the citizen principally depends."[29] The liberty of the constitution concerns "the government" and separation of powers, but the citizen's liberty mainly concerns particular laws and judicial procedures: "The knowledge already acquired in some countries, and yet to be acquired in others, respecting the surest rules one can observe in criminal judgments, concerns mankind more than anything else in the world." Indeed, it is "only on the practice of this knowledge that liberty can be founded."[30]

These emphatic declarations immediately point Montesquieu to proposed reforms of the categories and subjects of criminal law, moderating their reach and severity.[31] In the remainder of *The Spirit of Laws* he recurs to this judicial-legal spirit of moderation; sometimes explicitly, sometime by omission when noting the extremes to which politics descends in its absence. Thus in his portrait of the "extreme" liberty of English political culture in Book 19, with only the "two visible powers" seeming dominant, he recalls his characterization in Book 11 of the "invisible" power of judging and its capacity to moderate an extreme liberty.[32] It hardly seems accidental that Hamilton in *Federalist* No. 78, having invoked Montesquieu on the judiciary early in the essay, emphasizes precisely the moderating power of an independent judiciary in the new American constitutionalism.

Arguments throughout the *Federalist*, beyond Hamilton in No. 78 defending a federal judiciary with life tenure and a constitutional review power, show an American constitutionalism adapting the Montesquieuan philosophy on judicial power and moderation. Hamilton, Madison, and Jay were black-letter common law lawyers, trained in both Coke and Blackstone, and Jay became the first chief justice of the United States. Washington offered the office of chief justice to Hamilton upon Jay's retirement. It is not surprising, then, that the importance of an independent, federal judicial power arises early in and percolates throughout the *Federalist*, culminating in Hamilton's exposition in Nos. 78 to 83.[33] While Hamilton most notably emphasizes the judiciary in No. 9 and No. 78, Jay and Madison also voice Publius's emphasis on a national judiciary, including the costs of its absence under the Articles of Confederation (see, e.g., Nos. 3, 15, 22, and 37).

The scholarly focus on the argument in No. 78 for a power of constitutional review, now called judicial review, has led to neglect of the two other strands in Hamilton's exposition of judicial power. In the first, Hamilton defends an independent judiciary via the negative separation of powers, on the Montesquieuan premise that professional judges are bulwarks against the populist abuses likely arising from the legislative power in a republic. The second strand draws upon the spirit of Coke, Montesquieu, and Blackstone to argue that the Constitution implies a distinctly common-law character for the federal judiciary, a body of lawyers elevated to the bench and serving as a depository not of force or will but traditional legal judgment. The first strand justifies judicial review, but the second explains why common-law judges in a republic could have such a power and be entrusted with it, by shifting to the positive separation of powers. Hamilton's third strand, rarely noticed, amplifies both of these elements through a fully positive separation of powers and its spirit of moderation. Hamilton ultimately blends Montesquieu's juridical liberalism with an Aristotelian appreciation for practical legal wisdom: the judiciary as not only guardians of the Constitution but schoolmasters of this new constitutionalism of moderation.

Hamilton begins No. 78 modestly, however, by citing Montesquieu on liberty and a tripartite separation of powers, then defining a quietly influential judiciary as crucial to individual security and tranquility. He quotes "the celebrated Montesquieu" to insist that of the three powers "the judiciary is next to nothing."[34] Echoing the arguments of Nos. 9, 49, and 51, he declares appointment of judges during good behavior a crucial advance in the science of politics, not least because an independent judiciary is, in a republic, an "excellent barrier to the encroachments and oppressions of the representative body." Indeed, before citing Montesquieu Hamilton declares a professional judiciary "the best expedient which can be devised in any government, to secure a steady, upright, and impartial administration of the laws."[35] Montesquieu provides support, agreeing "there is no liberty, if the power of judging be not separated from the legislative and executive powers."[36] These premises lead him to argue that Article III and the entire Constitution imply a power to examine laws for constitutionality, of judicial review. Hamilton summarizes this first line of argument by declaring independent courts "the bulwarks of a limited Constitution against legislative encroachments."[37]

The larger moderating role of the judiciary arises in Hamilton's portrait of judges as disinterested legal experts, separated from the willful spirit of the political branches. To expect judges to check popular moves toward either "dangerous innovations in the government" or "serious oppressions of the minor party in the community" is to expect "an uncommon portion of fortitude in the judges to do their duty as faithful guardians of the Constitution."[38] Hamilton emphasizes, channeling Coke but also Montesquieu and Blackstone, that judges represent the rule of law itself—the depositories of legal learning and the benchmarks guiding the political order. Only if federal judges are truly independent can they be "the citadel of the public justice and the public security" the Constitution intends.[39]

This second strand of argument points to the third, the larger moderating influence of a judiciary, while remaining within the negative separation of powers, its prevention of injustice. Hamilton flips the traditional republican fear of such a semi-autonomous branch—not popularly elected, not easily removed from office—by emphasizing that only this independence will draw genuine legal experts to serve on the bench. Further, this common-law expertise provides security against judges abusing their office by drifting from judging toward legislating. Near the essay's close Hamilton makes this "weightier" argument for "permanency of the judicial offices," one "deducible from the nature of the qualifications they require."[40] His common-law reasoning borrows from Montesquieu and Blackstone by noting it is "frequently remarked" that "a voluminous code of laws is one of the inconveniences necessarily connected with the advantages of a free government." Such training protects liberty and the rule of law: "To avoid an arbitrary discretion in the courts, it is indispensable that they should be bound down by strict rules and precedents, which serve to define and point out their duty in every particular case that comes before them." Given numerous legal controversies, "the records of those precedents must unavoidably swell to a very considerable bulk, and must demand long and laborious study to acquire a competent knowledge of them."[41]

Hamilton's immediate point is that "but few men" will have "sufficient skill in the laws to qualify" as judges; then, "given the ordinary depravity of human nature," there will be a still smaller number "who unite the requisite integrity with the requisite knowledge." Even these few honorable, learned lawyers are human, however, since to entice such "fit characters" away from "a lucrative line of practice" they must be offered more security than a temporary tenure provides.[42] This emphasis on the extraordinary legal training of judges and presumed moral integrity to adhere to traditional rules rather than innovate directly prepares the third strand of Hamilton's analysis. He refers repeatedly to the "duty" such independent judges will have "to adhere to" the Constitution over a statute contravening it, "their duty as faithful guardians of the Constitution."[43] These ennobling references prepare for an argument combining the negative rationale, checking legislative and popular usurpations, with positive space for professionals needing independence to do their job:

> But it is not with a view to infractions of the Constitution only, that the independence of the judges may be an essential safeguard against the effects of occasional ill humors in society. These sometimes extend no farther than to the injury of the private rights of particular classes of citizens, by unjust and partial laws. Here also the firmness of the judicial magistracy is of vast importance in mitigating the severity and confining the operation of such laws. . . . This is a circumstance calculated to have more influence upon the character of our governments, than but few may imagine. The benefits of the integrity and moderation of the judiciary have already been felt in more states than one.[44]

Hamilton emphasizes that such judicial moderation of politics already "must have commanded the esteem and applause of all the virtuous and disinterested," of "considerate men of every description."[45] Such a "temper in the courts" will check any "spirit of injustice" that might arise in state or federal affairs under the new Constitution, if only through the subtle, indirect method of mitigating and confining unjust laws. All of this draws on separation of powers as propounded by Montesquieu and Blackstone, itself explicitly grounded in concepts of natural right and traditional common-law rights, entailing that judicial power eschew any legislating or innovating. Only with such strict distinctions will the independent judiciary, and the separation of powers system itself, achieve its moderating effect on politics.

American constitutionalism in its third century has substantially repudiated such moderation or balance—from our disregard for the initial understanding of and arguments about it, to our neglect of the practice of it. Distinct schools of scholarship or political factions instead emphasize some single element of modern liberal democracy and our globalized world at the expense of others, and of constitutionalism itself. Regarding judicial power, most draw on Holmes's legal realism, seeing no fixed meaning to any legal principle, thereby inviting judges to practice their elite legal reason in a spirit of innovation and progress. Today we must note: Either these innovating academic and legal elites are completely irrelevant to American public life, or, they bear some responsibility for the constitutional and civic disintegration besetting us. Familiarity with Montesquieu's more comprehensive, balanced philosophy would help us to rediscover the interrelations and larger whole that until recently had persisted in American constitutionalism, and to recover its balance and moderation.

One scholar rightly has called Montesquieu "the father of constitutions," preparing the ground for the waves of liberal democracies born in subsequent centuries.[46] All scholars of human affairs who see the importance not only of institutions and policies, but also of the broader political culture or spirit animating a constitutional politics, owe a debt to this capacious philosophy. These legacies among current statesmen and scholars persist to some degree even if, as now is likely, few have studied Montesquieu's works directly. Still, his influence has greatly declined, and the constitutionalism he helped to forge in America is beset by functional polarization and ignorance of its principles and spirit. Montesquieu had warned of the need for civic vigilance about the degeneracies produced by such complex constitutional forms themselves—including, at the close of his portrait of English political culture, the intellectual degeneracy of separation into narrow-minded sects, schools, and theories.[47] Yet we now hardly remember either the positive instructions or warnings. It is an important academic and practical question whether his progeny in the twenty-first century can recover and argue with his philosophy, as Tocqueville did in the nineteenth; and whether liberal modernity can be persuaded of its need to rediscover this philosophy of moderation and constitutional complexity.

Notes

1. For an elaboration of this argument and the sources consulted see my "Constitutionalist Political Science: Rediscovering Storing's Philosophical Moderation," *American Political Thought* 4, no. 2 (Spring 2015): 259–288.

2. A general diagnosis of our civic and constitutional condition is Richard Haass, *The Bill of Obligations: The Ten Habits of Good Citizens* (New York: Penguin Press, 2023), especially "Democratic Deterioration," 17–35. On American higher education's failure to prioritize a civic education in knowledge of constitutional democracy, see Ronald J. Daniels, Grant Shreve, and Phillip Spector, *What Universities Owe Democracy* (Baltimore, MD: Johns Hopkins University Press, 2021).

3. This chapter draws upon but substantially revises material from Paul Carrese, *The Cloaking of Power: Montesquieu, Blackstone, and the Rise of Judicial Activism* (University of Chicago Press, 2003); *Democracy in Moderation: Montesquieu, Tocqueville, and Sustainable Liberalism* (Cambridge University Press, 2016); also the long entry "Montesquieu, Charles de," in *The Encyclopedia of Political Thought*, ed. Gibbons (Wiley-Blackwell), 2014.

4. See Carrese, "Montesquieu, the Founders, and Woodrow Wilson: The Evolution of Rights and the Eclipse of Constitutionalism," in *The Progressive Revolution in Politics and Political Science*, ed. Marini and Masugi (Rowman & Littlefield, 2005).

5. Among many fine studies of Montesquieu and his constitutionalism drawn upon here see especially Thomas Pangle, *Montesquieu's Philosophy of Liberalism* (University of Chicago Press, 1973); Judith Shklar, *Montesquieu* (Oxford University Press, 1987); Anne Cohler, *Montesquieu's Comparative Politics and the Spirit of American Constitutionalism* (University Press of Kansas, 1988); Paul Rahe, *Montesquieu and the Logic of Liberty* (Yale University Press, 2009); Sharon Krause, "The Spirit of Separate Powers in Montesquieu," *Review of Politics* 62 (2000): 231–265.

6. See Donald Lutz, "The Relative Influence of European Writers on Late Eighteenth-Century American Political Thought," *American Political Science Review* 78 (1984): 189–97; James Muller, "The American Framers' Debt to Montesquieu," in Muller, ed., *The Revival of Constitutionalism* (University of Nebraska Press, 1988).

7. For the argument that American constitutionalism is not primarily shaped by the liberal rationalism of Hobbes and Locke, see James R. Stoner, *Common Law and Liberal Theory: Coke, Hobbes, and the Origins of American Constitutionalism* (Lawrence: University Press of Kansas, 1992).

8. Harvey C. Mansfield argues that Montesquieu's conception of an executive placed within a system of separated powers is a milestone in constitutionalism and greatly influenced the American framers; "Moderating the Executive," in *Taming the Prince: The Ambivalence of Modern Executive Power* (New York: Free Press, 1989).

9. Recent works emphasizing moderation, in one sense or another, in Montesquieu's philosophy include Aurelian Craiutu, *A Virtue for Courageous Minds: Moderation in French Political*

Thought, 1748–1830 (Princeton University Press, 2012); Dennis Rasmussen, *The Pragmatic Enlightenment: Recovering the Liberalism of Hume, Smith, Montesquieu, and Voltaire* (Cambridge University Press, 2013); Vickie Sullivan, *Montesquieu and the Despotic Ideas of Europe: An Interpretation of "The Spirit of the Laws"* (University of Chicago Press, 2017); Joshua Bandoch, *The Politics of Place: Montesquieu, Particularism, and the Pursuit of Liberty* (University of Rochester Press, 2017); Keegan Callanan, *Montesquieu's Liberalism and the Problem of Universal Politics* (Cambridge University Press, 2018). See also Leslie Rubin, *Aristotle, America, and the Politics of a Middle Class* (Baylor University Press, 2018).

10. On the complex constitutionalism of *The Federalist*, delineating negative and positive modes, see Harvey C. Mansfield, "Separation of Powers in the American Constitution," in *America's Constitutional Soul* (Johns Hopkins University Press, 1991).

11. Alexander Hamilton, John Jay, and James Madison, *The Federalist*, ed. Robert Scigliano (New York: Modern Library, 2000), 308.

12. Id. at 48.

13. Id. at 496.

14. Id. at 502.

15. See "Holmes and Judicialized Liberalism" in *The Cloaking of Power*, 231–56; and the long entry "Holmes, Oliver Wendell, Jr.," in *The Encyclopedia of Political Thought*, ed. Gibbons (Wiley-Blackwell), 2014.

16. All quotations are from Montesquieu, *The Spirit of the Laws*, translated A. Cohler, B. Miller, H. Stone (New York: Cambridge University Press, 1989); citing Book and chapter, with page number; here, 11.2 and 11.3, 154–55.

17. Id. at 11.3, 155.

18. Id. at 11.4, 155.

19. Id. at 11.4, 155–156.

20. Id. at 11.5, 156.

21. Id. at 11.6, 156–57.

22. Id. at 11.6, 157.

23. Id. at 11.6, 157.

24. Id. at 11.6, 158.

25. Id. at 11.6, 164.

26. Id. at 11.6, 166.

27. Id. at 11.7, 166–167.

28. Id. at 11.11, 169.

29. Id. at 12.2, 188.

30. Ibid.

31. Id. at 12.4.

32. Id. at 19.27.

33. Two contrasting analyses of Publius on judicial power are Stoner, "Constitutionalism and Judging in *The Federalist*," in *Common Law*, 197–211; Sotirios Barber, "Judicial Review and *The Federalist*," in *The Constitution of Judicial Power* (Johns Hopkins University Press, 1993), 26–65.

34. *The Federalist*, 496, quoting *Spirit of Laws*, 11.6.

35. Id. at 496.

36. Id. at 497, quoting *Spirit*, 11.6.

37. Id. at 500.

38. Id. at 500–501.
39. Id. at 497.
40. Id. at 502.
41. Id. at 502–503.
42. Id. at 503.
43. Id. at 500–501.
44. Id. at 501–502.
45. Id. at 502.
46. Judith N. Shklar, *Montesquieu* (Oxford, 1987).
47. *The Spirit of the Laws*, 19.27.

CHAPTER 6

John Adams and the Separation of Functions

Brigid Flaherty Staab

In the aftermath of Lexington and Concord, the American colonies hastened to draft republican constitutions in anticipation of their divorce from the English Crown. A main question directed the thought of state legislators: how to protect their established rights in a republic that ensured stability and security. Seeking to answer this question from late 1775 to spring 1776, legislators from North Carolina, Virginia, and New Jersey turned to a lawyer known throughout the colonies: John Adams.[1] The resulting publication, *Thoughts on Government,* offers a reflection on the proper design for republican government and puts forward the central components of Adams's thought: the rule of law, representation, bicameralism, and the separation of powers.

Scholars have regarded *Thoughts on Government* as influential during the Revolutionary period, particularly as a guide in the drafting of state constitutions and in its articulation of a general understanding of republicanism. However, it is often argued that Adams's influence waned as the United States emerged from the Revolutionary War and advanced toward the Constitutional Convention of 1787. Generally guided by Adams's *Defence of the Constitutions of Government of the United States of America,* written as a response to French radicals, Adams is presented as an early friend of republicanism who abandoned his revolutionary principles to defend the division of society into three orders that are balanced through a mixed constitution.[2] This evolutionary reading is generally considered to capture Adams's complete judgment on the separation of powers. The apparent change in his thought led to two general approaches to the study of Adams's political thought: the first attempts to makes sense of his changing opinion; the second, emphasizing the perceived change in his thought, finds Adams outdated for the constitutional issues of the late 1780s and thereby limits his role in shaping American political thought.[3] One advantage of this reading is its presentation of a clear contrast between the revolutionary views of Adams and French radicals.[4] However, by focusing on the disputed change within Adams's thought, scholars have left unconsidered key features of *Thoughts on Government* and its similarities with the following decade's constitutional debates.

This chapter reconsiders Adams's *Thoughts on Government* as an early articulation of the separation of functions. In doing so, it pushes against the conception of Adams as a thinker solely concerned with a balanced, mixed constitution.[5] A careful reading of the pamphlet, which tracks Adams's constitutional logic by analyzing his conception of each governmental branch, confirms the continued centrality of the rule of law, bicameralism, and representation while identifying these concepts as features of an institutional system rooted in the separation of functions. Thus, I link the scholarship on John Adams with the emerging field of the separation of functions and argue that a recognition of Adams's articulation of the separation of functions provides more continuity between the Adams of 1776 and the constitutional conversations of 1787. Moreover, returning to Adams's pamphlet offers textual evidence for the founders' account of the separation of functions—an account extrapolated by separation of functions scholars as an idea commonly understood at the founding but rarely tied to specific American texts outside of the *Federalist Papers*.

Separation of Powers as the Separation of Functions

Understanding the separation of powers as the separation of functions is a pressing concern in the study of American political institutions and American political thought. David Siemers articulates the founders' understanding of the separation of functions as directed toward two ends: effectual government and protection against encroachment.[6] The U.S. Constitution reflects these ends: Rather than a balanced, coequal division of powers that compete for shared power,[7] the framers distributed governmental duties through a "modified separation of functions." This separation protects against legislative overreach and provides internal moderation so that each branch can pursue its proper end. However, the separation of powers, as Jeffrey Tulis recognizes, is often stripped of its functional nature: "The term *separation of powers* has perhaps obstructed understanding of the extent to which different structures were designed to give each branch the special quality needed to secure its governmental objectives."[8] For Tulis and Siemers, the objectives of each branch—legislation, execution, and judgment—determine the separation of powers. Benjamin Kleinerman expands on Tulis, arguing that the American constitutional system "intentionally structures politics so that each institution best fulfills its function."[9] Understanding the separation of powers as the separation of functions, then, recognizes that each branch is structured to perform certain functions—that the form of the institution produces its effects.

A diligent reading of Adams's *Thoughts on Government* points to the functional end of his pamphlet. Adams designs his proposal in such a way that the concern to produce an effectual government directs the ends of each institution, and these functional ends dictate the relationships between the branches of government. In addition, Adams extends his concern for effective government by specifying secondary constitutional features that can be altered to fit the particularities of place and achieve better representation. These alterations show representation and the separation of functions are interrelated. Furthermore, Adams's discussion of the changeability of secondary constitutional features does not contradict his functional account but further emphasizes the importance—and permanency—of effectual government, protection from encroachment, and the rule of law in his system. The significance of the rule of law in Adams's account builds on the separation of functions literature. At times, some separation of functions scholars suggest a tension between the rule of law and effectual government.[10] However, this tension only appears at first glance; a full understanding of the functional ends of governmental powers allows for the use of discretionary action to limited ends and maintains the rule of law as the basis of republicanism. Returning to Adams's thought allows us to see how the republican principle of the rule of law is promoted by this functional account.

Interpretation of Adams

The delay in turning back to John Adams's 1770s work as a guide for later constitutional thought has roots in the two interpretations of Adams best articulated by Joyce Appleby and Gordon Wood. More recent scholarship has pushed against the standard description of Adams as irrelevant and aristocratic, but often does so within the confines of or in relation to Adams's *Defence*.

C. Bradley Thompson offers a contextual approach that situates Adams within a larger tradition of political thought, with the purpose of proving that Adams never veered from his commitment to republicanism.[11] Luke Mayville adds to Thompson's account by highlighting Adams's fear of oligarchic power.[12] Mayville's study is helpful for this project because it provides a fuller account of Adams's view of aristocracy. For Adams, an aristocrat is simply "every man who can command or influence two votes; one beside his own." Framing a constitution to ensure responsibility and efficiency requires that the draftsmen pay attention to the reality that political elites, either through "qualities of merit" or "qualities of fortune," could use their influence over fellow citizens to wield political power.[13] Adams's concern for this reality allows us to better understand his system of representation in *Thoughts on Government.*

While Mayville provides a thorough understanding of Adams's fear of oligarchy, he rarely considers *Thoughts on Government.* Richard Alan Ryerson provides a larger discussion of *Thoughts* through a chronological analysis of Adams's political ideas and provides two insights. First, as early as 1776, Adams—as the articulator of an American republican orthodoxy—was pushing against more radical egalitarian views of politics, especially Paine's *Common Sense*; second, Adams understood the basis for republican government as the rule of law and a representative assembly but recognized an "'inexhaustible variety' of republics arising out of the 'innumerable variations' in 'the possible combinations of the powers of society.'"[14] My analysis of Adams's representative system in *Thoughts on Government* will show that he does not put forward a method of representation that constructs a legislature representing three distinct orders, as many of the "mixed regime" Adams scholars suggest, but rather puts forward a theory of mirrored representation that aims to proportionally represent the distinct interests of the people.

Like Ryerson, Willi Paul Adams highlights the contrast between Paine and Adams, suggesting a real difference in 1776 between republican theorists like Adams, who put forward a moderated system of government directed toward stability, efficiency, and responsibility, and egalitarian thinkers.[15] To understand the difference between Paine and Adams, Willi Paul Adams suggests a dichotomy between principle and experience. However, *Thoughts* makes clear that John Adams's approach to politics was directed by both concerns. Adams's combination of principle and experience shows the influence of Montesquieu on the American thinker. *Thoughts on Government* suggests another Montesquieuan influence: the belief that constitutions are reflections of the people. In *Thoughts*, Adams articulates the necessary institutional features of republican governments while maintaining that a constitution ought to fit the people who adopt it. A reading of *Thoughts on Government* with an eye to the separation of functions shows why Adams recognized specific features of republican government as necessary to good—that is, effective—governance while other features were amenable to the particularities of place. Further, it points to the elevation of the rule of law as the basis for republican government within a separation of functions account.

Thoughts on Government, 1776

What follows is an analysis of *Thoughts on Government* as an articulation of the separation of functions. Directed by the structure of Adams's *Thoughts*, this analysis considers the three branches individually, with attention to the way that Adams crafts the institutions to produce and ensure specific ends: The legislature is directed toward making law for the public good, the unitary executive to administer the law and provide security, the judiciary toward judgment that provides protection for the individual through the consistent meaning of the law.

To begin his proposal, Adams defines the aim of a republican government by critiquing Alexander Pope's claim that the government "which is best administered is best." He argues, "Nothing is more certain, from the history of nations and the nature of man, than that some forms of government are better fitted for being well administered than others."[16] Against Pope's claim, Adams argues that the administration of government is dependent on the form of the regime. This dismissal at the start of *Thoughts* points to the purpose of his reflection: In devising a republican government, one must ensure, first, the republican form and, second, that the republic can produce good administration of the law. In short, Adams begins by directing his readers to the unity between the aims and effects of a republican system. He makes this unity clear: "The divine science of politics is the science of social happiness, and the blessings of society depend entirely on the constitutions of government, which are generally institutions that last for many generations."[17] For Adams, politics is a practical science that produces the effect of happiness, or "ease, comfort, security" through the structuring of institutions that promote that end.

Thus, against Pope's assertion, Adams contends that the best government is that which best provides for the happiness of the people. Adams, "like all sober inquirers after truth," suggests virtue as that which produces happiness.[18] In recognition that this pamphlet puts forward a practical goal for constitution-making, the meaning of governmental virtue must be considered. Following Montesquieu, Adams contrasts governments animated by the principles of virtue against those animated by fear or honor.[19] A recognition of this Montesquieuan influence offers two lessons. First, Montesquieu defines virtue as the love of the laws and of the country. Second, this virtue is attained by a government that is moderated through institutional design.[20] Moreover, the loss of virtue comes from a corruption of government or a government that has become immoderate: "In a popular government when the laws have ceased to be executed, as this can come only from the corruption of the republic, the state is already lost."[21] These lessons from Montesquieu are found in Adams's theory: first, in his commitment to republicanism as the rule of law and, second, in his institutional design that produces efficiency and prevents encroachment (immoderation).

Adams suggests that the recent experience of Americans "will convince any candid mind, that there is no good government but what is republican. That the only valuable part of the British constitution is so; because the very definition of a republic is 'an empire of laws, and not of men.'"[22] Therefore, he pairs his lessons from Montesquieu with James Harrington's definition of a republic. For Adams, the organization of a republican government must be directed toward producing the rule of law. Interestingly, Adams here suggests that the "only valuable part of the British constitution" is that it provides for the rule of law.[23] Yet, the British system is limited as it consists in other parts that do not produce republican ends. Therefore, Adams tempers his approval of the British system. Its sole value is the rule of law.

Adams further expands his initial definition of a republic: "That, as a republic is the best form of government, so that particular arrangement of society, or, in other words, that form of government which is best contrived to secure an impartial and exact execution of the law, is the best of republics."[24] A rule of law system structured on mere legislation is not enough; rather, the government must be arranged in such a way as to produce the efficient execution of the law. This concern for efficiency unites Adams's conception of constitutionalism with the separation of functions account articulated by David Siemers and others. Moreover, while Siemers acknowledges that the separation of functions has two ends—efficiency and protection against encroachment—he argues that the concern for encroachment has led to an overemphasis on checks and balances while neglecting the separation of functions organization of the separation of powers.[25] In *Thoughts on Government*,

Adams provides a blueprint for a republican form of government that seeks to achieve the two aims of a separation of functions constitution. A study of each branch will show how Adams's system does not fall into the checks and balances trap observed by Siemers but utilizes checks to support the separation of functions.

The Legislative Power

Following his definition of a republic, Adams asserts legislative power—making law—as the principal act of government. In structuring the legislature, Adams directs this power toward the public good through true representation, the moderating system of bicameralism, and frequent elections. First, the legislative power is paired with representation. To maintain the rule of law, the legislative power must create laws that equally apply to and are the product of the people. The best way to guarantee equal application is by making the legislative power a representative body: "In a large society, inhabiting an extensive country, it is impossible that the whole should assemble to make laws. The first necessary step, then, is to depute power from the many to a few of the most wise and good."[26] C. Bradley Thompson attributes the mischaracterization of Adams as a proponent of balanced government to his theory of legislative representation. For Thompson, although Adams did not put forward a theory of government based on the balance of different societal orders in all three branches, he did advocate for a division within the legislature rooted in "different orders of *offices*, but [not] of men."[27] This division, Thompson's "triple equipoise," produced a kind of moderation that could be understood as balance.[28] Thompson understands Adams's approach in *Thoughts* through a well-studied account of personal letters. However, the text of *Thoughts on Government* itself, especially as a pamphlet with influence beyond the three states that requested his help, reveals a deeper republican commitment.

The function of the legislative power is to make laws for the public good. To accomplish this, the legislature must comprehend the interests of the people. For Adams, representation, as a means of ensuring the rule of the people, "should be in miniature an exact portrait of the people at large. . . . That it may be the interest of this assembly to do strict justice at all times, it should be an equal representation, or in other words, equal interests among the people should have equal interests in it."[29] Of note, Adams does not here point to landed or other monied interests, but rather suggests mirror representation of the several interests found in the state. For Adams, true representation is produced not solely through fair and frequent elections but through the (fair and frequent) election of those who proportionally represent the diverse interests of the people. While this theory of representation acknowledges that there must be some reason for people to unite in choosing a representative—perhaps a recognition of their wisdom and goodness, or just their social influence[30]—the representatives themselves must represent based on interest. Proper representation is so vital for republican government that Adams stresses that the "greatest care" must be taken in designing this representative assembly.[31]

Adams's concern for true representation is further articulated in his discussion of the dangers that come from entrusting all the powers of government to a single assembly. This discussion highlights the basic logic of the separation of functions, namely that particular powers are granted to an institution because it is naturally best equipped to produce a particular outcome. According to Adams, a single supreme assembly entrusted with the legislative, executive, and judicial powers is unable to govern for the interests of the people. He opines, "I think a people cannot be free, nor ever happy, whose government is in one assembly."[32] A single assembly threatens both happiness as the end of government and the liberty promised by a republican government. In this, it threatens efficiency of government and produces the conditions for governmental encroachment. To explain this, Adams turns to his understanding of the regime as a reflection of the human person; the dangers of a single assembly are rooted in the "vices, follies, and frailties" of the human being. A single assembly will become "avaricious, and in time will not scruple to exempt itself from burdens, which it will lay . . . on its constituents," and "grow ambitious, and after a time will not hesitate to vote itself perpetual."[33] A single supreme assembly is almost, by definition, inefficient and threatens to become tyrannical.

In addition to the vices that may befall a single assembly, this structure of government lacks the institutional qualities necessary to accomplish the executive and judicial powers. A single assembly should not hold the executive power because it lacks "secrecy and dispatch." Likewise, it should not be entrusted with the judicial power because it is "too numerous, too slow, and too little skilled in the laws."[34] Combining these institutional deficiencies, Adams describes what dangers this single, supreme assembly might produce: "A single assembly, possessed of all the powers of government, would make arbitrary laws for their own interest, execute all laws arbitrarily for their own interest, and adjudge all controversies in their own favor."[35] This is the case even for a single assembly that is elected through proper representative means; the corrupting nature of governmental authority is too much for one body. Adams's illustration offers two key arguments. First, that the separation of governmental functions into different branches is necessary because a representative assembly, due to its size and deliberative manner, is ill-equipped to perform the executive and judicial functions. This is a central idea in the separation of functions literature.[36] Second, the legislative power itself must be moderated through a bicameral system to protect against the arbitrary use of power that grows from avarice and ambition. This moderation supports the efficient exercise of the legislative power.

Accordingly, Adams turns to evaluate bicameralism as a means of preventing the dangers of unicameral legislative power. Through bicameralism, Adams seeks to ensure that legislative action is directed toward the public good rather than the self-interest of the legislators. He writes, "If the legislative power is wholly in one assembly, and the executive in another, or in a single person, these two powers will oppose and encroach upon each other, until the contest shall end in war, and the whole power, legislative and executive, be usurped by the strongest."[37] In this assessment, Adams recognizes that the competition between the two political powers when the legislative power is united in one assembly is too volatile to be combated solely by the judiciary within a simple separation of powers system. Indeed, any intended check provided by the veto power, while a support against the legislature's susceptibility to avarice and ambition, is insufficient to negate the tendency toward usurpation. Moderation of the legislative power requires a "distinct assembly be constituted as mediator." Adams calls this "distinct assembly" a "council," which is chosen "by ballot, from among [the representatives] or their constituents, or both" to create "a distinct assembly."[38] Thus, the system of bicameralism provides for a smaller chamber to moderate the legislative power, which protects against the avarice and ambition that corrupt single assemblies and directs the representative body to craft law for the interests of the people.

The moderating effects of a second legislative chamber can also be found in the arguments at the Constitutional Convention and Publius's defense of the Senate. According to Madison's *Convention Notes*, Edmund Randolph argues that a second legislative chamber is necessary to "control" the legislative process and produce good laws. He argues, "A firmness & independence may be the more necessary also in this branch, as it ought to guard the Constitution against encroachments."[39] Randolph appears to share Adams's concern that a secondary legislative chamber provides for effectual government and protection against encroachment. Similarly, in *Federalist* No. 62, Madison discusses how the size of the Senate provides for an intra-legislative "salutary check" that "doubles the security to the people by requiring the concurrence of two distinct bodies."[40] While the Senate functions as a check to prevent encroachment and abuse, Madison also argues that the Senate's involvement in the legislative process produces the qualities of good government, "first, fidelity to the object of government, which is the happiness of the people: secondly, a knowledge of the means by which that object can be best attained."[41] The Senate's qualities surely develop through the negotiations at the Constitutional Convention and its age and representation requirements clearly differ with Adams's model. Nonetheless, central mechanical features of a system of bicameralism point to a shared constitutional logic. Both Adams's defense of bicameralism and the later arguments offered by Randolph and Madison in the 1780s reflect a concern regarding protection against encroachment and effectual, good governance.

The Executive Power

Adams's discussion of the executive power primarily extends his argument regarding the twofold purpose of the separation of functions. Similar to his analysis of the legislature, he shows that those offices entrusted with political power must be structured to ensure the execution of their particular function and prevent the growth of avarice and ambition. With this view, Adams focuses his discussion on frequent elections and the executive's relationship with the legislature. While Adams's discussion of the executive power may seem limited, it is important to remember that he is proposing executive powers on the state level. Nonetheless, it is noteworthy that Adams's executive plays a larger role in political decision-making compared to early state constitutions like Virginia's.[42] Unlike a simple republican constitution that entrusts the legislature with a majority of governmental power, Adams's system of separation of functions puts forward an executive branch that points toward the executive of Article II.

Adams shows that he understands the executive function primarily as carrying out the laws through his concern for frequent elections and the interbranch relationship between the executive and legislative powers. The executive is chosen when the two legislative chambers "by joint ballot choose a governor, who, after being stripped of most of those badges of domination called prerogatives, should have a free and independent exercise of his judgment, and be made also an integral part of the legislature."[43] While this initial presentation suggests a potentially controversial role for the executive, namely within the legislature, Adams uses this argument to provide further evidence that his system is designed to produce controlled, effectual government through the structuring of powers for particular ends: "As the governor is to be invested with the executive power, with consent of the council, I think he ought to have a negative upon the legislative."[44] The veto power is the sole legislative activity granted to the governor. This interbranch involvement ensures that the legislative power is employed for the public good in line with its representative purpose.

The veto power is often construed as an example of checks and balances to reconfirm the coequality of the distinct branches. This reading suggests that the separation of powers is intended for one purpose: protection against encroachment. Indeed, Siemers suggests that Adams's construction of the veto power may lead to this reading. For Siemers, Adams's veto is an example of "legislative-process coequality," an argument for an absolute veto that failed to win the day at the Constitutional Convention.[45] Yet, Adams's veto offers a lesson about the relationship between the two purposes of the separation of functions. Because a separation of functions system recognizes the predominance of the legislative branch, the executive and judicial branches are fortified to guard against legislative overreach.[46] Adams shows that this fortification is not solely defensive but also corrective.[47] As a check, the veto both protects the distinctive functions of the executive and leads to a better use of legislative power. Adams reminds us that legislative overreach can occur when the legislature attempts to take on executive or judicial action or when it expands its legislative function beyond the ends entrusted to the government. Far from working against efficient governance, the governor's veto provides a check against legislation that is opposed to the interests of the people. It encourages the legislature to better execute its function and thus supports effectual government.

Similarly, Adams is aware that a constitution must guard against executive usurpation. The principal way to control executive avarice and ambition is through annual election, which ensures that the governor "will always have so much reverence and affection for the people, their representatives and counsellors, that, although you give him an independent exercise of his judgment, he will seldom use it in opposition to the two houses, except in cases the public utility of which would be conspicuous."[48] While this comment is principally about the necessity of annual elections, it also points to Adams's recognition that the governor should be granted a certain leniency for discretionary power. The governor should be given "an independent exercise of his judgment" to be used for "public utility." Thus, while Adams emphasizes the centrality of legislation within his system, he recognizes the need for discretionary executive power, in addition to the veto, to protect against legislative misconduct and provide for the public good. He thus grants three additional powers to the governor: command over the militia and armies; pardons, which will be shared with the council; and the nomination and appointment of judges, justices, and "all other officers, civil and military," with the advice and consent of the council, unless the people decide in favor of a more popularly elected government.[49]

This expansion of executive power provides a fuller account of Adams's understanding that the function of the governor is to carry out the laws and provide security. This new articulation of executive power obliges one to consider the position of discretionary power within a rule of law system. Recognizing its Lockean origins, Benjamin Kleinerman describes discretionary action as "a crucial supplement to the constitutional order created by the standing laws."[50] Thus, for Kleinerman and other scholars of presidential prerogative, discretionary power is inherently outside the bounds of the constitutional or legal system.[51] Since Adams's definition of a republic is "a government of laws," discretionary power seems inherently in tension with his proposed system. But Adams suggests an alternative reading. When he grants the governor discretionary power, he limits its usage to particular actions: the pardon, command of the militia or army, and the legislative veto, and qualifies that executive action must be directed toward "public utility." These specific actions are not extraconstitutional but are central elements of the office of the governor. Moreover, he grants these powers to an officer subject to annual elections. Adams's discretionary power is limited compared to the powers put forward in Article II. This difference may be rooted in Adams's recognition that he is proposing a structure for state constitutions; nonetheless, it offers lessons for the separation of functions.

Found throughout Adams's proposal is a fear of arbitrary power that subverts popular sovereignty by directing governmental action to the interest of politicians rather than the interests of the people. This fear directs Adams to moderate the legislature. Now, by providing specific avenues for the use of executive discretion, Adams recognizes the necessity of flexibility, or dispatch, while ensuring that the executive remains responsible to the people. Simply put, Adams's system emphasizes that the governmental functions are separated for efficiency *and* that this separation empowers the branches to act lawfully in accord with the public good. The interests of the institution are good only insofar as they reflect the public interest.

This unity of interest between the people and their governmental officials directs Adams to extend the principle of annual elections to representatives and counselors. He writes, "there not being in the whole circle of sciences a maxim more infallible than this, 'where annual elections end, there slavery begins.'" Annual elections teach public officials "the great political virtues of humility, patience, and moderation, without which every man in power becomes a ravenous beast of prey."[52] By instituting annual elections, governmental officials are kept on a short leash to prevent the growth of ambition or avarice. Moreover, the people are allowed to practice political judgment via elections, which fosters democratic vigilance.

There is a complication in Adams's articulation of annual elections, however, since it seems to be contingent upon an abundance of virtuous citizens: "It would be attended, no doubt, with many advantages; and if the society has a sufficient number of suitable characters to supply the great number of vacancies which would be made by such a rotation, I can see no objection to it."[53] Therefore, while Adams crafts a constitutional system to maintain the proper functions of government, this maintenance is further dependent on the virtuous character of public officials. One infers that Adams realistically understands, like the Federalists a decade later, that the protections against the misuse of power cannot solely depend on ever-virtuous politicians since the tendency toward avarice and ambition is rooted in human nature. However, he does suggest that virtue is necessary for the noblest, highest, and most stable government. Thus, Adams's proposal seems to suggest a layered understanding of constitutionalism where the separation of functions is necessary but not sufficient for the highest aims of government. A secondary layer rooted in proper character is required for a government to pursue higher ends.

The Judicial Power

Adams's presentation of the judicial power seems to unite those higher governmental aims with his understanding of republicanism as the rule of law. He writes, "The dignity and stability of government in all branches, the morals of the people, and every blessing of society depend so much upon an upright and skillful administration of justice, that the judicial power ought to be distinct from both the legislative and executive, and independent upon both, that so it may be a check upon both, as both should be checks upon that." Though his analysis is brief, Adams offers a separation of functions understanding of the judiciary. The court must be independent from the political branches to perform its function, judgment. However, separation alone is not sufficient; Adams argues that the judiciary must be made further independent through specific character traits of the judges themselves.

Therefore, instead of reflecting on the need to control tendencies toward avarice, ambition, and self-interest, as is found in his discussion of the legislative and executive powers, Adams turns to consider the positive attributes that will empower the branch to judge well. For Adams, the branch furthest from the lawmaking process is least likely to fall to avarice and ambition. Judges must "be always men of learning and experience in the laws, of exemplary morals, great patience, calmness, coolness, and attention. Their attention should not be distracted with jarring interests; they should not be dependent on any man, or any body of men."[54] Adams puts forward three necessary attributes: first, knowledge and experience of the laws; second, exemplary morals; third, independence. The first of these attributes provides for efficient execution of the judicial function. To have a consistent standard of interpretation, judges must be well educated and experienced in the laws. The second attribute allows for permanency and stability. The third, plainly, independence: judges should "hold estates for life in their offices; or, in other words, their commissions should be during good behavior," and subject to impeachment by the legislature.[55] In this presentation of the judiciary, Adams shows how the "dignity and stability" of government, the rule of law, is protected by experienced, independent, and long-serving judges. Moreover, within this rule of law system, the judiciary secures the government of laws, which further ensures the protection of individual citizens—the judicial end identified by Kleinerman and Tulis.[56]

Possible Constitutional Modifications

The foregoing analysis followed the structure of Adams's pamphlet by highlighting the central features of his separation of functions account. Yet, found throughout *Thoughts* are suggestions that certain parts of the constitutional system are changeable. These modifications are secondary adjustments meant to promote the central principles of his system. After recognizing the separation of functions basis of his pamphlet, these modifications clearly aim at promoting an effective and representative government. Thus, Adams's suggestions regarding constitutional change are premised on the assumption that these changes will lead to a truer republican government that is more efficient and offers better protection against encroachment through a refined method of representation.

The first potential modification is in the election of the two legislative chambers. Adams acknowledges that the current crisis may limit the ability to design a system of representation based on interest. He suggests, for the time being, that the colonies proceed along "established modes" of election.[57] While he points to possible changes in the election system in the near future, the representative end and structure of the legislative power is permanent; changes ought to further the goal of a republican government. Therefore, these changes in representation should happen only if they produce a legislature that is better at making laws for the interests of the people. Additionally, Adams provides flexibility in the size and manner of the election for the upper chamber of the legislature. Again, the end and structure of the legislative power is supported by this change. In a similar way that election reform allows for better representation, changes to the council aim to empower the branch to perform is legislative function.

In a similar vein, Adams discusses possible modifications to the election of the executive. He identifies both the executive (i.e., the governor) and other officers within the executive branch. Again, he ties the possible change to the challenge of forming a government in emergency circumstances. He writes, "the present exigency of American affairs, when, by an act of Parliament we are put out of the royal protection, and consequently discharged from our allegiance . . . it has become necessary to assume government for our immediate security." Thus, for the present, the "government"—those executive officers necessary for carrying out the law and providing security, such as the governor, lieutenant governor, and treasurer—will be formed through a joint ballot of the legislative chambers.[58] If, in times of peace, however, this mode of election is found "inconvenient," the legislature can modify elections so that executive officers are chosen either by "the people at large," or "it may enlarge the term for which they shall be chosen to seven years, or three years, or for life, or make any alterations which the society shall find productive for its ease, its security, its freedom, or in one word, its happiness."[59]

This modification seems to contradict his defense of annual elections. Yet perhaps it is significant that this change is solely offered for executive officers, not lawmakers, and does not extend to the structural components of the office (e.g., unitary nature and powers). These modifications are suggestions to better achieve the efficient exercise of the executive power to serve the ends of government: ease, security, freedom, and happiness. The legislature is entrusted with this determination to secure those ends and prevent any antirepublican expressions of executive power. Moreover, while this legislative duty might suggest a greater role for the legislature, the change itself opens the possibility for a more independent executive—one who could be elected by the people or who serves for a longer term.

Adams's Republicanism

Considering Adams's constitutional system in terms of its essential and secondary, or changeable, features provides a better understanding of his republicanism. His comments regarding which parts of his proposed system are open to modification and silence about the changeability of other parts of the government reemphasize the central concerns of *Thoughts on Government.* First, representation in the legislative power is necessary for making laws conducive to the public good. This representation must reflect the interests of the people so that the legislature can truly be understood to make laws on behalf of the people. He suggests modifications to correct any misrepresentation caused by designing a system of government during wartime. Second, Adams suggests that some aspects of the council are changeable. Thus, he emphasizes bicameralism as a structure that moderates the legislative power to fully perform its legislative function while allowing flexibility in the size of the upper chamber to meet the needs of the different states.[60] Similarly, Adams's modifications to the executive point to his understanding that institutional arrangement can produce better representation, protection against encroachment, and enhanced execution of its governmental function.

While these modifications provide greater insight into his system, Adams's silence regarding other changes directs his readers to what he sees as the fundamental principle of republicanism: the rule of law. Whereas secondary changes to executive and legislative elections aim to better provide for an efficient and representative government, Adams reemphasizes the importance of an independent judiciary. Like many founders, Adams recognizes that the fidelity to the law that comes from an independent judiciary requires the appointment of judges rather than their election. Indeed, judicial independence, by way of lifelong appointments, is secured even if the people choose to have a more popular government through the direct election of the governor: "If you do, all officers, civil and military, may be chosen by joint ballot of both houses; or, in order to preserve the independence and importance of each house, by ballot of one house, concurred in by the other."[61] This change in appointment perhaps allows for a more "republican" government because those closest to the people vote by ballot; however, the process still elevates the judiciary above the demands of frequent election and provides for a refinement in choice through the bicameral process. Any concern that this would increase judicial dependence on the legislature is negated through lifetime tenure. Likewise, recognizing the representative foundation of Adams's account, the judges would further understand their obligation to protect individual rights. Yet, since this protection can only come from hearing actual cases, the judiciary is relatively weak compared to the legislature in Adams's account.

After analysis, Adams's *Thoughts on Government* is an early articulation of an American system of the separation of functions. As a student of Montesquieu, Adams separates the three branches not simply for a balance within the government but according to the function and nature of the powers. He pairs his understanding of the nature of each power with the recognition that governments can fall to the vices of avarice and ambition. Thus, he designs a system directed by the function of each power and infused with the proper checks—bicameralism and frequent elections—to better empower the branches to function well. Adams's design for the legislative and executive power is a moderated system that ensures that the government is rooted in the rule of law and that its power cannot be subverted by the will of officeholders.

As a whole, Adams's 1776 pamphlet articulates a republican government with three branches: a bicameral legislature formed to make laws for the interests of the people and refined through the presence of a smaller upper chamber; a unitary executive in the form of a governor with the attributes of secrecy and dispatch, a strong veto power to protect against legislative encroachment and misconduct, and discretionary power to provide for the public good; and an independent judiciary populated by men of wisdom and virtue whose governmental position is directed toward ensuring the protection of the people through the consistent application of the law. In 1787, a constitution with similar features is developed for the nation. Moreover, like the constitutional structure articulated throughout this paper, the separation of functions provides for efficient government and protection against encroachment through the primacy of the rule of law. That in turn produces a government that displays the virtues of effectiveness, stability, and responsibility. Adams's constitutional system in 1776 shares a similar structure *and* effect with the Federalist account of the US Constitution.

Shared Aims Found in the *Federalist*

Throughout the *Federalist*, Alexander Hamilton and James Madison discuss how the Constitution produces efficiency and protection from encroachment. The separation of functions literature has turned to the *Federalist*'s articulation of the separation of powers, especially found in *Federalist* No. 51, as proof against a coequal division of governmental power.[62] David Siemers has also pointed to *Federalist* No. 78 as an example of the separation of functions and its two effects.[63] The *Federalist*'s separation of functions understanding is not limited to those specific papers, however, and additional passages recall Adams's understanding of the effects of a separation of functions constitutional structure.

Hamilton is the great articulator of American governmental efficiency. Notably, in *Federalist* No. 68, he turns to discuss administration in the same way that Adams begins his discussion in *Thoughts*, by referencing Alexander Pope. While Hamilton refuses to "acquiesce" with Pope's claim that good administration ought to trump the form of government, he says that good administration is the "true test" of government.[64] This should not be read as a break from Adams since other papers, especially *Federalist* No. 39, have already established a republic as the only form of government "reconcilable with the genius of the people of America."[65] Rather, as Adams's *Thoughts on Government* shows, the respectability of a republican government comes from its promotion of the rule of law, efficiency, and the protection of rights. Therefore, *Federalist* No. 68 is proof that the Constitution aims to create good administration, an essential aspect of an efficient government. Thus, Adams and Hamilton articulate a constitutional logic that unites the aims and effects of government: a good constitution shows an "aptitude and tendency to produce a good administration."[66] In an essay concerning the merits of the Electoral College, Hamilton argues that this method of election provides for "a constant probability of seeing the station filled by characters preeminent for ability and virtue. And this will be thought no inconsiderable recommendation of the Constitution by those who are able to estimate the share which the executive in every government must necessarily have in its good or ill administration."[67] A good administration requires that the executive function be entrusted to a person of suitable character. The shared understanding between Hamilton and Adams is clear.

James Madison, who consistently addresses the Constitution's conformity to republican principles, best articulates its protection against encroachment. Like Adams, the protection against encroachment is tied to a government that is representative of the people and directed toward the public good. In *Federalist* No. 37, Madison acknowledges the difficulties encountered at the Convention in devising the Constitution, especially "combining the requisite stability and energy in government with the inviolable attention due to liberty and to the republican form."[68] Moreover, Madison recognizes a danger that attacks both energy and stability: the mutability of law. He writes, "An irregular and mutable legislation is not more an evil in itself than it is odious to the people; and it may be pronounced with assurance that the people of this country, enlightened as they are with regard to the nature, and interested, as the great body of them are, in the effects of government, will never be satisfied till some remedy be applied" to the turbulent state governments. This concern shows the relationship between the aims of Adams's articulation of the separation of functions and the Federalists'. First, Madison recognizes that the people are interested in both the nature and effects of the Constitution. Second, the rule of law is of paramount concern since energy, stability, and the confidence of the people are destroyed through ever-changing law. Third, the mutability of the law attacks both the efficiency of government, through improper administration, and representation since a government that no longer has the confidence of the people cannot represent their interests. These three conclusions have been put forward as lessons gleaned from *Thoughts*.

Before overselling the continuation of Adams's ideas, one should consider Madison's definition of a republic to ensure that the connection between Adams's articulation of republicanism in 1776 and the Federalist understanding in the 1780s is tenable. In *Federalist* No. 39, Madison states: "We may define a republic to be, or at least may bestow that name on, a government which derives all its powers directly or indirectly from the great body of the people, and is administered by persons holding their offices during pleasure for a limited period, or during good behavior."[69] At first glance, this definition is more particular than Adams's "government of laws." However, further consideration reconciles the thinkers' definitions. Madison expounds on his definition, showing which features are essential to a republican government and which features are sufficient to produce the needed outcome. It is essential that a republican government "be derived from the great body of society, not from an inconsiderable portion or a favored class." But this representation can be produced when "the persons administering it be appointed, either directly or indirectly, by the people; and that they hold their appointment by either" specific terms in office or during good behavior.[70] Thus, Madison seems to agree with Adams's recognition of the "inexhaustible variety" of republics.[71] Republics are structured so as to produce specific effects. Both thinkers structure their constitutions to produce an efficient government that protects against encroachment and preserves the rule of law.

Conclusion

This chapter has sought to provide a deeper look into John Adams's *Thoughts on Government* as an early articulation of the separation of functions. A careful examination of this 1776 pamphlet finds a system of the separation of powers directed by the functions of each branch of government. Moreover, this constitutional structure puts forward the rule of law as the defining feature of republican government. While asserting the rule of law as the animating principle for republican government, Adams does not diminish the need for discretionary executive power. Rather, he attempts to reconcile the rule of law with discretionary power. For Adams, a constitution that is animated by the rule of law secures effective government and protection against encroachment. Thus, Adams encourages study concerning the rule of law within the separation of functions—whether it emerges as a distinct third aim or is better understood as a necessary feature that ensures effectual government and prevents encroachment. This may lead to deeper insight concerning how a written constitution not only preserves liberty by preventing governmental encroachment but also empowers effective and efficient government.

Notes

1. *The Works of John Adams*, vol. 4, ed. Robert J. Taylor (Cambridge, MA: Harvard University Press, 1979), 65–68 (https://www.masshist.org/publications/adams-papers/index.php/view/PJA04dg2).

2. See Ben Peterson, "Republican Institutionalism for a 'Government of Laws': The Polybian Political Science of John Adams," *American Political Thought: A Journal of Ideas, Institutions and Culture*, vol. 8 (Summer 2019): 323–346.

3. For the first view, see Joyce Appleby, "The New Republican Synthesis and the Changing Political Ideas of John Adams," *American Quarterly* 25, no. 5 (Dec. 1973): 578–595; John R. Howe, *The Changing Political Thought of John Adams*, (Princeton: Princeton University Press, 1966). And, for the second, see Gordon Wood, *The Creation of the American Republic, 1776–1787* (Chapel Hill: University of North Carolina Press, 1969).

4. Timothy W. Burns, "Adams, Turgot, and the New Science of Politics," in *Classical Rationalism and the Politics of Europe*, ed. Ann Ward (Newcastle upon Tyne, UK: Cambridge Scholars Publishing, 2017), 197–229.

5. M. J. C Vile's definition of the four elements for a separation of powers theory points to Adams's *Thoughts on Government* as a strong example of the separation of powers. As we will, see, however, the pamphlet fits better with an account of the separation of powers as the separation of functions. For Vile's discussion of Adams, see: M. J. C Vile, *Constitutionalism and the Separation of Powers*, 2nd ed. (Indianapolis, IN: Liberty Fund, 1998), 14.

6. David J. Siemers, *The Myth of Coequal Branches: Restoring the Constitution's Separation of Functions* (Columbia: University of Missouri Press, 2018), 7.

7. Richard Neustadt puts forward a different reading of the separation of powers as "separate institutions *sharing* powers." Richard Neustadt, *Presidential Power and the Modern Presidents: The Politics of Leadership from Roosevelt to Reagan* (New York: Free Press, 1990), 29.

8. Jeffrey Tulis, *The Rhetorical Presidency* (Princeton, NJ: Princeton University Press, 1987), 42.

9. Benjamin Kleinerman, *The Discretionary President: The Promise and Peril of Executive Power* (Lawrence, KS: University Press of Kansas, 2009), 104.

10. See, for example, Tulis's discussion of the "dynamic" interbranch disputes and how presidents developed several ways around congressional deadlock: "Similar scenarios could be constructed for the other issues over which congressional and presidential claims to authority conflict, such as the use of executive agreements in place of treaties, the deployment of military force, or the executive impoundment of appropriated monies," Tulis, 45; Kleinerman puts it more directly, describing presidential discretion as a "crucial supplement to the constitutional order created by the standing laws." See Kleinerman, 7. This passage will be discussed in a later section; similarly, Clement Fatovic's analysis of executive power provides great insight. He argues that "the Federalists' theory of executive power is the idea that a constitution is a purposive and flexible instrument," which enables the president to respond to emergencies. Clement Fatovic, *Outside the Law: Emergency and Executive Power* (Baltimore, MD: Johns Hopkins University Press, 2009), 182.

11. C. Bradley Thompson, *John Adams and the Spirit of Liberty* (Lawrence, KS: University Press of Kansas, 1998).

12. See Luke Mayville, "Fear of the Few: John Adams and the Power Elite," *Polity* 47, no 1 (January 2015): 5–32; Luke Mayville, *John Adams and the Fear of American Oligarchy* (Princeton: Princeton University Press, 2016).

13. Mayville, "Fear of the Few," 18.

14. Richard Alan Ryerson, *John Adams's Republic* (Baltimore: Johns Hopkins University Press, 2016), 175.

15. Willi Paul Adams, *The First American Constitutions: Republican Ideology and the Making of State Constitutions in the Revolutionary Era* (Chapel Hill: University of North Carolina Press, 1980), 124.

16. John Adams, *Revolutionary Writings,* Selected and with a Forward by C. Bradley Thompson (Indianapolis: Liberty Fund, 2000, 287). This remark by Alexander Pope was frequently cited during the founding period. For example, in *Federalist* No. 68, Alexander Hamilton directly engages with this quotation. The difference between Adams's and Hamilton's usage of the quotation will be discussed in a later section.

17. Ibid.

18. Id. at 287–289.

19. Montesquieu, *The Spirit of the Laws*, ed. Anne M. Cohler, Basia C. Miller, and Harold S. Stone (Cambridge: Cambridge University Press, 1989), 21–28.

20. Montesquieu, 42.

21. Montesquieu, 22.

22. J. Adams, 288.

23. While one may ask why Adams would recognize that the British system produces the rule of law when its form of government is not the same as the republican system that he articulates here, Adams's claim can clearly be linked to Montesquieu. As demonstrated in *Spirit of the Laws,* Montesquieu recognizes that republics are animated by virtue. He also notes that republics come in two forms, democracy and aristocracy.

24. J. Adams, 288.

25. Siemers, 9.

26. J. Adams, 288.

27. Thompson, 247.

28. Id. at 221.

29. J. Adams, 288.

30. Mayville, 8.

31. J. Adams, 288.

32. Id. at 289.

33. Ibid.

34. Ibid.

35. Ibid.

36. See Siemers, 41; Tulis, 41–42.

37. J. Adams, 289–290.

38. Id. at 290.

39. James Madison, *Notes of Debates in the Federal Convention of 1787*, Bicentennial ed. (New York: Norton, 1988), 110.

40. James Madison, "*Federalist* No. 62," in *The Federalist Papers*, ed. Clinton Rossiter (New York: Signet Classics, 1961), 377.

41. Id. at 378.

42. This is especially interesting given Thompson's suggestion that Virginia's constitution was influenced by *Thoughts on Government* and the pamphlet's earlier iteration in a letter to Richard Henry Lee. See Thompson, 213.

43. J. Adams, 290.

44. Ibid.

45. Siemers, 46–47.

46. Id. at. 35.

47. Id. at 55. At times Siemers raises the protective nature of certain checks, like the veto, without fully articulating the corrective element—the element that allows for a better achievement of the governmental function.

48. J. Adams, 290.

49. Ibid.

50. Kleinerman, 7.

51. See also Fatovic's chapter on executive power and the American founding. Fatovic, 157–207.

52. J. Adams, 291.

53. Ibid.

54. Id. at 291–292.

55. Id. at 292.

56. See Kleinerman, 13; Tulis, 43.

57. J. Adams, 289.

58. Id. at 290.

59. Id. at 291.

60. C. Bradley Thompson makes the claim that Adams's argument here is necessarily malleable because of the property disparities in the several states he is advising. The difference between the states is not disputed. However, I contend that general constitutional principles can be gleaned from the features Adams puts forward as changeable. Through his presentation of a generalizable American constitutionalism, we can see further applications of Adams's ideas beyond New Jersey, North Carolina, and Virginia. See Thompson, 249.

61. J. Adams, 291.

62. See Siemers, 51–55; Kleinerman, 84–86.

63. Siemers, 53.

64. Alexander Hamilton, "*Federalist* No. 68," in *The Federalist Papers*, ed. Clinton Rossiter (New York: Signet Classics, 1961), 413.

65. James Madison, "*Federalist* No. 39," in *The Federalist Papers*, ed. Clinton Rossiter (New York: Signet Classics, 1961), 236.

66. Hamilton, 413.

67. Id. at 412–413.

68. James Madison, "*Federalist* No. 37," in *The Federalist Papers*, ed. Clinton Rossiter (New York: Signet Classics, 1961), 222.

69. James Madison, "*Federalist* No. 39," 237.

70. Ibid.

71. J. Adams, 288.

PART II

Applications

CHAPTER 7

"Not so with different Governments": Separation of Powers, Federalism, and the Limits of Constitutional Conflict

Connor M. Ewing

When the American political system is described or taught, three features usually loom largest: separation of powers, federalism, and checks and balances. These, in turn, are used as lenses to illuminate the more intricate and varied components that make up the American constitutional tapestry.[1] But as they are commonly explained, this triumvirate of constitutional identity quickly becomes muddled, soon appearing more like three dimensions of a single phenomenon than three distinct components. Separation of powers is portrayed as a means for institutions to check and balance each another, empowering political actors to thwart tyrannical designs of opposing institutions in defense of individual rights. Federalism is also seen in this light and accordingly described as a further embodiment of the checks and balances principle, a brake on potential abuses of power. This tendency is reflected in the common argument that federalism is itself a form of separation of powers, a vertical application of the horizontal relationships among national-level political branches.

This phenomenon is interesting in its own right, suggesting distinctive characteristics of political culture and patterns of constitutional development.[2] But it is consequential principally because of the constitutional claims it underwrites. If states stand alongside Congress, the president, and the courts in the definition and use of constitutional powers, then exercises of national power could be checked by state institutions. States, moreover, could claim constitutional sanction when rebuffing national determinations or directives. At a more general level, this would support the case for a normative constitutional commitment to strong-form federalism, up to and including a compact interpretation of the American regime and its state sovereignty rationale. From both a constitutional and a practical standpoint, then, the stakes are quite high.

This chapter takes up the question of federalism's relationship to separation of powers, arguing that the effort to draw a constitutionally consequential relationship between the two is intractably complicated by the nature of institutional relationships relevant to each. Whereas separation of powers entails reciprocal relationships organized around shared powers and purposes, federalism entails no such relationships. States and the federal government encounter each other not as partners in a constitutionally generative relationship but as "different Governments," in the words of James Madison. For this reason, their interactions cannot yield many of the benefits incident to interbranch relations at the national level. To get to this conclusion, though, we must first come to an understanding of the causes and consequences of constitutional conflict, for it is on this basis that federalism and separation of powers are most frequently equated. Federalism is like the separation of powers, the argument goes, because it enables states to engage in political contests with the national government over everything from the scope of national power to the substance of public policy. The equivalence is asserted in conflictual terms and for the sake of the goods produced by such conflict. Articulated by many of the contributors to this volume, a conflict-oriented understanding of the constitutional order emphasizes the agonistic nature of relationships between governing institutions and posits a set of resulting constitutional goods. In addition to bringing some structure to this emergent approach to American constitutionalism, outlining the basic claims of the conflictual account will provide the necessary leverage to evaluate the claim that federalism and separation of powers are similar in some constitutionally consequential way. In this respect, then, assessing the relationship between federalism and separation of powers requires coming to an understanding of the limits of constitutional conflict.

Conflictual Constitutionalism

In his conclusion to *The Limits of Constitutional Democracy*, Christopher Eisgruber observes that, despite the wide range of issues taken up in that volume, the essays shared a broad understanding of constitutionalism. At the center of that understanding was a phenomenon more frequently decried than praised: conflict. As Eisgruber put it, "They treat durable conflict as a sustaining element, a kind of animating tension, within constitutionalism."[3] This common approach across disparate applications led him to outline a broader argument, that constitutionalism itself was "an effort to sculpt a generative culture of argument."[4] So conceived, constitutional conflict is both a central component of empirical explanation and a standard for normative evaluation—a "view [that] better describes our constitutional practice, is normatively superior, and indeed is conceptually inevitable, given basic aspects of constitutional practice."[5]

This conflict-oriented account of constitutionalism has seen considerable development in recent years. Indeed, discernible in much contemporary scholarship on constitutionalism in general, and American constitutionalism in particular, is a distinctly conflictual approach to describing, explaining, and assessing constitutional politics. To be sure, this conflictual interpretation is less a discovery than a methodological clarification and reorientation—it claims not to be a novel approach to political analysis but a better and more accurate approach. An emphasis on conflict is evident in earlier scholarly treatments of American politics, going back at least as far as Corwin's description of the Constitution as "an invitation to struggle."[6] Although Corwin's characterization was limited to the specific context of American foreign policy, those who emphasize the role of conflict in the separation of powers—like many of the contributors to this volume—have identified, diagnosed, and formalized its broader applicability. More significantly, as a perusal of the growing scholarship quickly reveals, the roots of this approach lie deep in American political thought and history, finding especially clear expression in *The Federalist*, the proceedings of the Constitutional Convention and ratification debates, and subsequent contests over constitutional meaning. In this way, conflictual constitutionalism *is* our constitutionalism, and it always has been.

A principal advancement of the recent scholarship has been the clarification of the causes and consequences of constitutional conflict. As both are relevant to the relationship between federalism and separation of powers, we would do well to devote some attention to each. The causes of constitutional conflict range from the specific design of the American political system to the nature of political constitutions and, finally, the enterprise of constitutionalism itself. The consequences of constitutional conflict follow from these causes: the advancement of core constitutional commitments, the precipitation of political deliberation, and the generation of constitutional authority.[7] Each is discussed in the sections that follow, beginning with the causes of constitutional conflict.

Causes of Constitutional Conflict

The most comprehensive accounts of the origins of constitutional conflict contend that the American constitutional order is—and from the outset has been—predicated on differently structured institutions advancing different commitments. Conflict, according to this understanding, is a function of constitutional design. In their reinterpretation of American political development, Tulis and Mellow argue that the American constitutional order is a "mixed democracy," a political system "in which the desiderata of democracy itself were embedded in institutions designed to vindicate their competing perspectives on the democratic political project."[8] These desiderata are the fundamental goods of constitutional self-government—popular will, rule of law, individual rights, security. Moreover, these fundamental commitments are encoded into the constitutional order through institutional design, giving rise to processes and offices alike that are oriented toward their articulation. As Tulis puts it in an earlier work, "A crucial invention of the new American science of politics was to design institutions to represent different desiderata of democratic governance rather than to represent social orders or alternative regimes."[9] By connecting "the interests of the man . . . with the constitutional rights" of the office he inhabits, these institutions foster the expression of different perspectives on common goals.[10] Designed with distinctive governing capacities rooted in constitutionalism's ultimate ends, the component institutions of American constitutional self-government generate different views on questions of policy and power and, as a result, give rise to divergent arguments and actions in pursuit of these ends. Conflict, then, is the result of constitutional institutions operating in accordance with both their individual function and their larger purpose.

In his study of Congress, Joshua Chafetz presents an account of "separation of powers multiplicity" that complements the mixed democracy interpretation by foregrounding the ways in which political institutions foster multiple and overlapping claims of authority. There Chafetz writes, "Political institutions are involved in constant contestation, not simply for the substantive outcomes they desire, but also for the authority to determine those outcomes."[11] Echoing Tulis and Mellow's argument about the basic desiderata of good government, Chafetz emphasizes the incommensurability of political interests. Despite agreements that may exist on what interests are worth pursuing, there is enough variation in how those interests should apply to a particular issue to render comprehensive solutions both imprudent and practically impossible. Indeed, given the nature of the overlapping consensus embodied by liberal constitutionalism—as evidenced by our ability to speak of a defined set of constitutional goods—the accommodation of some measure of disagreement stands as a goal in itself.[12] As is true for individual interests, in the context of collective interests "we make local, one-off choices between incommensurate goods in an attempt to construct the sort of life that we would like to lead."[13] Even as there are multiple political ends—Tulis and Mellow's "desiderata"—no one political institution, much less actor, can reliably bring them all to bear in discrete political contests. And even if it were possible to construct a single institution capable of advancing different perspectives or interests simultaneously, doing so would both risk the subordination of certain views and preclude the possibility of refining the advantaged views through opposition. The multiplicity of governing institutions, while introducing the possibility of inefficiency and political tumult, enables the pursuit of political goods that cannot be reduced to a single spectrum nor fully articulated by a single institution. The differentiation, both functional and structural, that gives rise to this multiplicity thus reflects the commitment that "*no* legal form can transubstantiate *any* political institution of normal politics into We the People of the United States."[14]

Implicit in structural explanations of the origin of constitutional conflict is a second, deeper cause, one rooted in the nature of political constitutions. Regardless of their length or specificity, constitutions cannot account for every future contingency. Language is imprecise, disagreements among drafters often preclude the creation of detailed provisions, the objects addressed by constitutional language change over time—for these and many other reasons, constitutions cannot fully script the politics they are intended to structure. To put the point another way, constitutions leave questions unanswered. Such is the consequence of human attempts to impress meaning onto political forms and processes with language. This phenomenon was expressed perhaps most poignantly in *The Federalist* No. 37. In the course of explaining the challenges faced by the Constitutional Convention, Publius describes the specific difficulties that attended the construction of both separation of powers and the federal system. After addressing the vagueness of the "faculties of the mind," he turns to the artifices of government, identifying "three sources of vague and incorrect definitions: indistinctness of the object, imperfection of the organ of conception, inadequateness of the vehicle of ideas."[15] Beyond the inevitability of imprecision occasioned by the nature of constitutional language, there is also a measure of intention. In part for the reasons identified by the structural accounts discussed previously, constitutional designers often opt to craft general instead of precise provisions to promote resilience and durability.[16] After all, the Constitution's framers were charged with "render[ing] the federal constitution adequate to the exigencies of Government & the preservation of the Union." Experience had shown that exigencies and the means required to address them are more often than not unforeseen.

What Publius describes in No. 37 is the phenomenon of constitutional determinacy and its absence. Precisely because constitutional texts cannot account for all future contingencies, they will always be subject to questions of meaning and the politics they organize will confront the question of what fidelity to the constitutional enterprise requires. There are, moreover, two ways in which a constitutional text can lack determinacy. First, there is *indeterminacy*, according to which the possible meanings of the text, while not specified *a priori*, nonetheless can be exhaustively enumerated. That is, the meaning of a provision can be said to preexist a case or controversy, even if multiple meanings are possible. On the other hand, there is *underdeterminacy*. Whereas indeterminacy entails an equivalence between the set of possible meanings and the set of possible results, underdeterminacy entails nonoverlapping sets of meaning and result. In other words, a constitutional provision is underdeterminate if an outcome is not specified by relevant interpretive sources but is nonetheless legitimate. An "'underdeterminate' text constrains, without fully fixing, a legal outcome."[17] When constitutional language stops short of specifying the full set of possible applications or interpretations—that is, when it is not fully determinate—constitutional meaning must be constructed. Unlike judicial interpretations, constitutional constructions "do not pursue a preexisting if deeply hidden meaning in the founding document; rather, they elucidate the text in the interstices of discoverable, interpretive meaning, where the text is so broad or so underdetermined as to be incapable of faithful but exhaustive reduction to legal rules."[18]

The vagaries of constitutional determinacy are front and center in conflictual accounts of American constitutionalism, particularly those that focus on individual institutions or powers. In her study of the Constitution's war powers, for example, Mariah Zeisberg identifies the underdeterminacy of the relevant constitutional provisions as one cause of interbranch disputes over the power to initiate hostilities. Applying this insight to the state-federal relationship, Edward Purcell argues that the Constitution established a federal structure that was "doubly blurred, fractionated, instrumental, and contingent."[19] This understanding echoes Whittington's assertion, "Although the foundations for the ultimate structure are taken as given, political actors must bring external values and interests to bear in order to add specificity to an inherently indeterminate text and change received understandings of its implications."[20] The emphasis of these and other accounts on constitutional indeterminacy or underdeterminacy contradicts approaches to constitutional meaning that posit a considerably higher degree of constitutional determinacy. Where these determinate accounts see constitutional meaning as settled and, therefore, principally the domain of judicial inquiry, those attuned to a robust notion of constitutional conflict see room for political debate, creation, and meaning-making.

The third, and for our purposes final, cause of constitutional conflict is found not in the nature of particular constitutional structures or texts but in the nature of constitutionalism itself. Constitutional orders exist for the sake of particular substantive ends, and pursuing those ends requires deliberation over their meaning, requirements, and the means best calibrated to their achievement. While consensus is by no means impossible, more often than not there will be considerable disagreement on both the meaning of constitutional aspirations and how they are best secured. These disagreements are expressed via the procedures set forth in the polity's constitution, from intrabranch legislative and adjudicative processes to interactions between institutions to debates within the citizenry. John Finn expresses this point especially clearly in the context of his distinction between the juridic and civic constitutions. Whereas the juridic constitution privileges legal modes of constitutional understanding and thus "finds its identity in law," the civic constitution grounds the polity's aspirations and the resulting questions of legal meaning in the citizenry constituted by the constitutional text. "Its purposes," Finn writes of the civic constitution, "are to establish a community, a civic culture, that prizes questions about the fundamental principles and purposes of constitutional life, principles that include, among others, the meaning of liberty, equality, and justice."[21] An agonistic politics—both within the institutions of government and within the citizenry—is the natural outcome of taking these questions and principles seriously. From this vantage point, conflict emerges as the result of good politics—it is an indication that the appointed constitutional ends are being sought. Accordingly, constitutional conflict can serve as a sign of constitutional health and vitality. At the same time, the absence of conflict can be an indication of constitutional debility or even failure. As Sotirios Barber argues, "The chief measure of constitutional success is the quality of civic debate."[22] Further, that quality is assessed by reference to the apprehension of and progress made toward the positive ends of constitutional governance.[23] Beyond providing clear standards for evaluating political discourse, Barber's argument on this point makes clear that the characteristics often attributed to successful constitutional orders—peace, stability, widespread consensus—might actually portend constitutional failure. A healthy constitutional culture thus requires not only the capacity to provoke debate over fundamental questions but also the ability to acknowledge the legitimacy of the ensuing conflict, despite perceived and actual costs.

These, then, are three principal causes of constitutional conflict: the structure of political institutions, the nature of constitutional language, and the enterprise of constitutional self-government. Though brief, it should be clear from the preceding discussion that these causes intersect and run together, further emphasizing the pervasiveness of conflict in constitutional politics. Taken together, they point up the endemic nature of political contestation, particularly in a well-functioning constitutional order. But conflict is more than just an interesting phenomenon; it can also produce a range of beneficial results. To see this, we must turn from the causes to the consequences of constitutional conflict.

Consequences of Constitutional Conflict

The first consequence of constitutional conflict is the advancement of constitutional aspirations and commitments. If institutions operate well—that is, if the actors embedded in them make use of the tools at their disposal in service of constitutional ends—then the political process will be inflected with the multiple values that are central to constitutional democracy. Over the long run, this means that these fundamental commitments will retain their vitality, remaining near the surface of political debate and decision-making. In particular political episodes, this means that these commitments are brought to bear on the same set of facts and interests. This, in turn, channels the multiplicity of core constitutional commitments into productive dialogue by creating opportunities for the structured articulation of interests throughout the political process. Seen in this light, politics organized along these lines "can be conceived as an effort to give institutional voice to different democratically relevant concerns and perspectives."[24] We see here both a sequential and a substantive dimension to political conflict. The Constitution establishes a political process that arrays interest-bearing institutions in a particular order while also imbuing those institutions with distinctive perspectives and governing capacities, a phenomenon Jeremy Waldron terms "articulated governance." Reflecting on the successive steps by which laws are made, enforced, and contested, he writes:

> What matters is that the governmental action has become articulated and many of the stages in that articulation correspond to rule-of-law requirements, such as the principles of clarity, promulgation, the integrity of expectations, due process, and so on. Each of these elements embodies the concerns about liberty, dignity, and respect that the rule of law represents. . . . Severally and together, they represent the stepwise incorporation of new norms into the lives and agency of those who are to be subject to them.[25]

In virtue of institutional design and the sequencing of the political process, conflictual politics can give voice to a polity's abiding constitutional concerns and values. Related to the advancement of core constitutional commitments, constitutional conflict can also induce substantive deliberation. As described by the idea of "articulated" politics, the institutional expression of fundamental values is just one phase in what is both a multistep and iterated process. Because no single institution is empowered to give effect to its will without the concurrence of others, the political process necessarily involves multiple institutions. If those institutions are to act, they must cooperate. But each institution has the ability to frustrate the governing process by inhibiting or countering the actions of other institutions. The institutional interactions entailed by this process are shaped by the distinctive governing capacities discussed earlier—the attributes derived from the confluence of democratic inputs, formal powers, and political functions. As a result, the political process is structured around not only core constitutional values but their interaction with each other. Structured political conflict requires (or at least generates the expectation) that actors embedded in institutions will take seriously the arguments and actions issuing from other institutions. As Tulis shows, deliberation between or among institutions is importantly different from deliberation between or among individuals. Unlike interpersonal deliberation that is mediated by speech, institutional deliberation is (also) mediated by text: "In the construction and exchange of texts institutions address the merits of public policy and the best of these exchanges manifest the most important attribute of deliberation: reciprocal respect for, and responsiveness to, opposing arguments regarding the issue addressed."[26] As arguments are aired and engaged, there is the opportunity to improve the course of action in accordance with the reasons offered by different actors. Here it is essential to recognize that much of this process takes place in public before the citizens whose constitutional commitments these institutions enact. Indeed, constitutional conflict can advance constitutional ends rather than simply favor the strongest participant precisely because of this aspect of publicity. Politicians that ignore compelling arguments against their preferred positions or act without offering justifications for their decisions risk losing popular support or, at the very least, emboldening their opponents. Constitutional conflict and the deliberation it induces thus play important democratic functions, occasioning popular input and political adjustment as debate unfolds.

The final consequence of constitutional conflict is perhaps the most significant, at least when considered in light of the conventional understanding of the Constitution and the politics it structures. The dominant contemporary approach to constitutional meaning stresses the determinacy of constitutional text; questions of meaning or application are not only perceived to be answerable on constitutional terms but answerable by the constitutional text.[27] Constitutional authority, on this conventional view, is a function of the meaning discernible from the constitutional text and relevant historical sources. In contrast, conflictual accounts highlight the ways in which constitutional authority is an internal phenomenon of constitutional politics. Rather than being an *ex ante* condition of legitimate action, constitutional authority is a *product* of political contestation. On this view, constitutional authority does not exist independent of politics. It is "generated," "created," and "produced" by interactions between institutions.[28] To connect this consequence to its underlying cause, the generation of constitutional authority comes about through the resolution of constitutional indeterminacy and underdeterminacy, however contingent those resolutions may be. By elaborating constitutional meaning in these domains through interbranch deliberation and reason-giving, political processes produce "local and provisional settlements" of constitutional questions.[29] Unlike the claims of constitutional meaning and authority arising from more deterministic approaches, these settlements emerge from the political process. In this way, meaning and authority are endogenous to constitutional politics—they do not precede but are the outcome of constitutionally structured processes. This understanding of constitutional authority contrasts with the conventional Razian account, which holds that constitutional authority consists in reasons to obey that are independent of justificatory content.[30] Conflictual accounts of constitutional meaning, in contrast, are distinguished by their emphasis on the content-dependence of constitutional authority. Whereas the conventional account seeks the authority *by* which government actors act (i.e., the prescribed rules governing the exercise of power), the conflictual account seeks the authority *with* which they act (i.e., the substantive justifications animating the process by which authority is contested and power exercised).

Federalism and Separation of Powers

The conflictual approach to American constitutionalism advances two central points. First, the political system established by the Constitution is oriented toward contestation between the principal institutions of government over the fundamental ends of politics; and second, such conflict is an indication of constitutional health and holds the promise of a range of beneficial consequences. Conflict thus becomes not only an analytical frame with which constitutional politics can be assessed, but also a normative metric by which political practice can be evaluated. As noted at the outset, this conflictual understanding provides a robust account of constitutionalism in both its general and particular aspects. But how much of American constitutionalism does this account capture? If constitutionalism entails conflict, what kind of conflict is sanctioned and what kind is not? After all, even as conflict holds out the prospect of the beneficial consequences discussed earlier, it also holds the possibility of a host of more detrimental outcomes. What, then, are the limits of constitutional conflict? These questions have particular significance in the context of the American Constitution, where conflict has been identified as a characteristic feature of constitutional identity, one that unifies the central structural components of the constitutional order.

Consider, for example, the Supreme Court's opinion in *Printz v. United States*, a 1997 case declaring unconstitutional federal commandeering of state law enforcement officers. After citing Publius's discussion in *The Federalist*

No. 39 of the "distinct and independent portions of the supremacy" comprised by subnational political officials, the court addressed the relationship between separation of powers and federalism. Quoting an earlier decision vindicating state power, Justice Scalia wrote, "This separation of the two spheres is one of the Constitution's structural protections of liberty. 'Just as the separation and independence of the coordinate branches of the Federal Government serve to prevent the accumulation of excessive power in any one branch, a healthy balance of power between the States and the Federal Government will reduce the risk of tyranny and abuse from either front.'"[31] The majority opinion immediately proceeded to connect the liberty-protecting purpose of federalism to Publius's famous "double security" argument in *The Federalist* No. 51. Scalia concluded his analysis on this point by gesturing toward the dark possibilities beyond the bulwark of federalism, writing that without sufficient (judicial) enforcement of limits on national power "the power of the Federal Government would be augmented immeasurably."[32] As is made clear from the issue at stake in *Printz*, preventing the aggrandizement of federal power required states to be autonomous *so that they could resist encroachment and usurpation.* This negative function would not be possible if institutional boundaries were permitted to yield to expediency.

In addition to the prevention of tyranny, *Printz* made a further connection concerning the role federalism plays in preserving the integrity of separation of powers in the federal government. Echoing a familiar refrain in the Supreme Court's structural jurisprudence, the majority contended that the presence of independent political actors, subject to different political masters, protected "the separation and equilibrium between the three branches of the Federal Government."[33] Enforcement of state autonomy, the argument goes, will ensure that branches of the national government cannot get an advantage over each other. In this way, as Jessica Bulman-Pozen argues, federalism safeguards the separation of powers, preventing a national-level branch from enlisting the power and capabilities of an opposing subnational institution.[34] To the extent that the modern executive enjoys wide latitude to reconfigure state-federal relations, the advent of "presidential federalism" may reveal the consequences of eroded separations between governmental levels.[35] At the heart of the majority opinion in *Printz* is a conception of conflict that both cuts across and unites federalism and separation of powers. The autonomy of states, the court makes clear, is a means toward the ultimate end of resisting unconstitutional exertions of national power, and this resistance preserves "the healthy balance of power" both between levels of government and among institutions within the national government. Thus, if "federalism was the unique contribution of the Framers to political science and political theory," as Justice Kennedy wrote in a case two years before *Printz*, for the Supreme Court it nonetheless appears that it is a contribution fruitfully understood by reference to separation of powers.[36]

Even observers that are attuned to the role of conflict in constitutional politics have drawn a connection between federalism and separation of powers. For instance, in his defense of the civic constitution, Finn stresses both the horizontal and vertical planes of separation of powers. The institutional differentiation created by divisions within governments is similar to the differentiation created by divisions between governments because both create space for necessary civic and political action. Finn thus writes,

> The prescription that counsels robust (dialogical) separation of powers tells us also that the Civic Constitution favors an approach to federalism in which states and local governments can make significant contributions to the construction of constitutional meaning. A robust doctrine of civic federalism is especially important to the Civic Constitution because it provides for an immediately accessible public space in which citizens can be active in the political and constitutional life of the community.[37]

The observation of horizontal and vertical dimensions to the separation of powers is rather common in political science and legal scholarship. Some have even gone as far as arguing for a "unifying theory" of separation of powers in which federalism is construed as a species of the separation of powers.[38] At the root of this argument is the contention that the constitutional division of powers between the national and state governments "leave[s] somewhat open the identity of the political entity ultimately authorized to decide how contested power is to be exercised."[39] As we saw earlier, this "openness" is the result of constitutional underdeterminacy. Like the relationship between national-level institutions, the relationship between the states and the national government is not fully scripted by the Constitution. In the same way that this deficit of determinacy enables the elaboration of constitutional meaning and generation of constitutional authority in the context of separation of powers, so too, these scholars contend, in the context of federalism. That, I take it, is one reason why Finn sees states "mak[ing] significant contributions to the construction of constitutional meaning."[40]

Consider also Chafetz's study of "Congress's Constitution." While it is explicitly about separation of powers among national institutions, his central insight about constitutional multiplicity was developed first in the context of federalism.[41] Additionally, in elaborating the role that competing claims to constitutional authority play in preventing tyranny, he draws an explicit parallel between separation of powers and federalism.[42] It is perhaps here, in the prevention of tyranny, that the relationship between federalism and separation of powers is most frequently drawn. And as we saw earlier in the discussion of *Printz*, for a state to protect its citizens in this way it must be independent of federal control. Implicit in this argument is a robust notion of conflict that furthers fundamental constitutional commitments. Just as the promotion of liberty is a good sought by the federal and state governments alike, so too for other goods. Both levels of government are empowered to pursue basic political goods like peace, security, justice, and majoritarian governance. Identifying additional political ends, Purcell writes, "the Constitution conceived of both levels [of government] as counterpoised forces protecting the same vague and contested values—liberty, property, and republicanism."[43] As a consequence, conflict is an endemic feature of the American federal system.

There is, then, an argumentative strain running through both constitutional jurisprudence and scholarship that posits a consequential similarity between the division between governments and the division of institutions within governments—that is, between federalism and separation of powers. Moreover, this similarity goes beyond structure and reaches constitutional aims and purposes. At each juncture, constitutional conflict plays a role. In short, the equivalence between the two—the "unifying theory" of separation of powers—draws on each of the causes of constitutional conflict discussed previously and suggests that the same consequences can result. On this view, states play a legitimate and central role in the enterprise of constitutional self-governance, a role that includes both resisting exercises of national power and elaborating constitutional meaning.

The Limits of Constitutional Conflict

Central to the benefits promised by constitutional conflict are a set of mutually supporting phenomena—iterated debate, institutionally inflected discourse, argumentation centered on shared political goals, and a form of constitutional statesmanship, to name just a few. All of these, however, rest on a more fundamental commitment and practice: reason-giving between actors and institutions. In order for conflict to be productive rather than destructive, it must be rooted in the exchange of competing arguments, justifications for action, and rational accounts of why a particular course of action is preferable to others. Moreover, this reason-giving must be accessible to other actors, in that arguments are presented in order to persuade and justify rather than trump and conquer. It is here that we can begin to see the differences between federalism and separation of powers, differences that complicate the hope that interactions between governments can yield the same benefits as those between institutions within government.

Reason-giving between institutions, at least of the kind just described, depends on a particular kind of relationship. In order to generate the goods discussed earlier, institutions must play different roles in the exercise of a particular power and, in virtue of this arrangement, be jointly responsible for the actions taken. In this way, the checks between institutions make possible the promotion of their distinctive capacities. As Thomas Bell puts it, "Checks and balances, in this perspective, are not wielded merely to prevent the exercise or abuse of power but ultimately to advance the branches' different perspectives about politics, which are shaped by their differing institutional designs."[44] Because the executive has veto power over congressional acts, for instance, there is occasion for the articulation of the executive's unique constitutional voice. This is a common feature of conflictual accounts in the separation of powers context, one that provides much of the structure for more formalized presentations of constitutional contestation.[45]

While such powers and relationships are clearly present in the context of separation of powers at the national level, it is far less clear that they apply to the federal system. This is the case principally because, whereas institutional relationships at the national level are governed by a principle of formal equality, relationships between state and federal institutions are governed by formal inequality and subordination, as enshrined in the Supremacy Clause's guarantee that national law trumps contrary state law. The applicability of the Supremacy Clause begs the underlying question of whether national action in a particular area is consistent with the limitations, structures, and standards imposed by the Constitution. Here again we return to the phenomenon of underdeterminacy that underlies both federalism and the separation of powers. In both cases, the Constitution does not specify the precise contours of the relationship in question. But the two differ in a crucial respect.

While institutions of the national government exist in relationships structured by shared powers and oriented toward specified constitutional ends, the relationship between levels of government lacks both the shared powers and reciprocal relationships undergirding the beneficial consequences of constitutional conflict. Because they do not exist in formally equal, responsive relationships, state and national institutions do not exchange reasons so much as they trade claims of legality and constitutional authorization. The difference here is between the potentially deliberative and consultative relations among the branches of the national government, on the one hand, and the independence and completeness of each level of government, on the other. While the implications of this difference are frequently obscured in modern accounts of American constitutionalism, the distinction itself is far from novel. Writing to Thomas Jefferson in 1823, James Madison discussed a pressing and ongoing constitutional challenge: "After surmounting the difficulty in tracing the boundary between the General & State Govts. the problem remains for maintaining it in practice; particularly in cases of Judicial cognizance."[46] Madison quickly dispenses with the viability of popular resolution, exclusive state interpretive authority, and leaving matters to the disputing parties. He then comes to the possibility of a nonjudicial resolution between governmental levels, precisely the kind of process envisioned by those who see a role for intergovernmental deliberation in the definition of constitutional meaning. But the prospects here are no better than the other options he canvassed:

> Nor would the issue be safe if left to a compromise between the two Governments; *the case of a disagreement between Governments being essentially different from a disagreement between branches of the same Government*. In the latter case, neither party being able to consummate its will without the concurrence of the other, there is a necessity on both to consult and to accommodate. *Not so with different Governments, each possessing every branch of power necessary to carry its purpose into compleat* [*sic*] *effect*. It here becomes a question between Independent Nations, with no other *dernier* resort than physical force. Negotiation might, indeed, in some instance, avoid this extremity; but how often would it happen, among so many States, that an unaccommodating spirit in some would render that resource unavailing?[47]

The cost of subnational autonomy is the inability to truly deliberate between governments. For Madison, this difference made the intervention of the federal judiciary "the constitutional resort for determining the line between the federal & State jurisdictions."[48]

To clarify the distinction being drawn here we can consider an alternative constitutional mechanism, one that was proposed but ultimately defeated at the Constitutional Convention. Judicial review of state laws—Madison's answer to the question of how jurisdictional disputes would be resolved—was effectively established as a replacement for the national veto, which would have required state legislation to be reviewed by the national government before going into effect. The principle of consultation and accommodation identified earlier in Madison's description of separation of powers would have applied as well, though in a quite different way, to his proposed veto, which would have enabled Congress "to negative all laws passed by the several States, contravening in the opinion of the National Legislature the articles of Union."[49] The plan of government submitted at the Constitutional Convention by the Virginia delegation also called for a joint executive-judicial "council of Revision with authority to examine every act of the National Legislature before it shall operate, & every act of a particular Legislature before a Negative thereon shall be final."[50] There were, then, two stages to this process: the first involved review of state legislation by Congress; the second, review of (*inter alia*) Congress's negative by the "council of Revision." While the first of these steps would indeed entail the superintendence of one government by another, the second adds an element of deliberation and reciprocity to questions concerning the shape of the national union. In other words, it would elevate a local question to a national forum, requiring representatives with different constituencies and state allegiances to confront the larger question of federalism's meaning and purpose. Just as significant, it would remain a *political* question, giving weight to considerations of prudence and policy as well as constitutional meaning. Though states were formally excluded from this process, they would be in the position of "sending questions up" in the first place, creating a sort of agenda-setting role for the states that could be exploited to advance their interests.[51] Of course, the national veto was defeated at the Constitutional Convention. As Alison LaCroix documents in her study of the origins of the American federal system, the compensatory mechanisms the Convention selected were judicial resolution of state-federal boundary disputes and a clause explicitly establishing the supremacy of federal *law*.[52] But unlike the national veto, from the standpoint of guaranteeing the authority of the national government this legal process presents only a partial solution, in that it lacks the completeness and efficiency of a mechanism that routed *all* state legislation into a national forum *prior to* enforcement. Under the compromise that produced Article III, any state infringements of national authority (or actions impermissibly prejudicial to other states) would stand until judicial proceedings were commenced and an injunction staying or decision invalidating such action was handed down. As a consequence, state laws threatening national powers and prerogatives would be invalidated only retrospectively and, in many cases, only after a period of enforcement. Further, their invalidation would come in the language of law, complete with legal justification and elucidation of the constitutional text.

Whereas the national veto would have been a prophylactic device animated by political justification, national supremacy underwritten by judicial review is a remedial institution grounded in juridical processes and modes of reasoning.[53] This is profoundly consequential for the kinds of politics to which the Constitution would give rise. As an initial matter, it permits states to not only make abstract claims of sovereignty—rooted either in history or in an interpretation of the constitutional text—but also to back up those claims with authoritative actions, establishing policy regimes and enforcing laws reflective of the state governments' sentiments without any intermediation from the national government. It also frees them from the expectation, much less the requirement, of offering reasons to the broader polity about the desirability and legitimacy of their actions. So in addition to the constitutional arguments that could be made about the nature of the federal system and the proper understanding of sovereignty, claims about state sovereignty would be grounded as well in *political facts*—in the states' ability to act as they saw fit unless and until checked by the national government through the judiciary. Moreover, interpretations of the Constitution would be refracted through and influenced by the states' ability to act in this way, because state and national action would together construct the political and legal context in which the underdeterminate state-federal relationship would be articulated and (re)defined.

Returning to the nature of relations between levels of government, we can now see that the claim of state sovereignty, just like the assertion of national supremacy, presents a content-independent reason for obedience. That is, both depend not on the reasons underlying the claim of authority—the very reasons that fuel the advancement of constitutional ends and the generation of constitutional authority—but on the validity of the claim itself, whether or not the states are sovereign in a relevant respect or the national government is supreme. As a result, conflict between state and national institutions cannot produce the deliberative or authority-generating benefits that can follow from conflict between branches of the national government. Indeed, deliberation is not a feature of state-federal relations in the way that it is for relations between Congress, the president, and the federal courts. Where content-independence obtains, any appearance of responsive relationships will be the result of national discretion. It should, therefore, be unsurprising that the opportunities often identified for states to produce the goods of constitutional conflict—congressional testimony, high-level meetings between state and national officials, interaction between state and federal administrators—are entirely matters of national discretion.[54] Any powers that are "shared" between the two levels of government will similarly be the result of national discretion. Absent both truly shared powers and reciprocal institutional relationships, federalism lacks the central prerequisites for the inducement of deliberation and the corresponding production of constitutional authority.[55]

Conclusion

In an era when political conflict is frequently blamed for dysfunction and gridlock, the emergence of what I have called conflictual constitutionalism offers hope that constitutional politics can be redeemed. Identifying the causes and consequences of generative conflict is one step toward this possibility. But so is clarifying the limits of that conflict. One such limit concerns the range of its application. In the final analysis, it is clear that the institutional relationships relevant to the separation of powers within the national government are fundamentally different from those between the national and state governments. The goods produced by constitutional conflict—principally constitutional deliberation and the generation of constitutional authority—require responsive relationships organized around shared powers. While such relationships are present in the context of separation of powers, they are absent in the context of federalism. As a result, conflict between levels of government cannot yield some of the most significant benefits that are possible for conflict among the branches of the national government. Realizing the goods of constitutional conflict thus requires a defense of the national orientation of the discourse and relationships they entail.

Notes

1. See, for example, the structure and content of a sampling of introductory American politics texts: Joseph M. Bessette et al., *American Government and Politics: Deliberation, Democracy, and Citizenship* (Wadsworth, 2012), 31–96; Theodore J. Lowi et al., *American Government: Power and Purpose* (13th ed.) (W. W. Norton, 2014), 48–103; Samuel Kernell and Gary C. Jacobson, *The Logic of American Politics* (2nd ed.) (CQ Press, 2003), 30–99.

2. Some of these are discussed in Jeffrey K. Tulis and Nicole N. Mellow, *Legacies of Losing in American Politics* (University of Chicago Press, 2018), 29–33 and 66–67.

3. Eisgruber, "Conclusion: Constitutional Engagement and Its Limits," in *The Limits of Constitutional Conflict* (Jeffrey K. Tulis and Stephen Macedo, eds.) (Princeton University Press, 2010), 317.

4. Id. at 318.

5. Id. at 327.

6. Edward S. Corwin, *The President, Office and Powers: History and Analysis of Practice and Opinion* (New York University Press, 1940). Also see Jeffrey K. Tulis, *The Rhetorical Presidency* (Princeton, 1987); Louis Fisher, *The Constitution Between Friends: Congress, the President, and the Law* (St. Martin's Press, 1978), revised in *Constitutional Conflicts Between Congress and the President* (Princeton, 1984); and Bruce A. Ackerman, "The Storrs Lectures: Discovering the Constitution," 93 *Yale Law Journal* 1013 (1984).

7. As should be clear from this discussion, my focus is limited to the beneficial results of constitutional conflict—the promises held out by contestation between institutionally embedded political actors. There are, to be sure, undesirable consequences, just as there is conflict that would not yield the benefits I discuss.

8. Tulis and Mellow, *Legacies of Losing*, 54.

9. Tulis, "The Possibility of Constitutional Statesmanship," in *The Limits of Constitutional Democracy* (Jeffrey K. Tulis and Stephen Macedo, eds.) (Princeton University Press, 2010), 121–122.

10. *The Federalist*, 51:349.

11. Chafetz, *Congress's Constitution: Legislative Authority and the Separation of Powers* (Yale University Press, 2017), 18.

12. See Nathan Tarcov, "Constitutionalism Ancient and Modern," in *The Supreme Court and the Idea of Constitutionalism* (Steven Kautz et al., eds.) (University of Pennsylvania Press, 2009).

13. Chafetz, *Congress's Constitution*, 305.

14. Bruce A. Ackerman, "The Storrs Lectures," 93 *Yale Law Journal* 1013 (1984), 1026 (emphasis in original). Jeremy Waldron's account of bicameralism and separation of powers presents related arguments on this front. See his *Political Political Theory: Essays on Institutions* (Harvard University Press, 2016), 72–92.

15. *The Federalist*, 37: 235, 237.

16. See Cass R. Sunstein, "Incompletely Theorized Agreements," 108 *Harvard Law Review* 1733 (1995); and "Incompletely Theorized Agreements in Constitutional Law," *Social Research* 74(1): 1–24 (2007).

17. Zeisberg, *War Powers*, 5 n. 23. These definitions follow those formulated by Lawrence B. Solum in his "On the Indeterminacy Crisis: Critiquing Critical Dogma," 54 *University of Chicago Law Review* 462 (1987), 472–474. See also Chafetz, *Congress's Constitution*, 15–17. A related but distinct set of questions concerns vagueness and ambiguity. On that matter, see Ralf Poscher, "Ambiguity and Vagueness in Legal Interpretation," *Oxford Handbook on Language and Law* (Lawrence Solum and Peter Tiersma, eds.) (Oxford, 2011).

18. Keith E. Whittington, *Constitutional Construction: Divided Powers and Constitutional Meaning* (Harvard University Press, 1999), 5.

19. Edward A. Purcell, Jr., *Federalism, Originalism, and the American Constitutional Enterprise* (Yale University Press, 2007), 6.

20. Keith E. Whittington, "The Political Constitution of Federalism in Antebellum America: The Nullification Debate as an Illustration of Informal Mechanisms of Constitutional Change," *Publius* 26(2), 2 (1996). For similar takes on this dimension of federalism, see David Brian Robertson, *Federalism and the Making of America* (Routledge, 2012) and Connor M. Ewing, "Structure and Relationship in American Federalism: Foundations, Consequences, and 'Basic Principles' Revisited," 51 *Tulsa Law Review* 689 (2016).

21. Finn, *Peopling the Constitution* (University of Kansas Press, 2014), 2.

22. Barber, "Constitutional Failure: Ultimately Attitudinal," in *The Limits of Constitutional Democracy* (Jeffrey K. Tulis and Stephen Macedo, eds.) (Princeton University Press, 2010), 19.

23. See Sotirios A. Barber, *Constitutional Failure* (University of Kansas Press, 2014).

24. Jeffrey K. Tulis, "Deliberation Between Institutions," in *Debating Deliberative Democracy* (James S. Fishkin and Peter Laslett, eds.) (Blackwell Publishing, 2008), 209.

25. Jeremy Waldron, *Political Political Theory*, 64.

26. Jeffrey K. Tulis, "Deliberation Between Institutions," 200–201.

27. See Jonathan Gienapp's account of the "fixed" constitutional imagination in *The Second Creation: Fixing the American Constitution in the Founding Era* (Harvard University Press, 2018); see also Connor M. Ewing, "Publius' Proleptic Constitution," *American Political Science Review* 118(3): 1131–1144 (2024).

28. Zeisberg, *War Powers*, 37, 41, and 45, respectively.

29. Chafetz, *Congress's Constitution*, 24.

30. See, e.g., Joseph Raz, *The Morality of Freedom* (Oxford University Press, 1986), 38–60; and *The Authority of Law* (Oxford University Press, 2009).

31. *Printz v. United States*, 521 U.S. 898 (1997), 921–922, citing *Gregory v. Ashcroft*, 501 U.S. 452 (1991), 458.

32. Id. at 922.

33. Ibid.

34. Jessica Bulman-Pozen, "Federalism as a Safeguard of the Separation of Powers," 112 *Columbia Law Review* 459 (2012).

35. Nicholas F. Jacobs and Connor M. Ewing, "The Promises and Pathologies of Presidential Federalism," *Presidential Studies Quarterly* 48(3): 552–569 (2018).

36. *United States v. Lopez*, 514 U.S. 549 (1995), 575.

37. Finn, *Peopling the Constitution*, 61.

38. Bruce G. Peabody and John D. Nugent, "Toward a Unifying Theory of the Separation of Powers," 53 *American University Law Review* 1 (2003).

39. Id. at 21.

40. Finn, *Peopling the Constitution*, 61.

41. Joshua Chafetz, "Multiplicity in Federalism and Separation of Powers," 120 *Yale Law Journal* 1084 (2011).

42. Chafetz, *Congress's Constitution*, 311.

43. Edward A. Purcell, Jr., *Federalism, Originalism, and the American Constitutional Enterprise*, 191.

44. Thomas R. Bell, "Perverse Politics: Recess Appointments, *Noel Canning*, and the Limits of Law," *Presidential Studies Quarterly* 48(2), 380 (2018). On this point, see also George Thomas, *The Madisonian Constitution* (Johns Hopkins University Press, 2008), 16–21.

45. Zeisberg, for example, argues that one of the three structural conditions of the relational conception she offers is that institutions share powers and exist in responsive relationships. As I understand her argument, this is the central condition because it incorporates the other two (i.e., independent sources of authority and distinctive governing and epistemic capacities). See *War Powers*, 30–31. Similarly, Chafetz's "multiplicity based" conception of the separation of powers requires that contestation be nonhierarchical in nature. See *Congress's Constitution*, 18–19.

46. James Madison, Letter to Thomas Jefferson, 27 June 1823, *Letters and Other Writings of James Madison* (J. B. Lippincott & Company, 1884), 3:325 (emphasis added).

47. Id., 3:326.

48. Ibid. The invocation of Jefferson and Madison may bring to mind a pertinent episode of state-federal conflict in which both men were involved: the 1798–1799 Kentucky and Virginia Resolutions. Some may wonder why this, among other possible examples, does not stand as a counterpoint to my argument about the inability of conflict between governments to produce the benefits of constitutional conflict. While a full treatment of this important question is beyond the scope of the present chapter, I will note two aspects of that episode that bear directly on my argument (see also note 55). First, the fact that the Resolutions sought action not only by other states but ultimately by those states' representatives in the national government reflects the limitations of the relationship between levels of government that I emphasize here. Second, the Resolutions' main significance at the time was not constitutional but political, serving as a rallying point for Republicans, fueling the electoral victory in 1800 that enabled them to oversee the expiration of the Alien and Sedition Acts. Success thus required enlisting the national government in a manner consistent with the argument I advance. For treatments of these dimensions of the Resolutions, see Chafetz, "Multiplicity in Federalism and the Separation of Powers," 1107–1111; and Adrienne Koch and Harry Amon, "The Virginia and Kentucky Resolutions: An Episode in Jefferson's and Madison's Defense of Civil Liberties," *William and Mary Quarterly* 5(2): 145–176 (1948).

49. Virginia Plan, Art. 6. Max Farrand, *The Records of the Federal Convention of 1787* (Yale University Press, 1911), I:21 (May 29, 1787).

50. Id., Art. 8. Farrand, *Records*, ibid.

51. For a counterfactual exploration of the constitutional politics in a world where the national veto was included in the Constitution, see Alison L. LaCroix, "What if Madison Had Won? Imagining a Constitutional World of Legislative Supremacy," 45 *Indiana Law Review* 41 (2011). She concludes there that the "negative might have brought more centralization, but at the price of raising every conflict to a constitutional crisis decades before the Civil War" (59).

52. LaCroix, *The Ideological Origins of American Federalism* (Harvard University Press, 2010), 158–174.

53. For an elaboration of this distinction, see Jenna Bednar et al., "A Political Theory of Federalism," in *Constitutional Culture and Democratic Rule* (Cambridge, 2001), John Ferejohn et al., eds.

54. Peabody and Nugent, "Unifying Theory," 18.

55. The discerning reader will note that, with its focus on institutional deliberation and the generation of constitutional authority, the argument advanced here leaves unaddressed the role of intergovernmental conflict in advancing constitutional values or elaborating constitutional meaning. This reflects an important—and intended—limitation to the present argument, which would require more space than is available here to sufficiently address.

CHAPTER 8

What Does "War" Mean?

Mariah Zeisberg

The Constitution commits the power to "declare war" to Congress (Article I, Section 8). In Article II, the Constitution vests the presidency with command of the military and requires of it an oath to "protect and defend," language that seems to license defensive military authority of some kind. A conventional understanding of the Constitution is that this text grants Congress the power to authorize war, and the president the power to repel (some) threats. In this essay, I refer to that understanding as the "Article I system."

The Article I system is often called the "traditional" or "original" construction of war powers, and it serves as a standard against which departures are assessed. Its logic evokes a deeper constitutional vision, articulated in *Federalist* Nos. 47, 48, and especially 51, of independent branches keeping each other in their "proper places" through mutual checks of each other's trespasses.[1] This idea, that rivalry between officeholders could keep branches appropriately aligned, evokes the possibility that Congress's jealousy of its Article I power to authorize war would lead it to retaliate against presidential manipulations that would aggrandize the executive branch at the cost of Congress's constitutional powers. By slashing funds, blocking appointments, or wielding impeachment as a last resort, Congress can reign in aggrandizing presidents and maintain the balance of the Article I system.[2]

We know today that things did not quite work that way. So much scholarship testifies to the problem of a passive Congress failing to insist on its Article I prerogatives, in war and beyond.[3] But, while we all know today that the "checks and balances" vision of warmaking in the Article I system is not a good depiction of contemporary interbranch security processes, there is an imagined past—pre-1952, specifically—when an appropriately mobilized Congress did produce meaningful and legitimate interbranch oversight, thereby protecting a public's negative liberties from an aggrandizing executive branch.

This kind of scholarship implicitly sustains the idea that separation of powers as imagined in the Article I system "works" to protect liberties and improve public policy—for example, it blocked public policy that would impair liberties (e.g., the Cold War) and protected the nation from terrible public policy (e.g., the Vietnam War). According to this line of thinking, the real problem we face is a contemporary departure from the Article I standard, most evidenced by the rise of an imperial presidency that views itself authorized to engage war whenever and however it likes.

This perspective hinges on a certain scholarly imaginary wherein interbranch contestation prior to 1952 both depended upon, and maintained, the word "war" as a transhistorical, empirically stable reference for ascertaining the boundary line between presidential and legislative empowerment laid out in the Article I system. For it is Congress's power to "declare war" that serves as a linchpin for any kind of neat division of war powers between the branches.

Many scholars argue that Korea was the "single most important precedent" in constitutional war powers—a rupture to the Article I system, wherein actions that look like war (sending armies, dropping missiles, enacting military blockades) were renamed in order to allow them to escape from the deliberative structure that separated powers (in the Article I imaginary) requires. In this account, that singular precedent launched a transfer of power from Congress to the presidency that defined a twentieth-century trajectory.[4] Scholarship on the Constitution and the Cold War often bemoans the extent to which war was named otherwise by presidents including Truman, Kennedy, Nixon, Johnson, and Reagan. This approach, epitomized by a decades-long project of Louis Fisher, expresses hopefulness about an original age when the concept of war was not subject to manipulation, but was ascertained through a process involving institutional checks, thereby producing constitutionally legitimate policies around war.[5]

This story of a Korean War rupture with the past involves a conversation about the meaning of the term "war." It was, in part, Truman's naming of the Korean War as a "police action" that took it outside of the Article I system. According to this line of scholarship, it was also other branches' deference to that naming that destroyed the stable meaning of "war" that had existed previously. In the wake of the imperial presidency, "war" has become whatever the president says that it is. This renders Article I's allocation to *Congress* of the power to declare war quite meaningless.

Empirical war powers scholarship is not the only place with investments in the idea that the meaning of war has, or once had, a stable empirical reference point. Dominant theories of interbranch decision-making on war—legitimacy models, the block war model, and intelligence/deliberation models—also treat "war" as a concept with a transhistorical meaning.[6] It is an open question what to make of these models, if, as I shall claim here, "war" is *both* endogenously defined through the very processes of accountability that these scholars seek to theorize *and* has been such since well before 1952.

The most important claim of this essay is that the pre–Korean War golden age is an imagined past. History does not interact with the text in quite the way that much contemporary war powers scholarship suggests. Although it is true that nineteenth-century presidents believed that "wars" were to be authorized by Congress, so too did Nixon and Reagan. The crux is this: What counts as "war," as well as historical constructions of war powers, have both been messier than what the Article I system claims.

Even during the founding, there was a consensus that not all military strikes amounted to "war." President Washington sent federal troops to put down Native American resistance to white settlement of the Pacific Northwest, and to the extent that this was authorized by law it was not through Congress's Article I war powers but rather through its appropriations powers and its Article IV powers to govern territories.[7] President Jackson paid militiamen to repel attacks by Native Americans in Missouri, Michigan, and Indiana without specific legislative authorization.[8] Federal army units were dispersed throughout the West during the Indian Wars of the mid-nineteenth century. Congress appropriated funds for these and other similar ventures, sometimes characterizing them not as war, but rather as "the repressing of hostilities."[9] Public officials did not always conceive of these hostilities as "war" despite treaties with Native American tribes that implicitly recognized some sovereignty.[10] But in the context of the expansion of a white settler state, what really distinguished "defend[ing] the frontier" from war?[11]

The answer that officials give to the question "what is war" is historically inflected. What I want to emphasize is not a unique Korean War turning point, but an institutional structure that—consistently through time—empowers officials to define "war" in ways that are responsive to their specific ends. From this vantage point, the word "war" does not have an objective and fixed transhistorical meaning. Rather, it is defined through the very constitutional processes that it is then called upon to govern.

I will concretize these suggestions by showing how the "System of 1896" was able to pursue projects of military aggression outside the Article I system. The Panama Canal gives an illuminating window into patterns of political behavior through which actors within the System of 1896 were able to generate independent presidential warmaking outside of Article I. By creating military capacity, developing suggestive legal treaties, and advancing bellicose rhetoric, Congress sidestepped the Article I system in pursuit of expansionist goals. Gordon Silverstein has shown how the post-Korea security order amounts to Congress trading authority for influence.[12] We see a similar pattern here wherein Congress permits, even invites independent presidential warmaking, even as it also seeks to influence the target, timing, and goals of that bellicosity.

In this chapter, I do not draw explicit parallels to the Korean War or Cold War system, although Truman and the State Department did cite the behavior of Presidents McKinley, Roosevelt, Taft, and Wilson.[13] Rather, my exploration of Panama is suggestive. We should view strategic manipulation of the Article I system as a predictable feature of the constitutional politics of war. Scholars should therefore try to explain departures, rather than compliance, with that logic.

Constitutional Structure

Why do I believe that it is predictable for the language of "war" to vary in its concrete signification through regimes? The first reason is because it is common for language itself to change through time. The intrinsic malleability of language and the way such malleability makes stable linguistic meanings themselves a vulnerable target for political ambition was an evocative theme for Thomas Hobbes and James Madison alike, and this observation continues to generate valuable analysis denaturalizing words like "war," "crisis," and "emergency."[14]

But in addition to the intrinsic vulnerability of language to politics, there is a way that constitutional structure itself *sets up* the language of war to vary through time due to how it positions the branches. For not only does the Constitution give power over war to two elected branches who are responsible for governance, but it also makes the word "war" a dividing line for institutional empowerment. A variety of dynamics between the branches thus would find a quite natural outlet in varying political dynamics around operationalizing the word "war." The Constitution also fails to identify any outside agent to adjudicate important war powers controversies, including the meaning of the term "war" when that is contested. It seems to be entirely in the hands of the president and Congress themselves—as well as the public—to self-monitor in accordance with the Constitution's war powers system.[15] As such, it seems quite plausible that "war," or what an Office of Legal Counsel memo calls "war in the constitutional sense," would be constructed politically by the branches in their responses to their various goals.[16] If their goals change, or the nature of their interbranch relationship changes, it would seem entirely predictable for the word "war" to be pressured in its operational meaning to accommodate that change. Consider George W. Bush's behavior in seeking authorization for war in Iraq, which was surprisingly appropriate given the nature of the war itself. Arguably, a cooperative Congress staffed with his co-partisans made a war declaration a piece of low-hanging constitutional fruit.[17]

Two points are worth emphasizing here. First, the fact of changing dynamics between branches (sometimes cooperative, sometimes contestatory, sometimes both) does not, on its own, mean that language will change. In a stable environment, including a stable linguistic environment, strategic interbranch behavior may well lead officials to behave similarly over time. Second, and crucially, the fact that the Constitution launches a set of strategic dynamics around defining the term "war" does not mean that "war" has a completely indeterminate meaning. The relationship between strategic behavior and the meanings of words must be at least in part an open empirical question. But the dynamics surrounding the status of the term "war" in the Constitution's politics do suggest that interbranch political processes should be expected to translate their goals into the Article I system in ways that potentially destabilize the empirical referent of the word "war" across regimes through time. "War" in this separated powers system is a constitutional idea with endogeneity problems.

In the discussion to follow, I will argue that the empirical possibility of stability even despite dynamic interbranch relationships has not actually played out in American political development. Change, induced both through interbranch contestation and coordination, has been an ordinary feature of the meaning of "war." In my research on war powers, I have found that whether an act of military aggression is named "war" or "not-war" has less to do with empirical features of the violence at hand—for example, whether it is defensive or offensive; scale; whether combatants are sovereign states; types of weaponry used; whether ground troops, naval forces, or only air troops, are in play. It has more to do with the possibilities and consequences associated with using the Article I system given a specific interbranch configuration.

I will illustrate this claim by discussing the Roosevelt Corollary to the Monroe Doctrine, specifically as it played out in the acquisition of the Panama Canal. The (Theodore) Roosevelt Corollary to the Monroe Doctrine stepped outside of the Article I system to license independent presidential acts of war.[18] The process of acquiring the Panama Canal followed a very specific template that was common to military action during the period of Republican-led imperialism, and historians working through the Wisconsin school have done a great service in tracing this pattern out in some detail.[19]

Importantly, the template did not involve legislative passivity. It was established in the context of Congress's *non*-deferential behavior. Those legislators challenging the newly empowered presidency were, in many cases, also driving a foreign policy agenda that entailed independent presidential warmaking. This shows how interbranch contestation can help to *consolidate* new powers in the presidency through a massive interbranch collusion in shifting the operational meaning of the term "war." Congress was active in inviting the presidency to exercise warmaking powers, and interbranch conflict over the scope of that invitation ultimately served to expand, not contract, the national government's warmaking posture. Congress combatively invited the president into acts of independent warmaking while attempting to influence the direction of that bellicosity. Shifts in the operational meaning of the constitutional term "war" are produced, then, not by contestation or cooperation on their own, but by distinctive dynamics that vary through time.

The Roosevelt Corollary to the Monroe Doctrine

The Roosevelt Corollary to the Monroe Doctrine emerged from the Fourth Party System, what Schattschneider called the "System of 1896." A series of depressions (most importantly the Depression of 1893) sparked an initial transformation followed by the realignment of 1894–1895. This realignment culminated in the emergence of the Republican Party as the party of business and capitalist development, together with a series of Republican presidential wins—with the notable exception of Woodrow Wilson—until 1932. Republicans also dominated Congress through this period.

The Populist movement responded to economic dislocation in this era with proposals for reform in banking, monetary, and labor policy.[20] Perhaps if Populists had won control of the presidency or of Congress, they might have forced a deeper conversation on the best response to these depressions. But they did not. Wisconsin School historians have traced how US elites outside the Populist movement diagnosed their contemporary economic problems not in domestic economic policy, but rather in the overproduction of agrarian materials. Their solution was to create new demand by cultivating foreign markets.[21] From this goal for foreign policy, a variety of entanglements emerged: the Spanish-American War, with its Treaty of Paris (1898) giving the US control over Puerto Rico, Guam, and the Philippines; the annexation of Hawaii; and the construction and eventual control of the Panama Canal were all among the goals of a Republican regime seeking oceanic stepping stones that could be leveraged to expand US markets.

Transforming the nation's foreign policy away from its historic isolation from European powers and toward engagement with present or past European colonies entailed developing new ideology about the place of the United States in the world. The Roosevelt Corollary to the Monroe Doctrine articulated a rationale for intervention that, coincidentally or not, served the economic expansionist goals of the System of 1896. In his 1904 message to Congress, Republican Theodore Roosevelt invoked a fear that instability in the Western Hemisphere could pave the way for European economic dominance, a concern that, according to him, licensed military interventions abroad:

> Chronic wrongdoing, or an impotence which results in a general loosening of the ties of civilized society, may in America, as elsewhere, ultimately require intervention by some civilized nation, and in the Western Hemisphere the adherence of the United States to the Monroe Doctrine may force the United States, however reluctantly, in flagrant cases of such wrongdoing or impotence, to the exercise of an international police power.[22]

This transformed the Monroe Doctrine from a doctrine of isolation into one of intervention.[23] It also had constitutional implications. Invoking an "international police power" implied presidential authority to use the military outside of Congress's Article I power to authorize war. President Roosevelt promised that such action would come "only in the last resort, and then only if it became evident that their inability or unwillingness to do justice at home and abroad had violated the rights of the United States or had invited foreign aggression to the detriment of the entire body of American nations."

Events during the late nineteenth and early twentieth centuries are easily decipherable through the Roosevelt Corollary; consider the 1893–1894 deployment of warships to Brazil to suppress a European-supported revolutionary moment; Grover Cleveland's incursion into Panama in 1885; and Roosevelt's support for the Panamanian revolution and US acquisition of the Panama Canal Zone in 1903.[24] Indeed, presidents explicitly cited the corollary as a premise for incursions into the Philippines, Cuba, Nicaragua, Haiti, and the Dominican Republic.[25] This ideology was applied in 1905 when Roosevelt forced the Dominican Republic to accept an American economic advisor as the financial director of that state, and in the formation of a provisional government in Cuba in 1906.[26]

Were these bellicose actions also acts of war? If so, then independent presidentialism here amounted to a violation of the Article I system. Scholars Louis Fisher, E. Corwin, and Arthur Schlesinger have resisted such a conclusion on the grounds that these early twentieth-century military interventions were "modest in scope."[27] But other war powers scholars insist that the Article I system covers "little wars," or, in Jules Lobel's words, "small military invasions and quick strikes" no less than big ones.[28] Fisher himself cites Jefferson's reluctance to engage in even limited combat with pirates without specific congressional authorization as evidence for reading the Article I system as the original conception of war powers.[29]

More important than the best reading of the Article I system, though, is to notice that the distinction between little and big wars replicates the perspective of early twentieth-century imperialists, who worked to obscure how independent presidentialism under the Roosevelt Corollary implicated Article I. Claiming that an act of military aggression is *small* was one of the defenses that President Roosevelt's co-partisans offered on his behalf after his Panamanian incursion when a few legislators challenged his war powers violation. We see a parallel logic with Harold Koh, who was once highly concerned that little-war presidentialism threatened the overall Article I framework.[30] Koh's tune changed dramatically when he was called to justify the use of the Air Force in Libya during Obama's presidential administration. In an about-face, Koh defended these small actions as not rising to the level of "war for the purposes of Article I of the Constitution."[31]

The important consideration for my purposes is not whether little wars are included in the Article I system. Rather, it is noticing the political conditions that render a conversation about scope salient in the first place. During the early twentieth-century period of American imperialism, it was precisely the struggle to define "war" in the context of an interbranch system featuring Republican ambitiousness to access foreign markets that *led* actors into a conversation about whether these deployments of the Navy activated Article I requirements. It is the repetition of that struggle over definition, in the context of new political goals, that I want to emphasize.

A Co-Created Politics of Presidential Bellicosity

I would like to draw attention to three means by which presidents and their Republican Congresses together constructed a regime of independent presidentialism to gain access to Latin American markets. By building military capacity, developing politically suggestive legal architectures, and then advancing bellicose rhetoric, Congress and the president co-constructed a regime of independent presidentialism.

They did so using ordinary tools of governance found in Article I and Article II. Indeed, appropriations for a military, negotiating and passing treaties, and floor debate are all noncontroversial constitutional powers. Crucial to notice, however, is that Congress's specific *use* of these powers created a suggestive politics that invited the president into independent bellicosity.

When the president did engage in acts of war, members of Congress ignored the fact or even criticized him for being too passive. Some of the president's challengers—most notably, Senator Morgan (D)—wanted to use the military to open (different) foreign markets, so Republican acts of presidential warmaking were not conflict-free events. And yet, through this pattern of interbranch relation, almost all agents failed to define these hostile acts as "war." The problem was not one of deference. Congress was conflictual with presidents over foreign policy. But Congress did not challenge presidents along the lines that would be suggested by adherence to the Article I system. Instead, these nineteenth-century Congresses seemed to be acting from the "influence vs. authorization" schema that Gordon Silverstein suggests anchors the post-Korea system.[32]

My story of Congress inviting the president into bellicosity starts with Congresses of the 1890s and their decisions to create military capacity. While the 1890s is often spoken of in terms of "modernization," that word obscures the political choices that were being made about national investment. The military wasn't simply being "modernized"; rather, it was being equipped to intervene in areas connected to the United States through water.[33] The choice and structure of armaments itself reveals something about what officeholders were imagining in US force.

The modern Navy originated in the Appropriations Act of 1883, which authorized unarmored cruisers equipped for hit-and-run operations. The ships authorized between 1885 and 1889 were small.[34] But in the early 1890s, as the landed frontier closed, a group of public intellectuals and political elites—A. T. Mahan, William McKinley (R), Theodore Roosevelt (R), Henry Cabot Lodge (R), and others—emphasized the value of a commercial frontier across the ocean. Mahan evoked a merchant marine and battleship navy that could deter European competitors from the oceans, which he described as highways, not barriers. These leaders wanted to influence other nations in order to secure steppingstones to Asian and Latin American markets. They did not want to "colonize" Latin America or Asia so much as extend markets and secure them with military power.[35] They contemplated that this strategy would embed the nation in military violence.[36]

In a series of congressional debates between 1889 and 1892, other imperial expansionists came to the same conclusion: Military confrontation would be an element of expanding US power. In 1890, a Republican Congress authorized the buildup of the first battleships, vessels that could go far out to sea rather than stay close to the coast for immediate defense.[37] The system's orientation toward the Article I system is obvious in Secretary of the Navy Benjamin Tracy's reassurance that the "sole purpose" of the naval buildup was defense.[38] By 1905, the size of the Navy had about quadrupled.[39] On the other hand, the United States did not heavily invest in an army, which would be necessary to repel a land invasion of its own territory or even to subdue colonial populations over a long term.

The creation of military capacity is a hallmark of a transformed war powers system, and Stephen Griffin describes it as an important feature of war powers post-Korea.[40] What is important in this buildup, whether during this period or during the Cold War, is not simply the new capacity for intervention that presidents obtained as a consequence. It is also the political vision that attended the buildup and the political vision that new technologies suggested. A set of new political goals were evident in the structure of armaments that were developed: no longer simply defense and isolation from

European powers, but also the ability to engage through the water. This happened through the perfectly ordinary and legal use of Congress's Article I appropriations tools.

However procedurally regular the military buildup was, it took on a specific meaning in the context of other congressional acts that, taken together, oriented the interbranch system away from the Article I system. Specifically, Congress's participation in developing suggestive legal structures and bellicose rhetoric, as well as its staging of accountability moments that subsumed the implications of independent presidential action for the Article I system, all suggested a buildup for warmaking outside of Article I. Each of these behaviors (military appropriations, suggestive treaties, bellicose rhetoric, and presidential challenge) are ordinary, not unusual, exercises of constitutional power. Yet taken together, they created a politics and a field of meaning in which independent presidential aggression was an obvious entailment.

The next step in the pattern was treaty-making, which created the context for US interests to take legal form in target countries. All of the military operations conducted under the Roosevelt Corollary were at least pretextually connected to treaties between the United States and the nation in question. In ratification processes, these treaties were usually discussed in terms of their commercial value. For example, in Panama, Senate debate on the issue of a canal through Central America noted the "vast . . . material interests of the people" at stake and specifically, the value of an isthmus canal, "which will be of incalculable benefit and advantage to commerce generally and especially in the interest of our own great nation."[41]

Key treaties for Panama included the Bidlack Treaty of 1846—between Colombia and the United States—which guaranteed rights of transit for a railroad crossing the isthmus and which resulted in the introduction of a US military presence into Panama.[42] Expansionist President James Polk (D) had argued that the treaty would "constitute no alliance for any political object, but for a purely commercial purpose," and by the turn of the century, the United States had intervened with force multiple times to suppress Panamanian secession from Colombia.[43] Such interventions in support of Colombian sovereignty were discussed by Congress not as acts of war requiring legislative authorization, but rather as acts guaranteeing neutrality and property rights by securing Colombian sovereignty.[44]

In the early months of the Grover Cleveland administration, though, Congress found a more heated rhetoric to express its aims. The president had sent a Navy landing force to Panama to pacify a local revolt. Congress was adjourned during this intervention, and when it returned, it found much to criticize in the president's behavior; it attacked the president as "weak" and "puerile" for his too-early withdrawal from the region.[45] Here, while Congress was willing to hold the president accountable for missteps in his use of military force, their concern did *not* include his use of the military outside of congressional authorization. Congress, here, was not jealous or protective of its Article I prerogatives; rather, Congress was combative toward the presidency for what it viewed as an insufficient independent use of the military.

In fact, from the Clayton-Bulwer Treaty (1850) to the Hay-Pauncefote Treaty (1901), the Senate exercised consistent pressure on the president to negotiate agreements expanding the scope for US military presence and power in the region. Senate pressure first led the president to negotiate a right to construct and control a Central American canal under sole US authority and then to drop neutrality guarantees around the governance of that canal. These developments culminated in a treaty that permitted US fortifications and discretion over the canal in times of war, as well as a guarantee of US protection over the canal.[46] Importantly, through various drafts and revisions, neither the Clayton-Bulwer Treaty nor the Hay-Pauncefote Treaty were amended to include any enforcement mechanisms for their guarantees, and the Senate did not suggest or propose any legal remedy to this omission. As such, the treaties in both their content and their political sequencing suggest a Senate that was inviting the presidency to act independently to advance goals pertaining to the canal that were ever broader and ever more accommodating of US interests.

In mid-1902, Congress finally authorized the president to build a canal in Panama if a favorable treaty could be arranged with Colombia, but to otherwise turn to Nicaragua. The story of the rejected Hay-Herrán Treaty (1903), which was the administration's first effort to enact the Senate's goal, is a fascinating window into how separated powers dynamics can accelerate rather than block the movement toward independent presidential war. In this case, congressional rhetoric and treaty design both became elements of independent presidential warmaking. The Hay-Herrán Treaty was an agreement that Secretary of State Hay, on behalf of President Theodore Roosevelt, negotiated with Colombia to construct the Panama Canal with some compensation to Colombia. That treaty granted the United States control of a canal zone as well as a "sole and absolute" option to build, collect tolls, exercise police and administrative powers, and intervene militarily in the isthmian region.[47] Though the Senate at the time appears not to have, *we* should notice a lingering open question in such a treaty's design: How would the treaty's suggestion of military intervention be squared with Congress's prerogatives in the Article I system?

The Senate was dissatisfied with this treaty, but not because the Senate wanted to hold fast to its Article I prerogatives. During the treaty's consideration on the floor, congressional rhetoric both destroyed the chances of Colombian acceptance of the treaty and also invited presidential warmaking, even as it challenged and rebuked the presidency. Senator Morgan, a Democrat also committed to imperial expansion, had been an advocate for an alternative Nicaraguan route for the canal, and he used the ratification process of the Hay-Herrán Treaty to call the president's treaty negotiations a "brilliant coup d'état."[48] Far from seeking to restrict the domain of independent presidentialism, Morgan's many proposed amendments would have broadened the scope for US military intervention in the zone, advocating control of the zone "in perpetuity" rather than for a renewable 100-year lease; the right to use and fortify several surrounding islands;[49] creating US military tribunals in addition to regular courts;[50] and granting a right for the United States "at all times and in its discretion, to use its police and its land and naval forces for these [protective] purposes."[51] In Senate debate, Morgan compared the Hay-Herrán treaty to what in his view was a more favorable Nicaraguan treaty with its *more* emphatic guarantee of US powers of intervention.[52] The Senate's debates in executive session apparently featured suggestions that the United States should just go to war "once we have a foothold there under this treaty." Morgan called this "derogatory to our country," but his own suggestions for treaty design hardly suggested a limited scope for the projection of US military power.[53]

Senator Cullom, chair of the SFRC and an Illinois Republican, responded to Morgan on the Senate floor. He argued that much of the scope for US military intervention Morgan sought was already implicit in the treaty at hand: while "Colombia agrees to provide the armed forces necessary for the protection of the canal . . . [t]he United States will determine what are exceptional circumstances and unforeseen or imminent danger. Those terms are susceptible of a very broad construction."[54] Thus both the challenge to the treaty and the defense offered by the president's allies centered on the question of expanding the scope for independent presidentialism in the use of military force.

Senator Morgan and the opposition that clustered around him never objected that the treaty would unconstitutionally shift powers to the presidency. His lengthy objections included no concern that the treaty's security guarantee or his bellicose amendments would have any implications for the war powers of Congress and the president.[55] This is what it looks like for the Senate to participate in a construction of constitutional authority whereby military strikes in foreign lands, and then governance of those lands, are not acts of war requiring Article I authorization by Congress. Ultimately, the Senate ratified the Hay-Herrán Treaty—without any of Morgan's broadening amendments—by a vote of 73 to 5.[56]

Importantly, although the Congress was a full participant in constructing a legal architecture that would politically (but not legally) license independent presidential bellicosity, this is not because Congress was deferential to the president. The Senate response to the Roosevelt administration's Hay-Herrán Treaty with Colombia was highly contentious; both treaty defenders and critics were bellicose. Indeed, bellicose and contemptuous rhetoric on the floor precipitated the conditions for independent presidential warmaking. Senator Morgan, who was later to become one of McKinley's fiercest critics over the military's actions in Panama, spoke openly about his view of Colombians as a "degraded, dissatisfied, turbulent, mixed, and filthy" population.[57] Leading senators, including the chair of the Foreign Relations Committee, Shelby Cullom, "publicly suggested the unilateral appropriation of the canal zone as a 'universal public utility,' with compensation to be arranged after the fact."[58] Senatorial impatience apparently entered as an element of communication in Roosevelt's diplomacy with Colombia.[59] These comments, as well as the poor terms of the treaty, rendered the treaty "not only unacceptable but offensive" to the Colombian Senate, which then unanimously defeated it.[60]

Instead of turning to Nicaragua as required by law, Roosevelt coordinated military activities with an insurrectionary movement in Panama, backing a real coup d'état on behalf of a revolutionary government that was willing to invite the United States into the canal zone. In the State Department, John Bassett Moore developed a memorandum legally justifying a unilateral seizure of the canal zone, and Roosevelt began to prepare for a November special session to urge Congress to endorse seizure.[61] Even while deploying Marines to Panama in preparation for a revolution, Roosevelt was drafting a message to Congress recommending occupying the zone using the legal justification of the Moore memo.[62] Presidential bellicosity had not been authorized by Congress, but the politics of the moment demonstrated that neither the president nor his critics were overly interested in how the Article I system intersected with their goals.

On November 2, 1903, the executive branch sent orders to an American gunboat in the canal zone to "prevent the landing of any armed forces with hostile intent, either government or insurgent."[63] The next day, a second American warship dispatched four hundred Marines to block Colombian claims to the canal zone. On May 6, the United States formally recognized the new Republic of Panama, and the Navy was ordered to form a blockade making it impossible for Colombian vessels to intervene.[64] The Senate quickly ratified a treaty with the new Republic of Panama granting US control of the canal zone. Roosevelt is famous for bragging, "I took the canal zone and let Congress debate,"[65] but the legislature largely endorsed his claims and went on to ratify the Hay–Bunau-Varilla Treaty (1903) that further entrenched US legal and military control of the area.

The Hay–Bunau-Varilla Treaty included a US security guarantee to Panama, as well as a guarantee that the United States could exercise "all the rights, power and authority . . . which the United States would possess and exercise if it were the sovereign of the territory . . . to the entire exclusion of the exercise by the Republic of Panama of any such sovereign rights, power, or authority."[66] Despite this language, and despite some senators' expressed concerns about the president's constitutional violations, not a single senator indicated that this language implied presidential enforcement action, and that presidential discretion in enforcement could amount to acts of war. And once again, not a single senator argued that requiring domestic implementation of legislation might serve to discipline future presidents.

This is not to say that there was no contention over this treaty. Far from it. Senator John Tyler Morgan again spearheaded the opposition. And among others, Senators Morgan, Tillman, and Carmack raised a series of constitutional challenges to the president, with resolutions being put on the floor seeking information about the president's role in the revolution; condemning the president for his violation of the Constitution and of war powers; and condemning the president's violation of international law.[67] Here, an observer trained by the *Federalist Papers* to look for institutions jealously guarding their prerogatives might be excited to finally find the Senate behaving as expected.

In the face of this challenge, Roosevelt's supporters defended the constitutionality of the president's exercise of a purely discretionary power to "recognize" a foreign nation, rhetorically sidestepping the issue of armed intervention.[68] When challenged that deploying Marines to block Colombian ships was hardly an act of "recognition,"[69] presidential advocates argued that the president's conduct was not war because it had been necessary to protect US citizens;[70] or because it was required by the 1846 treaty's guarantee to protect the rail;[71] or because it was required by the "law of exhausted patience."[72] Presidential defenders also argued that it was not an act of war under international law, but rather an act of *preventing* war.[73]

Senator Hoar ultimately backed down, stating, despite his ferocious statements of presidential misconduct, that there was no war powers violation and he could vote for the treaty.[74] Senator Morgan maintained his opposition, but even while Morgan was willing to criticize the president for unlicensed war, he emphasized his preference for the Nicaraguan route for a canal and continued to advocate treaties that implied a continued policy of independent presidential warmaking without explaining this discrepancy or being challenged on it.[75] Morgan's openness to an alternate scheme even more bellicose than the one he challenged undermines the argument of those who would read his contributions as a meaningful defense of the Article I system. Ultimately, after this confusing debate, the Republican Senate voted 66 to 14 in approval of the Hay–Bunau-Varilla Treaty that President Roosevelt had negotiated with the newly recognized state of Panama.[76]

Conclusion

The Senate's Panama debates were characteristic of legislative politics for some time. While some relatively limited criticisms of presidential empowerment were generated by anti-imperialists, anti-imperialists' loss on the annexation of the Philippines in 1899 and on the Spanish-American War left them disorganized and marginalized.[77] Ultimately, despite limited opposition, the System of 1896 constructed a politics wherein presidential use of military force to foster expansive commercial development was not "war in a constitutional sense." The system did this by constructing a large naval establishment, organizing treaties that could create pretexts for action, neglecting to create implementing legislation that would organize treaty commitments according to the Article I system, rhetorically encouraging presidential bellicosity, and failing to render accountability for presidential warmaking,

Scholars who call the Article I system the "traditional" or "original" structure for constitutional war powers and who lean on the idea of institutions jealously guarding their prerogatives from one another should expect to find presidents seeking to aggrandize their war powers and Congresses resisting. But in this case, the branches did not challenge each other in ways that could have held the meaning of "war" to an objective, transhistorical meaning. In this case, the operational meaning of "war" came to exclude military mobilizations that installed new governments. This is a meaningful shift from "war" in Jefferson's presidency.

An obvious rejoinder is that I have simply shown that the branches are capable of violating the Constitution. Some even fear that historically or regime-inflected constitutional studies in general risks eliminating the normative core of constitutional studies,[78] displacing questions about the "health and maintenance of the polity" with a value-free social science that simply notices change through time.[79] In other work I have tried to argue that the Constitution's normativity saturates the political process in such a way that both change and normativity can be addressed in the Constitution's war powers system. Here, I limit myself to illuminating a more circumscribed point: Regardless of its stakes for normative interpretive processes, the Constitution's interbranch war powers system establishes *change* to the meaning of "war in the constitutional sense" as a constitutive feature.

Where does this leave us in terms of the themes of this volume, which aspires to challenge the idea of separation of powers as legalistic, as a feature of negative constitutionalism, and as a bar to effective government action? The answer, perhaps appropriate for a volume that wants to "*defamiliarize* the separation of powers—to make it into an object of inquiry and curiosity," is messy.[80] I will say that, in the context of the expanded Monroe Doctrine, what Tulis calls the "separation of powers system"—separate institutions sharing overlapping powers in order to advance government purposes—was indeed associated with effective, but (to my eyes) morally wrong political action and public policy. I mean by this that the United States was able to "effectively" purchase some version of "security," as well as "effectively" enrich its national treasure, through exploitative relations with other nations. Representative institutions were able to converge on common purposes and work through the separated powers system to achieve those aims. In some sense, the goals of the Preamble for governance that secures a "common defence" and the "general welfare" of "We the People" was advanced, albeit at the cost of respectful relations with foreign nations. Indeed, the Constitution's warmaking system, messy as it may be, has overall proven effective at extracting national wealth from foreign and indigenous publics alike. This may speak to a need to consider whether the version of a "common good" that is realistic from within the Constitution's scheme of representation is still appropriate for today.

Notes

1. *Federalist* No. 51. Clinton Rossiter, ed., *The Federalist Papers: Hamilton, Madison, Jay* (New York: New American Library–Mentor, 1961).

2. Provocatively on this theme, see Josh Chafetz, *Congress' Constitution: Legislative Authority and the Separation of Powers* (New Haven: Yale University Press, 2017).

3. E.g., Louis Fisher, *Congressional Abdication on War and Spending* (College Station: Texas A&M University Press, 2000); Jeffrey Tulis, *Congressional Abdication* (Princeton: Princeton University Press, forthcoming).

4. Louis Fisher, "The Korean War: On What Legal Basis Did Truman Act?" *American Journal of International Law* 89:1 (1995): 21–39.

5. John Hart Ely, *War and Responsibility* (Princeton: Princeton University Press, 1995); Louis Fisher, *Presidential War Power* (Lawrence: University Press of Kansas, 1995); Stephen Griffin, *Long Wars and the Constitution: From Truman to Obama* (Cambridge: Harvard University Press, 2013); Gordon Silverstein, *Imbalance of Powers: Constitutional Interpretation and the Making of American Foreign Policy* (Oxford: Oxford University Press, 1996); Arthur Schlesinger, *The Imperial Presidency* (Mariner Books reprint, 2004).

6. For legitimacy models see Tara Ginnane, "Separation of Powers: Legitimacy, not Liberty," *Polity* 53(1) (2021): 132–159; Geoffrey Brennan and Alan Hamlin, "A Revisionist View of the Separation of Powers," *Journal of Theoretical Politics* 6 (1994): 345–68. For block-war models, see Alexander Hamilton, "Federalist 69: The Real Character of the Executive," *Federalist Papers*; William Howell and Jon Pevehouse, *While Dangers Gather: Congressional Checks on Presidential War Powers* (Princeton, NJ: Princeton University Press, 2007); Bruce Ackerman and Oona Hathaway, "Limited War and the Constitution: Iraq and the Crisis of Presidential Legality," *Michigan Law Review* 109 (4) (2011), 447–517. For intelligence/deliberation models see Joseph Bessette, *The Mild Voice of Reason: Deliberative Democracy and American National Government* (Chicago: University of Chicago Press, 1997); Griffin (2013); Sarah Burns, "Legalizing a Political Fight: Congressional Abdication of War Powers in the Bush and Obama Administrations," *Presidential Studies Quarterly* 51(3) (2021): 462–491.

7. See Paul Frymer, *Building an American Empire: The Era of Territorial and Political Expansion* (Princeton: Princeton University Press, 2017), 58–60.

8. Henry Bartholomew Cox, *War, Foreign Affairs, and Constitutional Power 1829–1901* (Cambridge, MA: Ballinger Publishing, 1976), 16.

9. Cox, War, *Foreign Affairs, and Constitutional Power* 17 (1976): 17.

10. But see the higher level of concern in Congress when military actions implicated great power interests, as for instance Jackson's conduct against the Seminole people implicated Spain in the First Seminole War. David S. Heidler, "The Politics of National Aggression: Congress and the First Seminole War," *Journal of the Early Republic* 13(4) (1993): 501–530.

11. Cox, *War, Foreign Affairs and Coonstitutional Power* 65 (1976): 65.

12. Silverstein (1996); 123–4, 156.

13. Undersecretary of State Nicholas Katzenbach, "Hearings Before the Senate Committee on Foreign Relations," U.S. Commitments to Foreign Powers, 90th Cong., 1st sess., (1967): 126; Jack Werkley, "Truman Says He Can Send Troops to Palestine Without Congress," *New York Herald Tribune* (April 23, 1948).

14. Dara Z. Strolovitch, *When Bad Things Happen to Privileged People: Race, Gender, and What Makes a Crisis in America* (Chicago: University of Chicago Press, 2023); Mary Dudziak,

War Time: An Idea, Its History, Its Consequences (Oxford: Oxford University Press, 2012); Bonnie Honig, *Emergency Politics: Paradox, Law, Democracy* (Princeton: Princeton University Press, 2011).

15. Common assumptions in American politics include that political actors pursue goals, including both policy goals and electoral goals, and that political actors behave strategically with reference to their goals.

16. Caroline D. Krass, Office of the Legal Counsel, "Authority to Use Military Force in Libya" (April 1, 2011), p. 37, https://www.justice.gov/olc/file/2011-04-01-libya-deployment/download (accessed February 24, 2023).

17. Consider also Bill Clinton, who faced a different kind of calculus around hostilities in Yugoslavia.

18. Walter LaFeber, "The Evolution of the Monroe Doctrine," in *Redefining the Past: Essays in Diplomatic History in Honor of William Appleman Williams*, ed. Lloyd C. Gardner (Corvallis: Oregon State University Press, 1986), 123, 132.

19. William Appleman Williams, *Empire as a Way of Life* (New York, 1980). An essay by Marc-William Palen, "The Imperialism of Economic Nationalism, 1890–1913," *Diplomatic History* 39(1) (2015): 157–185 contextualizes the Wisconsin school's contributions within a broader historiography of empire.

20. See Gretchen Ritter, *Goldbugs and Greenbacks: The Antimonopoly Tradition and the Politics of Finance in America, 1865–1896* (Cambridge: Cambridge University Press, 1999).

21. Walter LaFeber, *The New Empire: An Interpretation of American Expansion, 1860–1898* (Ithaca, NY: Cornell University Press, 1963), xxv. Peter Trubowitz, from political science, echoes LaFeber in stating that elites perceived foreign markets as a "safety valve." See his *Defining the National Interest: Conflict and Change in American Foreign Policy* (Chicago: University of Chicago Press, 1998), 34, 36.

22. Theodore Roosevelt, "1904 Annual Message to Congress" (December 6, 1904). Available at http://www.infoplease.com/t/hist/state-of-the-union/116.html (accessed June 11, 2012). See also his "First Annual Message to Congress" (December 3, 1901).

23. Theodore Roosevelt, "1904 Annual Message to Congress." See also his First Annual Message to Congress.

24. Daniel H. Wicks, "Dress Rehearsal: United States Intervention on the Isthmus of Panama, 1885," *Pacific Historical Review* 49:4 (1980): 581–605, 582; LaFeber (1963), 210.

25. Thomas Andrew Bailey, "A Latin American Protests (1943)," in *The American Spirit: Since 1865*, David M. Kennedy and Thomas Andrew Bailey, eds. (Boston: Houghton Mifflin, 1998), 199. Such incursions were often recognized in terms of the Monroe Doctrine even if the doctrine was not explicitly cited. See Hiram Bingham, *The Monroe Doctrine: An Obsolete Shibboleth* (New York: Da Capo Press, 1976).

26. The approach to World War I featured a projection of American power into Central and South America, but its legitimating source was Wilsonian ideas about law and order rather than Monroe Doctrine commitments to resisting European influence (and hence should be construed either as part of a different security order, or as orderless acts). For more on the difference in these presidents' uses of the war power, see James R. Holmes, *Theodore Roosevelt and World Order: Police Power in International Relations* (Washington, DC: Potomac Books, 2006), 83.

27. Fisher, *Congressional Abdication*, 20; Edward S. Corwin, *Presidential Power and the Constitution: Essays* (Ithaca, NY: Cornell University Press, 1976); Henry P. Monaghan, "Presidential

War Making," *Boston University Law Review* 50:1 (1970): 26–27; Schlesinger, *Imperial*. See too Jules Lobel, "'Little Wars' and the Constitution," *University of Miami Law Review* 50:1 (1995): 61–79. Fisher's resistance is confusing given his emphasis that Obama's Libya incursion is "war" regardless of scope. See Louis Fisher, "Military Operations in Libya: No War? No Hostilities?'" *Presidential Studies Quarterly* 42:1 (2012): 176–89. On the other hand, Senator Connally argued that "the Atlantic Pact is but the logical extension of the principle of the Monroe Doctrine." U.S. Senate, Committee on Foreign Relations, 81st Cong., 1st sess., *Hearings on the North Atlantic Treaty* (1949), 231.

28. Lobel, 61, 67. See too Jane C. Stromseth, "Understanding Constitutional War Powers Today: Why Methodology Matters," *Yale Law Journal* 106:3 (1996): 845–915.

29. Fisher, *Presidential War Power* (1995), ch. 2.

30. Harold H. Koh, *The National Security Constitution: Sharing Power After the Iran-Contra Affair* (New Haven: Yale University Press, 1990).

31. Harold H. Koh, Legal Advisor, US Dept. of State, "Libya and War Powers: Hearings Before the Senate Committee on Foreign Relations," 112th Cong. (2011), at https://2009-2017.state.gov/s/l/releases/remarks/167250.htm (accessed February 24, 2023), 13.

32. Silverstein (1996).

33. For a reading of military capacity and the Roosevelt Corollary, see Wicks (1980), 603.

34. LaFeber (1963), 59, 123–24.

35. LaFeber (1963), 91.

36. David McCullough, *The Path Between the Seas: The Creation of the Panama Canal, 1870–1914* (New York: Simon & Schuster, 1977), ch. 6.

37. LaFeber (1963), 124–25.

38. Richard Collin, *Theodore Roosevelt's Caribbean* (Baton Rouge: Louisiana State University Press 1990), 45, citing Benjamin Franklin Tracy, House Executive Documents, 51st Cong., 1st Sess., No. 1, pt. 3, Serial 2721, 3–4.

39. Trubowitz (1998), 3.

40. Griffin (2013).

41. Sen. Bacon, Congressional Record, 58th Cong., 2nd sess. (February 23, 1904), 2245; Cullom, Congressional Record, 58th Cong. (March 17, 1903), 110. See also Depew, Congressional Record, 58th Cong., 2nd sess. (January 14, 1904), 758–61.

42. McCullough, *The Path Between the Seas: The Creation of the Panama Canal, 1870–1914*, 136.

43. James K. Polk, "Special Message to the Senate" (February 10, 1847). Available at http://www.presidency.ucsb.edu/ws/index.php?pid=67954#axzz1veUUAsYn (accessed February 24, 2023).

44. On US intervention under the terms of this treaty, see Collin (1990), 237; E. Taylor Parks, *Colombia and the United States, 1765–1934* (Manchester, NH: Ayer Company Publishers, 1970), 218–28; see Senator Morgan's discussion of the enforcement of this guarantee in debate over the Hay-Herrán Treaty. *Congressional Record*, 58th Cong. (March 14, 1903): 92.

45. Wicks (1980), 598.

46. Robert E. Hannigan, *The New World Power: American Foreign Policy, 1898–1917* (Philadelphia: University of Pennsylvania Press, 2002), 26; Dwight Carroll Miner, *The Fight for the Panama Route: The Story of the Spooner Act and the Hay-Herrán Treaty* (New York: Columbia University Press, 1940), 97. The Senate Foreign Relations Committee's first report is printed in Sen. Docs, 56th Cong., 1st sess., no. 268; McCullough (1997), 256–59.

47. Hannigan (2002), 28.

48. Congressional Record, 58th Cong. (March 9, 1903), 22; see also 18–19. On Morgan see Joseph A. Fry, "John Tyler Morgan's Southern Expansionism," *Diplomatic History* 9(4) (1985): 329–346.

49. Congressional Record, 58th Cong. (March 9, 1903), 14.

50. Congressional Record, 58th Cong. (March 9, 1903), 14, 15.

51. Congressional Record, 58th Cong. (March 9, 1903), 15.

52. Congressional Record, 58th Cong. (March 17, 1903), 111, 119–20.

53. Congressional Record, 58th Cong. (March 9, 1903), 22; Collin (1990), 219–33.

54. Congressional Record, 58th Cong. (March 17, 1903), 109.

55. Congressional Record, 58th Cong .(March 9, 1903), 22; see also 18–19.

56. McCullough (1997), 332.

57. Congressional Record, 58th Cong. (March 9, 1903), 15–16.

58. Collin (1990), 199 and 243.

59. Collin (1990), 216.

60. Congressional Record, 58th Cong. (March 9, 1903), 15–16; Collin (1990), 219, 243.

61. Collin (1990), 252.

62. Collin (1990), 258.

63. Dispatch from president to commanders. As cited in Joseph C. Freehoff, *America and the Canal Title: Or, an Examination, Sifting and Interpretation of the Data Bearing on the Wresting of the Province of Panama from the Republic of Colombia by the Roosevelt Administration in 1903 in Order to Secure Title to the Canal Zone* (Ithaca: Cornell University Library, 2009) (original ed. 1916), 11.

64. Stephen Kinzer, *Overthrow: America's Century of Regime Change from Hawaii to Iraq* (New York: Times Books, 2006), 61.

65. E.g., Peter Irons, *War Powers: How the Imperial Presidency Hijacked the Constitution* (New York: Metropolitan Books, 2005), 97.

66. McCullough (1997), 393.

67. Sen. Gorman offered Senate Resolution 73. Congressional Record, 58th Cong., 2nd sess. (Jan 13, 1904), 703; Sen. Morgan, Congressional Record, 58th Cong., 2nd sess. (December 9, 1903), 112; Sen. Stone, Congressional Record, 58th Cong., 2nd sess. (January 13, 1904), 702. The resolution submitted by Sen. Morgan was Sen. Res. No. 66, Congressional Record, 58th Cong., 2nd sess. (December 19, 1903), 399; Sen. Bacon, Congressional Record, 58th Cong., 2nd sess. (January 12, 1904), 614; Sen. Newlands, Congressional Record, 58th Cong., 2nd sess. (January 22, 1904), 1033.

68. See Congressional Record, 58th Cong., 2nd sess.: Sen. Lodge (January 5, 1904), 459–65; Sen. Quarles (January 14, 1904), 756; Sen. Simmons (February 23, 1904), 2249–50.

69. Sen. Carmack, Congressional Record, 58th Cong., 2nd sess. (January 13, 1904), 705–706.

70. Ibid. (January 19, 1904), 867.

71. Congressional Record, 58th Cong., 2nd sess. (February 22, 1904), 2203.

72. Sen. Dolliver. Congressional Record, 58th Cong., 2nd sess. (January 22, 1904), 1031.

73. See exchange between Foraker and Daniel, Congressional Record, 58th Cong., 2nd sess. (January 12, 1904), 616–18.

74. Sen. Hoar, Congressional Record, 58th Cong., 2nd sess. (February 22, 1904), 2195.

75. The alternative Nicaraguan treaty that Morgan advocated guaranteed the US military power to enter the canal zone "for the protection of life, liberty, and property, and for the preservation of peace and good order." Morgan, Congressional Record, 58th Cong. (March 17, 1903), 119.

76. Sen. Morgan, Congressional Record, 58th Cong. (March 17, 1903), 285, 292–93.

77. For their criticisms, see Robert David Johnson, *The Peace Progressives and American Foreign Relations* (Cambridge: Harvard University Press, 1995), 26.

78. George Thomas, "What Is Political Development? A Constitutional Perspective," *Review of Politics* 73 (2) (2011), 275–294.

79. Thomas, "Political Development," 276.

80. See introduction to this volume (Charles Zug, "The Purposes of Constitutional Conflict").

CHAPTER 9

The Strange Case of the Legislative Veto: The Legal Undermining (and the Persistence) of Constitutional Politics

Thomas R. Bell

There is little doubt that the legislative veto was one of the most consequential constitutional innovations in the history of American government before it was invalidated by the Supreme Court in *INS v. Chadha* (1983) in one of the most sweeping judicial acts in American history. The legislative veto was a mechanism by which Congress delegated legislative power by statute to the executive branch or to bureaucratic agencies while retaining the ability to veto executive actions or proposed bureaucratic rules in particular instances. Congress used several variants of the legislative veto, including joint resolutions that required the president's signature (or veto). However, the most controversial legislative vetoes—the vetoes at issue in and invalidated by the court in *Chadha*—were those that, in the court's telling, did not meet the Constitution's requirements for lawmaking (bicameralism and presentment). For example, Congress could pass a concurrent resolution of approval, thus requiring that both houses approve a proposed rule before it could go into effect. Alternatively, Congress could allow proposed rules to go into effect after a specified period of time (usually 60 days) unless one or both houses disapproved by passing either a simple or concurrent resolution of disapproval.

The purpose of this chapter is to show that the legislative veto, while characterized by the Supreme Court as a departure from the literal strictures of the constitutional text, was actually emblematic of the dynamism of the

Constitution's separation of powers, an attempt to realize the energy of the executive branch while balancing that efficiency with the aims of republican government. Indeed, the legislative veto, itself authorized by a statute passed by both houses of Congress and signed by the president, merely altered the order of interbranch action without fundamentally changing the substantive involvement of the two branches in lawmaking. The legislative veto thus accompanied legislative delegation, allowing the executive branch to engage in the lawmaking function reserved to Congress while ensuring that such rules (which are themselves legally binding on citizens) only go into effect so long as both houses of Congress agreed. Given the need to delegate in an increasingly complex world, the political branches invented the legislative veto in order to reconcile such delegation with the constitutional structure.

Although the Supreme Court invalidated legislative vetoes nearly four decades ago, the court's decision in *Chadha* merits reconsideration. This is especially true as doubts about the constitutionality of legislative delegation gain traction on the Supreme Court. Both the majority in *Chadha* and the advocates of reviving a version of the nondelegation doctrine share a common, and flawed, premise: that it is the judiciary's role to ensure that each of the branches of government only exercise the type of power assigned to it. This legalistic and judiciary-centered approach to the separation of powers not only fundamentally misunderstands the type of political system the Constitution set into motion, it also risks convincing Americans that their Constitution is outdated, incapable of governing in the contemporary world.

Separation of Powers and the Problem of Means and Ends

Before evaluating the legislative veto and its invalidation by the Supreme Court, it is first important to understand the type of political system the Constitution set into motion, and how that system should be maintained. The argument of this essay is that the Constitution establishes a dynamic political order in which the boundaries of the branches are worked out in politics. This, however, is not the dominant understanding today. Indeed, while there is considerable disagreement about which interpretive methodologies should be utilized, it is hardly a contested proposition that the Supreme Court, utilizing the ordinary tools of legalism, should superintend the Constitution's separation of powers.[1] Such judicial enforcement, however, reveals a problem of ends and means.

The court's separation of powers jurisprudence largely alternates between two competing approaches often referred to as formalism and functionalism.[2] Formalism emphasizes the Constitution's strict separation between the branches, or the notion that the Constitution assigns particular types of power to the appropriate branches such that "Congress's grants of legislative power must enable it to legislate, the President's grant of executive power must enable him to execute all federal laws, and the federal judiciary's grant of judicial power must enable the federal courts to decide certain cases and controversies."[3] The literal strictures of the constitutional text interpreted in light of original intent or original public meaning are of the utmost importance, and the court gives little to no weight to governmental needs induced by changed circumstances or to broad objectives such as good or efficient government.[4] Given the importance of defining with legal precision the powers of the different branches, formalist legal scholars, in an effort to guide the judiciary in its line-drawing, utilize textual and historical analysis to determine the extent and limitations of the various clause-bound powers appropriately exercised by the different branches.[5]

The other dominant strand of the Supreme Court's jurisprudence, functionalism, emphasizes checks and balances. One of the guiding insights of the functionalist approach is that it is impossible to define the powers of the different branches with the precision that the formalist approach requires.[6] Rather, indeterminacy and imprecision are inherent in the Constitution's scheme of government.[7] Given this fundamental indeterminacy, the judicial task is to maintain the relative balance between the branches so that no branch encroaches on the core functions of another branch.[8] And yet, reasoning from structural qualities, like balance, that have no explicit basis in the constitutional text allows for a great deal of judicial discretion. As Elizabeth Brown notes, "In order for the functionalist system to work, someone must determine what values or functions are central to the constitutional structure, and must define the extent to which changed circumstances should be permitted to influence that determination."[9] Although in theory functionalism allows for more judicial discretion than the formalist approach, in practice the court's functionalist opinions have been far more deferential to the political branches.

The problem with the court's competing approaches is that judicial resolution of interbranch boundaries is primarily oriented to protecting the separation of powers itself through judicial enforcement of the constitutional text. Whether the court ensures strict textual separation or maintains the relative balance between the branches, the goods (primarily liberty) generated in the abstract by judicial superintendence are merely derivative consequences of enforcing the separation of powers itself. This, however, misunderstands the fundamental nature of the constitutional order and how its governing system is the means to the polity's various and politically contingent ends. While each legal approach represents something partially true about the constitutional system, separation and checks and balances are only ancillary components of a larger political architecture.

The Federalist explicitly rejects the fully judicialized, or overly legalistic, version of the Constitution. Rather, Madison argues that legal strictures (parchment barriers) are insufficient to ensure constitutional fidelity.[10] Rather than rely on legal boundaries, the Constitution creates independent institutions (separation), provides them with tools to resist encroachment (checks and balances), and, finally, relies on human ambition as the primary mechanism by which those checks and balances are utilized to protect or press institutional prerogatives against the other branches.[11] In this way, the Constitution governs not in the sense that it is primarily a text enforced as law by the court. Rather, it governs in the sense that it establishes the institutional forms of the polity, and the central feature of the Constitution's design is its self-enforcing nature. As Madison writes in *Federalist* No. 51:

> To what expedient, then, shall we finally resort, for maintaining in practice the necessary partition of power among the several departments, as laid down in the Constitution? The only answer that can be given is, that as all these exterior provisions are found to be inadequate, the defect must be supplied, by so contriving the interior structure of the government as that its several constituent parts may, by their mutual relations, be the means of keeping each other in their proper places.[12]

What should be clear from the preceding discussion are the ways in which such a self-enforcing political design significantly blurs the legal boundaries between the branches, placing it at odds with the formalists' strict separation account. The boundaries between the branches are not enforced by the court, but through political conflict between the branches. In fact, Madison makes clear in *Federalist* No. 37 the theoretical and practical impossibility of demarcating interbranch boundaries with legal precision in the first place,[13] and as Jeffrey Tulis notes, *The Federalist* never undertakes such a task. Rather, the political science of *The Federalist* details the ways in which differently designed institutions can serve positive functions in the constitutional order by bringing to bear different functional qualities and perspectives on politics through conflict within and between them.[14] For example, the plurality of Congress is meant to induce the deliberative spirit that aids it in performing its republican function of enacting laws that represent the reflective views of the political majority. The independence and unity of the executive branch makes more likely the vigorous administration of governance and responsiveness to the unforeseen problems that confront the polity. And life tenure insulates the judiciary from public opinion so that it can ensure that individual citizens are protected by law. Insofar as these different aims come into conflict, interbranch politics is the mechanism by which these different perspectives are brought to bear on the political questions that confront the polity.

This political design also transcends mere balance of power as the different branches perform distinct functions that empower them at different points in time.[15] Political power is thus far more dynamic and diffused than a particular snapshot in time could possibly reveal. Unforeseen circumstances might require the president to act in ways unanticipated by Congress when it passed a particular law, requiring constitutional justification by the president. Congress, in turn, has tools to contest presidential use of authority through oversight hearings, budget processes, and ultimately impeachment and removal from office.[16] Uses of power are often context dependent, requiring political and constitutional justification.

Given the inherent limitations of law to speak to the unforeseen contingencies that are endemic to political life, interbranch conflict between Congress and the president regarding the extent of their respective powers is a central feature of the Constitution's political design, enabling it to endure and adapt to the various crises of the ages. Judicial enforcement of the boundaries between Congress and the president disrupts this dynamic process and is superfluous given the political branches' institutional tools vis-à-vis each other. More problematically, judicial superintendence of interbranch boundaries represents a fundamental misunderstanding of the nature of the constitutional system insofar as it extracts the Supreme Court from the constitutional system, placing it above rather than within the separation of powers. Rather than defending its own prerogatives or safeguarding the rights of particular individuals, the court becomes the arbiter of the other branches' respective powers in ways that undermine a robust constitutional politics. The enforcement of the constitutional text becomes the primary aim rather than the polity's politically contingent ends sought through its political system. The court's invalidation of the legislative veto is a prime example of this phenomenon.

The Problem of Delegation

Article I of the Constitution explicitly states that "all legislative Powers herein granted shall be vested in a Congress of the United States." Even so, legislative delegation of rulemaking and adjudicatory power to administrators was a central feature of the national government almost as soon as the Constitution was ratified in 1789.[17] Congressional delegation skyrocketed in the twentieth century as Congress increasingly found itself incapable of legislating effectively given the vast array of complex issues on the national agenda. The national government's role expanded into complex and increasingly technical issues like transportation, communication, employment, wages and prices, labor relations, race relations, and the environment, among others. Although Congress had been better equipped to handle the comparatively simple tasks of nineteenth-century government, it increasingly delegated broad legislative powers to the executive branch and to bureaucratic agencies.

From a practical perspective, of course, such delegations of legislative power are justifiable for a number of reasons, especially if the national government is to have the ability to deal effectively with issues of national concern.[18] First, given the number of issues on the legislative agenda, Congress can delegate to alleviate its workload, prioritizing and focusing on issues it deems especially important. This is particularly important given the number of federal regulations that reach into nearly all facets of American life. In 2016, for example, the Federal Register included 3,853 final rules, taking up 38,652 pages, exceeding the previous record set in 2013 by 46 percent. While page counts provide an imperfect assessment of the number of annual regulations, they do underscore the massive level of federal regulation that has existed for much of the past century, at an ever-increasing pace. Without the ability to delegate, the national government would clearly be unable to deal with all of the issues that Congress deems of national importance. Second, many issues require expertise that average legislators are unlikely to have, especially given the wide range of issues confronting Congress in the modern world. Hence, while Congress can legislate with general goals in mind, it is often best to leave the specifics to those with the appropriate training and expertise. For example, it is not hard to imagine the difficulty with which Congress would write, say, nuclear power plant safety regulations (and perhaps even less difficult to imagine why most citizens would not want Congress to undertake such a task!). Delegation to entities that have resources in both time and expertise, therefore, allows Congress to ensure that federal regulations are adapted well to the various nuances and contingencies of specific problems, a task that surely exceeds the capabilities of a deliberative body of generalists.[19]

However, such delegation has not come without significant controversy. Even if legislative delegation to the executive branch and administrative agencies is a necessity for modern government on the scale with which it has existed during the past century, this does not necessarily entail that widespread delegation is an unqualified good, its benefits for governmental capacity and efficiency notwithstanding. In fact, delegation is deeply problematic from the perspective of democracy and public accountability. Insofar as Congress delegates its legislative authority to other entities, it diminishes its own constitutional role, placing lawmaking power in the hands of less democratic and electorally accountable actors.[20] As the Supreme Court argued in *Schechter Poultry Co. v. United States* (1935), the last case in which the court struck down a statute on nondelegation grounds, Congress can certainly delegate to others the responsibility for "the making of subordinate rules within prescribed limits," but the "necessity and validity of such provisions, and the wide range of administrative authority which has been developed by means of them, cannot be allowed to obscure the limitations of the authority to delegate, if our constitutional system is to be maintained."[21] In other words, delegation of legislative power to the president or administrative agencies in ways that allow Congress to avoid choosing between political alternatives (as opposed to merely administrative or logistical options) subverts the constitutional design by leaving lawmaking authority in entities that are not electorally accountable or representative of the range of diverse interests in the general public. The court's ruling in *Schecter*, however, proved to be an outlier in American constitutional history, one of only two instances where the court invalidated a law for violating the purported doctrine. In fact, while in the nineteenth and into the twentieth century the judiciary often at least rhetorically invoked a nondelegation principle, courts rarely if ever invalidated delegations on such grounds, leading two prominent scholars to characterize the notion of a judicially enforced nondelegation doctrine as a myth.[22]

While the current Supreme Court seems poised to reintroduce some version of a nondelegation doctrine, recent scholarship casts significant doubt on the constitutional pedigree of a judicially enforced nondelegation doctrine.[23] First, the mythic quality of the doctrine obscures the fact that delegation was widespread at the outset of American governance and provoked little if any controversy.[24] Given the extraordinary propensity of the first Congresses to extensively debate the Constitution's meaning and limitations on governmental action,[25] its willingness to delegate without sparking even a hint of constitutional controversy is striking.[26] Second, the fundamental premise undergirding a nondelegation principle is unapologetically formalistic, resting on the notion that different types of power are easily differentiated by their natures and assigned to and exclusively exercised by the appropriate branch, so that only the legislature can wield legislative power, and so on.[27] This formalistic notion, as argued above, hardly comports with founding-era conceptions of power. As Mortenson and Bagley argue, echoing Madison in *Federalist* No. 37, "sophisticated discussions of the founding recognize that efforts to classify government action in the abstract are irreducibly indeterminate."[28] Finally, from a practical perspective, the judicial enforcement of a nondelegation doctrine suffers from many of the same pitfalls of subjectivity that animate the concerns of those who oppose open-ended grants of delegated legislative authority. As Adrian Vermuele put it, writing in the wake of the Supreme Court's ruling in *West Virginia v. EPA* (2022), "the doctrine displays the same vagueness of standards that the Court finds objectionable, under the nondelegation rubric, when authority is granted to agencies. What is constitutional overreach for unelected bureaucrats in the agencies is constitutional virtue for the unelected bureaucrats on the bench."[29] The inherent subjectivity in criteria, and the concomitant unpredictability of judicial action in enforcing such a doctrine, thus invites lawsuits targeting all aspects of the administrative state, easily frustrating the ability of the government to regulate key aspects of American life. Such judicial action, and its accompanying chaos, is a poor substitute for political choice made by the people's representatives.

To make the case against a *judicially* enforced nondelegation doctrine, however, is not to unqualifiedly dismiss the core tenets of its political insight. Indeed, the key insight of the nondelegation doctrine is that delegations risk writing Congress, the most democratic and politically accountable institution in the government, out of the lawmaking process, leaving the lawmaking function in the hands of unelected and unaccountable administrators. While there are clear benefits to delegating to an expert administration for the sake of addressing particular policy questions with efficiency and the requisite expertise, expertise is no substitute for the political choices that a self-governing community must make. In other words, there is not necessarily a "correct" answer to many public policy questions that an expert administrator will be able to produce outside of the political process.[30] Nearly all of the questions of political life are certainly aided by expertise, but expertise is no substitute for the balancing of the various commitments and political trade-offs that are inherent in a government run by popular opinion. For example, vague congressional mandates to the EPA to issue regulations that ensure "clean air" (which assuredly a vast majority of Americans think is something worth having) do not answer the question of how to balance the need for clean air with, say, ensuring that businesses are not overly burdened by regulations to ensure a vibrant economy (also something that Americans surely want). Expertise, in other words, cannot fully account for the political trade-offs inherent in any policy choice.

In sum, while delegation might be necessary, it can only go so far before it undermines core constitutional values. The energy essential to good government must be held in tension with the need for public accountability. Although there is little basis in the constitutional text or founding-era history to support a judicially enforced nondelegation doctrine, a Congress motivated by its constitutional prerogatives should ensure that delegations comport with political principles deduced from the Constitution's allocation of power. Prior to its invalidation by the Supreme Court, the legislative veto was a mechanism that performed this vital function.

The Political Solution to Delegation: The Legislative Veto

Congress invented the legislative veto in response to the need to delegate, and in so doing showcased the dynamism of the Constitution's political framework. Confronted with the need to delegate, Congress employed the legislative veto to ensure oversight over its delegated powers. Legislative vetoes were thus part of a political arrangement negotiated by the two branches whereby Congress agreed to enact a statute delegating its legislative power to the executive branch (or to independent agencies) while reserving the right to approve or disapprove specific exercises of that legislative power.

For example, legislative vetoes were first included in laws granting the president the power to reorganize the executive branch by executive order rather than having to wait for Congress to legislate such plans. The legislative

Types of Legislative Vetoes	*Explanation*
Concurrent resolution of approval	Regulations only go into effect if both houses vote to approve
Concurrent resolution of disapproval	Regulations go into effect (usually after 60 days) unless both houses vote to disapprove
Simple resolution of disapproval	Regulations go into effect (usually after 60 days) unless one house votes to disapprove
Committee approval or disapproval	Regulations go into effect based on committee approval or disapproval

process is cumbersome and slow, and competing congressional pressures and compromises often stymied reorganization efforts rather than ensured that such efforts actually realized the overarching goal of efficient administration of the government, especially since opponents of any plan (perhaps agencies that will be discontinued or consolidated) could use all of the procedural mechanisms and hurdles of the legislative process to ensure defeat of a bill. Congress's deliberations on whether to delegate reorganization authority to the president were extensive and highly controversial as many members of Congress worried such a grant of authority to the executive branch would result in congressional abdication of its constitutional role.[31] When Congress finally granted the president reorganization authority in 1939, it only agreed to delegate power by also attaching a legislative veto provision that would allow reorganization plans to automatically go into effect after 60 days unless Congress passed a concurrent resolution of disapproval.[32]

While the reorganization delegation greatly empowered the executive branch in this area, Congress's veto power gave it negotiating leverage (much like the president's veto power in the normal legislative process) to ensure that plans reflected Congress's own set of priorities. All in all, 102 executive reorganization plans were submitted to Congress from 1939 until the mid-1980s; Congress disapproved 19 of them, demonstrating that Congress still had the final say even as it offered the president a more efficient alternative to the normal lawmaking process. The fundamental logic of the legislative veto in the executive reorganization case translates easily to other substantive areas where it was employed by Congress, especially in bureaucratic rulemaking. As the regulatory powers of the national government skyrocketed during the middle of the twentieth century, Congress increasingly delegated its lawmaking function to the executive branch and administrative agencies subject to a legislative veto.

What should be clear from the preceding is that legislative vetoes accompanied delegations of legislative power that greatly empowered the executive branch, ensuring that such delegations did not amount to congressional abdication of its constitutional function. Critics of the veto, however, worried that its exercise violated the Presentment Clause (Article I, Section 7), which stipulated that every "order, resolution, or vote" that required the concurrence of both chambers must be submitted to the president.[33] However, it is easy to dispense with such arguments for two reasons. First, the president's veto power was not implicated because legislative proposals came from the executive branch. Presumably the president would not veto his own legislative proposals. This was the position taken by Griffin Bell, attorney general for President Jimmy Carter, regarding executive reorganization. Such proposals were constitutional, according to Bell, because reorganization statutes permit the president to "submit to Congress only those plans which he approves."[34]

Although Bell attempted to distinguish executive reorganization vetoes from other types of legislative vetoes, executive control would seemingly extend to legislative vetoes more generally. For example, presidential control extends to bureaucratic rulemaking because the president enjoys significant political control of the bureaucracy through the power to appoint (with advice and consent) and fire subordinates within the executive branch. The Constitution also gives the president the power to request "the Opinion, in writing, of the principal Officer in each of the executive Departments, upon any Subject relating to the Duties of their respective offices."[35] This, as Javits and Klein argue, allows the president to require that any proposed policy action or subsidiary law be submitted to the president before prior review.[36] In fact, before the Supreme Court invalidated the legislative veto in *Chadha*, the executive branch required that all proposed final rules be submitted to the Office of Management and Budget (OMB) for review and approval before they were transmitted to Congress.[37] Since that time, executive control over bureaucratic rulemaking has increased.[38] In sum, while the president cannot micromanage all aspects of the bureaucracy, the potential for control is there, especially on issues that are particularly important for the administration.

Second, legislative vetoes did not violate the Presentment Clause because they were not instances of substantive legislation. Rather, Congress merely approved or disapproved (without amendment) specific rules or regulations issued by those wielding Congress's delegated power.[39] Hence, congressional invalidation of a proposed administrative action merely maintained the status quo. If Congress vetoed a proposed regulation before it went into effect, the executive branch had to go back to the drawing board, so to speak, and submit another rule. In short, legislative vetoes, authorized by delegation statutes, essentially reversed the substantive involvement of the branches in lawmaking. Congress's delegated powers exercised by the executive branch were ultimately subject to congressional approval or disapproval. Legislative vetoes thus reconciled the need to delegate in the contemporary world with constitutional structure, ensuring, at least in an attenuated sense, congressional involvement in the lawmaking process.

However, legislative vetoes have not been immune to political criticisms. Indeed, Jessica Korn, in an award-winning book on the legislative veto, argues that legislative vetoes were merely symbolic of congressional power rather than serving as a potent political weapon by which Congress maintained its political role in the constitutional order.[40] For example, Korn shows how in one issue area (Pell grants) Congress began to legislate more specifically after the veto was invalidated in *Chadha*. The Supreme Court invalidation of the veto, therefore, "made it easier for members to fulfill that aspect of their representative function that requires them to make Congress explicitly responsible for broadly supported public policies."[41] This, however, is ultimately not convincing when considered against the full backdrop of delegation and the vast amount of federal regulations issued each year (3,853 final rules in 2016 alone). Even if Congress was able to micromanage the needs-analysis formula for Pell grants, it certainly could not similarly micromanage *every* policy area it deemed important unless it was to do substantially less. Of course, many vocal opponents of the legislative veto, such as Antonin Scalia before he joined the Supreme Court, advocated just this type of return to a limited role for the national government with more specific legislation and more traditional oversight through hearings and the appropriations process.[42]

Contrary to Korn, other scholars have demonstrated that the legislative veto was a more effective tool of congressional oversight than traditional methods. After reviewing five agency programs during the 1970s, Harold Bruff and Ernest Gellhorn concluded that the legislative veto significantly altered "the working relationship" between Congress and bureaucratic agencies, making those agencies far more responsive to congressional views than they would be absent a legislative veto provision.[43] Traditional forms of legislative oversight, such as authorization renewal and appropriations hearings, provided ad hoc and sporadic opportunities for oversight, whereas the legislative veto ensured "regular and systematic examination of the substantive details of an agency's program."[44] Moreover, the legislative veto gave congressional committees negotiating power with agencies that helped bring final rules and regulations into alignment with congressional preferences.

Martha L. Gibson similarly found that the legislative veto protected congressional prerogatives on foreign policy issues, and that the viable threat of a veto fostered a cooperative spirit between the branches.[45] Without the legislative veto, Congress could only viably mobilize against the executive branch on issues that were of high political salience for the public at large, especially since congressional action absent a legislative veto often required supermajorities to overcome a presidential veto. The viable threat of a legislative veto, on the other hand, fostered a cooperative spirit between the branches that made it more likely congressional views would be taken into account earlier in the formation process.

Chadha and the Legal Undermining of Constitutional Politics

The legislative veto was a working political arrangement agreed upon by the political branches for several decades. This arrangement greatly empowered the executive branch by delegating lawmaking power while ensuring that the laws that govern citizens were only made in accordance with the deliberative will of the people expressed through Congress. The legislative veto, therefore, merely reversed the order of interbranch action while retaining the substantive political involvement of the two branches. The Supreme Court, however, invalidated the legislative veto in *INS v. Chadha* (1983) for its failure to abide by the Constitution's requirements for legislation: bicameralism and presentment. Writing for the court, Chief Justice Warren Burger declared that although the legislative veto was clearly a useful and efficient tool for congressional oversight of the executive branch, "the fact that a given law or procedure is efficient, convenient, and useful in facilitating functions of government, standing alone, will not save it if it is contrary to the Constitution."[46] Much can be said about the court's decision in *Chadha*, but the discussion here will focus on two particular concerns: the court's flawed and legalistic premises, which led it to fundamentally mischaracterize the legislative veto and the interbranch power dynamics it fostered, and the court's conflation of a particularly problematic legislative veto concerning the adjudication of an individual's legal status with legislative vetoes more generally.

The Court's Legalistic Premises

The Supreme Court characterized the legislative veto as a mechanism by which Congress stepped out of its legislative role to usurp executive functions in violation of the basic purposes of the separation of powers. The legislative veto, therefore, proved problematic because it empowered Congress vis-à-vis the executive branch, flying in the face of the framers' "profound conviction" that the powers of the legislative branch needed to be the "most carefully circumscribed" lest Congress dominate the constitutional system.[47] The question, then, is why the court viewed the legislative veto as *legislation* such that the constitutionally prescribed mechanisms for legislation—presentment and bicameralism—applied. This is an especially important question since such a view fundamentally mischaracterizes the interbranch power dynamics at issue. The legislative veto was a mechanism by which Congress retained its constitutional role in an attenuated sense as it greatly expanded presidential power through delegation. Congress could merely approve or disapprove substantive legislative proposals from the executive branch without amendment, thus ensuring that Congress's exercise of the legislative veto did not itself entail substantive legislation that avoided a presidential veto.

The court's legalistic premises about the separation of powers, however, led it to mischaracterize the power dynamics between the branches, and, ultimately, to undermine the robust constitutional politics sustained by the legislative veto. Indeed, the court asserted that the "Constitution sought to divide the delegated powers of the new federal government into three defined categories, legislative, executive, and judicial, to assure, as nearly as possible, that each Branch of government would confine itself to its assigned responsibility."[48] While not "'hermetically' sealed off from one another," the court contended that when any branch acts it is "presumptively exercising the power the Constitution has delegated to it."[49] In other words, when an executive official acts, that action is presumptively "executive," and when Congress acts it acts in a presumptively legislative way. This, of course, as indicated above, is a problematic presumption given the inherent difficulty of defining types of power with legal precision.

Beyond this problematic presumption, the court concluded that the legislative veto must be characterized as an act of lawmaking for two additional reasons. First, the legislative veto was "essentially legislative in purpose and effect" because it altered the "legal rights" of citizens outside the legislative branch in ways that would not have occurred absent congressional use of the veto.[50] As Justice White observed in his dissent, however, this ignores the fact that when the executive branch wields legislative power delegated to it by Congress, such as in bureaucratic rulemaking, the exercise of this legislative power by executive officeholders alters the legal rights of citizens, and this action is accomplished without the constitutional safeguards of bicameralism and presentment. While the court acknowledged this difficulty in a footnote, it brushed it aside by claiming that "executive action under legislatively delegated authority that might resemble 'legislative' action in some respects is not subject to the approval of both Houses of Congress and the President for the reason that the Constitution does not so require."[51] In other words, such actions are "presumptively" executive and, therefore, do not require bicameralism and presentment.

Second, the court asserted that the legislative veto had to be considered an act of lawmaking because there are only four constitutional provisions that allow one house of Congress to act outside of the legislative process.[52] But the question is not whether the Constitution specifically authorizes legislative vetoes, but whether Congress can enact a statute delegating legislative power subject to a legislative veto. If the legislative veto is derivative of a statute, then it does not matter that the Constitution does not explicitly provide for it. The court explained, however, that the Necessary and Proper Clause does not give Congress the power to review exercises of its delegated power with a legislative veto because the legislative veto was not a "constitutionally permissible means" of implementing its power.[53] This, of course, begs the question, especially given that one of the reasons the court asserted that the legislative veto was impermissible—and, therefore, could not be authorized by a statute under the Necessary and Proper Clause—was that the Constitution did not *directly* sanction this type of congressional action as one of the four ways in which Congress could act nonlegislatively.

What is particularly peculiar about this, as Justice White pointed out in his dissent, is that the Supreme Court was inconsistent on the question of whether Congress has the power to enact veto statutes based on its authority under the Necessary and Proper Clause. In fact, the court had long upheld actions similar to the legislative veto so long as those vetoes were exercised by nongovernmental entities. For example, in *Currin v. Wallace* (1939) the court upheld a statute that allowed certain restrictions on agriculture commodities to go into effect once a prescribed majority of affected farmers voted for it. Similarly, in *United States v. Rock Royal Cooperative* (1939) the court upheld a statute that gave producers of certain commodities the right to veto marketing orders issued by the secretary of agriculture. Hence, Congress could delegate legislative power subject to a veto from a specified interest group, but it could not reserve to itself the power to approve or disapprove exercises of its delegated legislative power. Evidently, the court believed that the Framers were so fearful of a powerful Congress that Congress cannot even modify its own powers in response to the modern fact of executive-dominated government. According to the court's logic, Congress can only act in a strictly legislative way and cannot take any action to oversee its delegated lawmaking functions outside of enacting a new statute. This, even as other entities are not subject to the same constraints for the mere fact that those entities are not Congress.

The court's formalism gave the illusion that Congress was stepping outside its constitutionally prescribed role in an attempt to encroach on executive prerogatives when, in fact, the legislative veto was a tool that allowed Congress to empower the executive branch to make law while ultimately ensuring that laws governing citizens still retained the consent of Congress. The court's failure to consider the legislative veto in light of delegation (in fact, the majority opinion does not mention delegation or the administrative state except in a passing footnote) kept it from recognizing that the legislative veto, far from undermining constitutional structure, was a political response to the problem of delegation that incorporated basic separation of powers values into the practice of contemporary government.

The court's ruling in *Chadha*, therefore, ultimately and perversely undermined separation of powers values. Categorizing delegated legislative power as executive solely because it is wielded by an executive branch official, and then narrowly defining the powers of Congress, actually frees the executive branch and bureaucratic agencies from separation of powers constraints such that they end up wielding legislative, executive, and judicial powers—the very definition of tyranny according to Madison. The court's inconsistent and futile attempt to confine different types of power in the appropriate branch led to the consolidation of power in the administrative state, unmoored from the political controls of the larger separation of powers framework.

Legislative Versus Adjudicatory Legislative Vetoes

What is also deeply troubling about the court's decision in *Chadha* is that it invalidated an entire class of legislative veto statutes based on a problematic and easily differentiated action. Consequently, the court irresponsibly issued a ruling far more sweeping than the case necessitated. This is an important point to dwell on, especially since the court's majority opinion collapsed the issues together, allowing a particularly pernicious congressional action to indict a legitimate governmental practice. The particular veto at issue in *Chadha* concerned whether one house of Congress could pass a resolution overturning an order of the attorney general to suspend a deportation over a finding of hardship.[54] Jagdish Rai Chadha was an immigrant from Kenya who lived in the United States on a student visa. Chadha was scheduled for deportation but requested that the Immigration and Naturalization Service (INS) suspend his deportation because he met the statutory criteria for residence in the United States because of the hardship he would face if deported. INS granted Chadha's request after a hearing and, as required by law, reported to Congress the names of 339 other persons, along with Chadha, who also had their deportations suspended for meeting the statutory criteria. Congress thus had the opportunity to exercise its veto to overturn any of the INS decisions it deemed improper. After reviewing the list, the House Committee on the Judiciary determined that six of those people, including Chadha, did not meet the statutory criteria, and it introduced a resolution to the House floor stating that "the House of Representatives does not approve the granting of permanent residence in the United States to the aliens hereinafter named." The House then passed the resolution without further explanation and without a recorded vote.[55]

The problem with this application of the legislative veto in the immigration context is that it was adjudicatory, altering the legal rights of particular individuals, rather than serving as a mechanism by which Congress oversaw its delegated and generally applicable legislative power. As Justice Powell argued in his concurring opinion, "The House did not enact a general rule; rather it made its own determination that six specific persons did not comply with certain statutory criteria."[56] Hence, the House of Representatives (acting like an appellate court) took on functions generally reserved to the judiciary without providing any of the safeguards normally afforded to citizens in judicial contexts, such as the right to counsel and the right to a hearing before taking legal action. While noting the imperfect parallel, Justice Powell argued that the "effect on Chadha's personal rights would not have been different in principle had he been acquitted of a federal crime and thereafter found by one House of Congress to have been guilty."[57] Such trial by legislature, Justice Powell observed, is anathema to separation of powers values: "[The Bill of Attainder Clause], and the separation of powers doctrine generally, reflect the Framers' concern that trial by a legislature lacks the safeguards necessary to prevent the abuse of power."[58]

Given the adjudicatory nature of the specific legislative veto at issue in *Chadha*, then, it is easily distinguished from legislative vetoes as such. As Lawrence Tribe argued, "If exercise of the legislative veto is objectionable because it amounts to a trial by legislature, that objection persists even if bicameral action and presentment to the President are assured."[59] In other words, Congress could not have overturned the decision of the INS and deported Chadha even by going through the full legislative process. The Supreme Court's holding with regard to Chadha was the right decision given that the application of law to specific individuals should only occur within adjudicatory settings that provide proper legal safeguards. The court erred, however, in failing to distinguish this particular congressional action from traditional forms of the legislative veto that did not pertain to the application of law to specific individuals in adjudicatory settings but, rather, were merely mechanisms by which Congress ensured that the generally applicable laws that govern citizens retain the consent of their representatives in Congress.

The Persistence of the Separation of Powers

The Supreme Court's ruling in *Chadha* dramatically curtailed Congress's ability to formally oversee its delegated powers. If Congress disagrees with a particular executive action, or a rule or regulation issued from an agency, it has to mobilize and go through the full legislative process to overturn by law the specific rule or action at issue. Given that Congress is seeking to overturn exercises of its delegated legislative power wielded by executive officials, such congressional action is far more susceptible to a presidential veto, and thus often requires supermajorities to overturn. The Congressional Review Act (CRA), passed in 1996, displays the difficulty of using the full legislative process to oversee delegated powers. The CRA required that all final rules be presented to Congress 60 days before going into effect, thus providing Congress time to review and then possibly overturn agency regulations by passing a joint resolution of disapproval.[60] Between its enactment in 1996 and 2016, however, only one regulation was overturned, and only 5 percent of regulations ever resulted in resolutions introduced on a chamber floor. The main success of the CRA has been in combating "midnight rulemaking."[61] Congressional Republicans and Republican President Donald Trump were able to use the CRA to subsequently overturn a number of last-minute rules promulgated during the last months of the Obama administration. The CRA, however, is largely ineffective when the political branches disagree.

The court's invalidation of the legislative veto has also at times made it less likely that Congress will delegate authority in ways that make government better and more efficient. Stripped of the legislative veto, Congress has at times chosen to rescind or change the mechanisms by which it oversees its delegated powers. For example, after *Chadha* Congress still granted the president the power to reorganize the executive branch, but rather than subject the president's proposals to a simple resolution of disapproval (meaning that the plan went into effect after a certain period of time *unless* one house mobilized to veto the plan) Congress subjected the reorganization plan to a joint resolution of approval. This is a far more onerous process, and one that made it far more difficult for the president to get plans approved. Given this, presidents stopped requesting reorganization authority soon after *Chadha*, and Congress has rarely taken on reorganization efforts itself. When it does act, it does so generally only as a response to major crises rather than with the kind of proactiveness that came with executive leadership.[62]

However, it can be easy to overstate the impacts of the *Chadha* decision on the practice of interbranch politics by looking at formal exercises of the legislative veto. While the concurrent and simple resolutions have all but disappeared from the congressional arsenal, Congress has continued to attach legislative veto provisions to bills. Most often such legislative vetoes are included in appropriations bills, requiring, in fairly standard language, that specified actions may not be executed without the "prior approval of the Committees on Appropriations of both Houses," or that the appropriations committees for both houses must be notified (generally 15 days) in advance.[63] The White House has often objected to the presence of such vetoes—claiming that they violate the court's *Chadha* decision. As Louis Fisher has noted, however, it is one thing for the president to condemn such legislative veto provisions as unconstitutional, but "agencies have a different attitude. They have to live with their review committees, year after year, and have a much greater incentive to make accommodations and stick by them. . . . Agencies cannot risk . . . collisions with the committees that authorize their programs and provide funds."[64]

Similarly, Congress can insert report-and-wait provisions in bills, which require that agencies keep Congress informed of new rules and regulations. Although report-and-wait provisions do not contain formal mechanisms to veto specific executive action or rulemaking, they make it more likely that executive actions or agency regulations comport with congressional views. If executive officials diverge too far from congressional preferences, they imperil important relationships with their oversight committees.

Critics of report-and-wait provisions hoped to see them invalidated because they perform the same function as formal legislative vetoes invalidated by the court. At first, the US Court of Claims did just this, striking down the report-and-wait provisions as a violation of separation of powers. While it found report-and-wait provisions to be "facially inoffensive," it was evident "from congressional and agency practice" that such provisions operated as "a *de facto* . . . congressional veto." On appeal, however, the Appeals Court upheld the distinction between formal and informal vetoes. The court noted that "committee chairmen and members naturally develop interest and expertise in the subjects entrusted to their continuing surveillance. Officials in the executive branch have to take these committees into account and keep them informed, respond to their inquiries, and it may be, flatter and please them when necessary." Even so, "there is nothing unconstitutional about this: indeed, our separation of powers makes such informal cooperation much more necessary than it would be in a pure system of parliamentary government." The difference between these informal legislative vetoes and the formal ones invalidated by *Chadha* is that the latter mechanism, according to the court, violates the Constitution's procedural requirements for lawmaking. In most other respects, however, they largely foster the same kind of interbranch politics that opponents of the legislative veto found so objectionable in the first place. Indeed, the logic of *Chadha* is strict separation, which makes even informal oversight or control suspect and certainly cannot make sense of the ways in which the branches consistently work together.

Conclusion

The artificial and static notion of separation of powers imposed by the Supreme Court in *Chadha* has ultimately proven undesirable and unworkable for both branches. The framers constructed a separation of powers system in which the branches would negotiate the limits of their respective powers in ordinary political disputes rather than according to static legal rules. The legislative veto is a prime example of interbranch politics wherein both branches negotiated the limits of their powers and came up with a working relationship that, while changing the order of interbranch action when it comes to lawmaking, maintained the substantive involvement of the branches. The court's formalistic focus missed these larger political dynamics that, far from being contrary to the Constitution, are, rather, the product of it. Given this, it is hardly surprising that such interbranch negotiation has continued despite the court's intervention. The court's notion of separation of powers articulated in *Chadha* can thus best be understood as layered on top of a working political order, disrupting the practice of healthy politics, but not entirely displacing it. The fact that interbranch politics has persisted points to the vitality of the Constitution's political architecture, albeit significantly diminished, despite the negative effects of bad judicial reasoning.

Notes

1. Nikolas Bowie and Daphne Renan, "The Separation of Powers Counterrevolution," *Yale Law Journal* 131, no. 7 (2022): 2024–25.

2. Peter L. Strauss, "Formal and Functional Approaches to Separation of Powers Questions—A Foolish Inconsistency?," *Cornell Law Review* 72, no. 3 (March 1987): 488–526.

3. Steven G. Calabresi and Saikrishna B. Prakash, "The President's Power to Execute the Laws," *Yale Law Journal* 104, no. 3 (1994): 544.

4. Rebecca L. Brown, "Separated Powers and Ordered Liberty," *University of Pennsylvania Law Review* 139 (1991): 1524; John F. Manning, "Separation of Powers as Ordinary Interpretation," *Harvard Law Review* 124, no. 8 (2011): 1939–2040.

5. See for example: Michael W. McConnell, *The President Who Would Not Be King* (Princeton: Princeton University Press, 2020); Manning, "Separation of Powers as Ordinary Interpretation"; Saikrishna B. Prakash and Michael D. Ramsey, "The Executive Power over Foreign Affairs," *Yale Law Journal* 111 (2001): 231–356; Saikrishna Prakash, "The Essential Meaning of Executive Power," *University of Illinois Law Review* (2003): 701–820; Saikrishna Prakash, "The Sweeping Domestic War Powers of Congress," *Michigan Law Review* 113, no. 8 (June 1, 2015): 1337–96.

6. Aziz Z. Huq, "Separation of Powers Metatheory," *Columbia Law Review* 118 (2018): 1530; Martin S. Flaherty, "The Most Dangerous Branch," *Yale Law Journal* 105, no. 7 (May 1996): 1755.

7. Peter L. Strauss, "The Place of Agencies in Government: Separation of Powers and the Fourth Branch," *Columbia Law Review* 84, no. 3 (April 1984): 603.

8. See Justice White's dissent in *Bowsher v. Synar* 478 U.S., 776. "[T]he role of this Court should be limited to determining whether the [act in issue] so alters the balance of authority among the branches of government as to pose a genuine threat to the basic division between the lawmaking power and the power to execute the law."

9. Rebecca L. Brown, "Separated Powers and Ordered Liberty," 1528.

10. Alexander Hamilton et al., *The Federalist Papers*, ed. Clinton Rossiter, 1st ed. (New York, NY: Signet, 2003), No. 48.

11. Hamilton et al., No. 51.

12. Hamilton et al., No. 51, 317–18.

13. Hamilton et al., No. 37, 228. "Experience has instructed us that no skill in the science of government has yet been able to discriminate and define, with sufficient certainty, its three great provinces the legislative, executive, and judiciary; or even the privileges and powers of the different legislative branches. Questions daily occur in the course of practice, which prove the obscurity which reins in these subjects, and which puzzle the greatest adepts in political science."

14. See Tulis's similar argument in this volume.

15. David J. Siemers, *The Myth of Coequal Branches: Restoring the Constitution's Separation of Functions* (Columbia: University of Missouri, 2018).

16. Josh Chafetz, *Congress's Constitution: Legislative Authority and the Separation of Powers* (New Haven: Yale University Press, 2017).

17. Jerry L. Mashaw, *Creating the Administrative Constitution: The Lost One Hundred Years of American Administrative Law* (New Haven: Yale University Press, 2012); Julian Davis Mortenson and Nicholas Bagley, "Delegation at the Founding," *Columbia Law Review* 121, no. 2 (2021): 277–368.

18. James M. Landis, *The Administrative Process*, Storrs Lectures on Jurisprudence 1938 (New Haven: Yale University Press, 1966); Jonathan H. Adler, "Placing Reins on Regulations: Assessing the Proposed Reins Act," *New York University Journal of Legislation and Public Policy* 16 (2013): 9–10; David H. Rosenbloom, *Building a Legislative-Centered Public Administration: Congress and the Administrative State, 1946–1999* (Tuscaloosa: University of Alabama Press, 2000), 133–34.

19. See *Mistretta v. United States* (1989): ("[I]n our increasingly complex society, . . . Congress simply cannot do its job absent an ability to delegate power under broad general objectives.").

20. Gary Lawson, "Delegation and Original Meaning," *Virginia Law Review* 88, no. 2 (2002): 327–404.

21. *Schechter Poultry Corp. v. United States*, 295 US 495 (1935).

22. Keith Whittington and Jason Iuliano, "The Myth of the Nondelegation Doctrine," *University of Pennsylvania Law Review* 165, no. 2 (January 1, 2017): 379.

23. Eric A. Posner and Adrian Vermeule, "Interring the Nondelegation Doctrine," *University of Chicago Law Review* 69 (2002): 1721–62; Julian Davis Mortenson and Nicholas Bagley, "Delegation at the Founding."

24. Mashaw, *Creating the Administrative Constitution*; Julian Davis Mortenson and Nicholas Bagley, "Delegation at the Founding," 332–66.

25. David P. Currie, *The Constitution in Congress: The Federalist Period, 1789–1801*, 1st ed. (Chicago: University of Chicago Press, 1999).

26. Julian Davis Mortenson and Nicholas Bagley, "Delegation at the Founding," 333–34.

27. Gary Lawson, "Delegation and Original Meaning," 342–43. "However difficult it may be to distinguish the legislative, executive, and judicial powers at the margins, the Constitution of 1788–89 clearly places such a distinction at the center of its structure. There are constitutional lines that the executive and judicial powers may not cross."

28. Julian Davis Mortenson and Nicholas Bagley, "Delegation at the Founding," 315.

29. Adrian Vermeule, "Perspective | There Is No Conservative Legal Movement," *The Washington Post*, July 6, 2022, https://www.washingtonpost.com/outlook/2022/07/06/epa-roberts-conservative-court-libertarian/.

30. Roger A. Pielke, *The Honest Broker: Making Sense of Science in Policy and Politics* (Cambridge: Cambridge University Press, 2007).

31. Richard Polenberg, *Reorganizing Roosevelt's Government: The Controversy Over Executive Reorganization, 1936–1939* (Cambridge: Harvard University Press, 1966), 129, 166.

32. Subsequent reorganization authorizations in later years used different variations of the legislative veto that shifted the balance between the two branches. For example, at times plans went into effect unless one house passed a resolution of disapproval.

33. Robert W. Ginnane, "The Control of Federal Administration by Congressional Resolutions and Committees," *Harvard Law Review* 66, no. 4 (February 1953): 594–99.

34. Letter of the attorney general to the president, in response to an inquiry on the constitutionality of section 906(a) of the executive reorganization statute, 5 U.S. Code, Sect. 901*ff*.: 43 Opins. A.G. 10 (1977), quoted in Murray Dry, "The Congressional Veto and the Constitutional Separation of Powers," in *The Presidency in the Constitutional Order*, eds. Jeffrey K. Tulis and Joseph M. Bessette (Baton Rouge: Louisiana State University Press, 1981), 195–223, 209.

35. U.S. Constitution, Article II, Section 2, Clause 1.

36. Jacob K. Javits and Gary J. Klein, "Congressional Oversight and the Legislative Veto: A Constitutional Analysis," *New York University Law Review* 52 (1977): 487.

37. Id., 487–90.

38. Steven Croley, "White House Review of Agency Rulemaking: An Empirical Investigation," *University of Chicago Law Review* 70 (2003): 821–86.

39. Javits and Klein, "Congressional Oversight and the Legislative Veto," 486.

40. Jessica Korn, *The Power of Separation: American Constitutionalism and the Myth of the Legislative Veto*, Princeton Studies in American Politics (Princeton, NJ: Princeton University Press, 1996).

41. Id., 90.

42. Antonin Scalia, "The Legislative Veto: A False Remedy for System Overload," *Regulation: AEI Journal on Government and Society*, 1979.

43. Harold H. Bruff and Ernest Gellhorn, "Congressional Control of Administrative Regulation: A Study of Legislative Vetoes," *Harvard Law Review* 90, no. 7 (1977): 1420.

44. Id., 1423.

45. Martha Liebler Gibson, "Managing Conflict: The Role of the Legislative Veto in American Foreign Policy," *Polity* 26, no. 3 (1994): 441–72.

46. *INS v. Chadha*, 462 US 919 (1983).

47. Id., 462 US at 947, 951.

48. Id., 462 US at 951.

49. Id., 462 US at 951.

50. Id., 462 US at 952.

51. Id., 462 US at 952, fn 16.

52. The House of Representatives alone was given the power to initiate impeachments (Art. I, Sec. 2, Cl. 2); the Senate alone was given the power to conduct trials following impeachment on charges initiated by the House and to convict following trial (Art. I, Sec. 3, Cl. 5); the Senate alone was given final unreviewable power to approve or disapprove presidential

appointments (Art. II, Sec. 2, Cl. 2); and the Senate alone was given the unreviewable power to ratify treaties negotiated by the president (Art. II, Sec. 2, Cl. 2).

53. *INS v. Chadha*, 462 US at 940–41.

54. Barbara Hinkson Craig, *Chadha: The Story of an Epic Constitutional Struggle* (New York: Oxford University Press, 1988), 3–35; Michael J. Berry, *The Modern Legislative Veto: Macropolitical Conflict and the Legacy of Chadha* (University of Michigan Press, 2017), 61–65.

55. *INS v. Chadha*, 462 US at 963–64. (Powell, J., Concurring).

56. Id., 462 US at 964–65.

57. Id., 462 US at 965, fn 8.

58. Id., 462 US at 962.

59. Laurence H. Tribe, "The Legislative Veto Decision: A Law by Any Other Name," *Harvard Journal on Legislation* 21 (1984): 16.

60. Morton Rosenberg, "Congressional Review of Agency Rulemaking: An Update and Assessment of The Congressional Review Act after a Decade," Report (Washington, DC: Congressional Research Service, May 8, 2008); Maeve P. Carey and Christopher M. Davis, "The Congressional Review Act (CRA): Frequently Asked Questions" (Congressional Research Service, November 12, 2021).

61. Paul J. Larkin Jr., "Reawakening the Congressional Review Act," *Harvard Journal of Law and Public Policy; Cambridge* 41, no. 1 (Winter 2018): 187–252.

62. John W. York and Rachel Greszler, "A Model for Executive Reorganization" (Heritage Foundation, November 3, 2017), 2, https://www.heritage.org/political-process/report/model-executive-reorganization.

63. Berry, *The Modern Legislative Veto*, 97.

64. Louis Fisher, "The Legislative Veto: Invalidated, It Survives," *Law and Contemporary Problems* 56, no. 4 (Autumn 1993): 288.

CHAPTER 10

The Constitutional Significance of the Eisenhower-McCarthy Standoff

Charles U. Zug

Congress has grown increasingly deferential toward the president and the federal courts since the mid-twentieth century. Building on the pathbreaking work of Jeffrey Tulis, I try to explain what this development means for the American constitutional system through an analysis of the 1954 constitutional standoff between Senator Joseph McCarthy and President Dwight Eisenhower over access to agency information and personnel, a standoff that resulted in a then-unprecedented assertion of executive privilege by the president.[1] Seen from the perspective of broader historical developments in executive-legislative relations, the Eisenhower-McCarthy standoff—along with similar separation of powers conflicts, such as the Steel Seizure Case[2]—can be interpreted as part of a broader development culminating in the so-called unitary executive and imperial presidency. Yet the same conflict can also be interpreted normatively as a subversion of the logic of the Constitution's separation of powers system. I leverage both interpretations—political development and constitutional theory—to argue that the Eisenhower-McCarthy standoff is perhaps best understood as a symptom of congressional dysfunction manifested in abdication by the Senate.

Lead-Up to the Standoff

As the other chapters of this volume demonstrate, the topic of separation of powers can be studied from several different perspectives, including the history of political thought (Paul Carrese and Brigid Flaherty Staab) and comparative constitutionalism (George Thomas). The two perspectives I choose to inhabit here are constitutional theory and American political development (APD), and in this regard my chapter's approach most closely resembles Mariah Zeisberg's. Whereas constitutional theorists try to understand the meaning and nature of the constitution itself (an endeavor that requires a significant degree of abstraction from history and contingency, and that invariably involves normative judgements),[3] APD largely focuses on the ways in which constitutional politics are constructed historically.[4] Because their priorities and background assumptions differ, scholars embedded in these disciplines will give important moments from the history of separation of powers—the subject of this volume—very different interpretations. One of my aims here is to deploy the insights of both disciplines in order to offer an analysis of the Eisenhower-McCarthy standoff that is attentive to political development and normative constitutional theory.[5] I call this style of analysis "diagnostic," by which I mean a method of interpreting political decisions and developments in light of a self-consciously articulated holistic standard of constitutional health—that is, through diagnostics of the health of the whole polity in question.

The analytical value-added of a diagnostic approach is that it self-consciously does what all other political science methods do (albeit without necessarily realizing it), namely spell out and interrogate the theoretical assumptions on which underlying judgments about political functionality are based.[6] The political diagnostician does not jump directly to questions like "What causes Congress to be dysfunctional?" or "What has made the modern presidency so powerful?" but instead lingers on the background theories on which such questions are implicitly based. What standards do we have in mind when we make claims such as, "Congress is dysfunctional," and "the presidency is too powerful"? What does it mean for Congress to function *well*? What is the right kind and degree of presidential power? Broadly, in light of what picture of institutional and constitutional health do statements like these make sense?[7] The diagnostic method refines and develops the answers to these questions into a theory of systemic functionality that can be leveraged to diagnose the overall health of a political regime on the basis of individual cases.[8]

Before proceeding with my analysis, let me offer a brief sketch of the historical and political context in which the Eisenhower-McCarthy standoff took place. In the spring of 1953, Senator Joseph McCarthy (R-WI) initiated a public campaign against the United States Army and other government agencies, alleging that these agencies had been infiltrated by Communist agents and that senior military officials had undertaken a conspiracy to protect, and even assist, the alleged spies. His campaign culminated in the infamous Army-McCarthy hearings, whose broadcast over national television in 1954 gave many American households their first up-close picture of McCarthyism at work. As is well known, congressional Republicans had been leveling similar allegations against the New Deal federal bureaucracy since the 1940s.[9] Yet it was McCarthy who launched the second full-fledged "Red Scare" in a speech to the Ohio County Republican Women's Club in Wheeling, West Virginia, on February 9, 1950. At one point in that speech, McCarthy held up a piece of paper on which he claimed were the names of fifty-seven "individuals who would appear to be either card-carrying members or certainly loyal to the Communist Party, but who nevertheless are still helping to shape our foreign policy."[10] Leveraging the frantic public response, McCarthy initiated a series of congressional investigations into the federal agencies in question, investigations that would drag on for several years. McCarthy's most effective weapon during these investigations was the committee hearing, a venue that provided him with the opportunity to bully and humiliate the various witnesses who felt compelled to appear before the Senate. McCarthy's popularity and influence in the years following the Wheeling speech ebbed and flowed; despite the reservations that many of his Senate colleagues maintained, none of them were willing to mount organized opposition against him. During the early 1950s, McCarthy wielded the Senate's investigatory power with relative impunity.[11]

Roughly three years after the Wheeling speech, McCarthy initiated an investigation into the internal operations of the US Army. As had been the case in his previous investigations, one of McCarthy's aims was to use the Senate's oversight authority over federal agencies to compel their personnel to testify before the Senate, where McCarthy could bully and humiliate them. As part of his investigation, McCarthy publicly demanded that White House officials appear before his Senate committee, the Committee on Government Operations' Permanent Subcommittee on Investigations. The ball was then in the president's court, and initially, Eisenhower sought the advice of his aides: "In March, [Eisenhower] asked the Attorney General if the President could order federal personnel to not appear before McCarthy on the grounds that they were being abused. The reply was that there was no such precedent. On May 3 and 5, Eisenhower asked for further briefs on his power to withhold confidential information from Congress."[12]

Evidently, the brief that appeared most satisfactory to Eisenhower was a 1949 law review article authored by Assistant US Attorney Herman Wolkinson.[13] Going beyond the assertions of Franklin Roosevelt or Harry Truman, Wolkinson's article concluded that "presidents and heads of departments have an uncontrolled discretion to withhold the information and papers [that Congress requests] in the public interest," and that when past presidents had acquiesced to congressional demands, they had done so "only in a spirit of comity and good will, and not because there had been an effective means to compel them."[14] The bottom line of Wolkinson's argument was that Congress has no legitimate competing claim to agency information that Congress believes the public interest requires making public. Rather, in matters of administration, the president has ultimate constitutional authority to decide what is in the public's interest.

On May 17, President Eisenhower issued an order to the secretary of defense directing *all* agency personnel—not just high-ranking officials—not to provide relevant information in response to the subcommittee's subpoenas.[15] Earlier that day, the president had told other high-ranking Republican officials: "Any man who testifies [before a congressional committee] as to the advice he gave me won't be working for me that night. I will not allow people around me to be subpoenaed and you might as well just know it now."[16] Eisenhower's claim was unqualified and unconditional. The order begins by acknowledging that Congress has a constitutional right to information pertinent to congressional committees. Yet Eisenhower immediately qualifies this right: "It is essential to the successful working of our system that the persons entrusted with power in any one of the three great branches of Government shall not encroach upon the authority confided to the others." For Eisenhower's claim, the final line of the paragraph in question is decisive: "The ultimate authority for the conduct of the Executive Branch rests with the President." Eisenhower accompanied his order with a memorandum by Attorney General Herbert Brownell—a memorandum that borrows language directly from Herman Wolkinson's original article.[17] According to one scholar, Harry Truman's Justice Department had examined the Wolkinson argument, "found it unsupported by law and by court cases," and "discarded it as of no value."[18] Though it is certainly plausible that what motivated the Truman administration to dismiss the Wolkinson rationale was a sense of legal and constitutional integrity, the political circumstances under which Truman's administration refused to avail itself of that rationale differed considerably from those that inspired Eisenhower to adopt it. Truman, a Democrat, faced Republican majorities in both the House and the Senate and suffered consistently low approval ratings during his second term.[19] In sharp contrast, Eisenhower had consistently high approval ratings during his entire presidency and had Republican majorities in both chambers in 1954, the year he issued his order embracing Wolkinson.

Perhaps more important, Eisenhower seemed to sense that his adversary McCarthy was in a precarious—indeed, vulnerable—position vis-à-vis both the Senate and the public at large, and that the time was therefore ripe for an aggressive and novel assertion of presidential power. Four days before Eisenhower issued his order, an article in the *New York Times* had reported that McCarthy and his right-hand man, Roy Cohn, had attempted to coerce the Army into giving "special privileges" to their colleague G. David Schine. The article concluded that "[McCarthy] and his friends have now truly been hoist with their own petard. They are at last on the defensive."[20] Three days later, on March 16, the Senate turned the tables by initiating hearings for the "Special Senate Investigation on Charges and Countercharges," now scrutinizing *McCarthy* for reckless accusations he had previously made against the Army, as well as for unethical requests McCarthy and his staff had made of Schine.[21] Though some senators had expressed disapproval of McCarthy from the very outset of his campaign against the government, as this event suggests, a significant number now felt comfortable publicly organizing against him.[22]

If these were Eisenhower's suspicions in May 1954, he was correct. When Eisenhower issued his order on May 17, the Senate refused to rally around McCarthy and follow up on his demands for subpoenas. Indeed, on May 18, Senator Wallace F. Bennett, a Republican, used the Army-McCarthy hearings (which were then being televised) as an example of how the broadcasting of Senate business would incentivize the kind of pandering that McCarthy had been so successful at leveraging in the preceding years:

> Mr. President, the present public hearings of the McCarthy-Army dispute have again brought the Senate face to face with a problem we should begin to resolve, the problem created by television. . . . Commercially sponsored telecasting would have its effect on Senators. It would put a premium on demagogery [*sic*] and would reward brashness. This could only result eventually in a lowering of the respect of the people of America for the Senate and for our system of government.[23]

McCarthy's standing with the broader public proceeded to collapse, as well. Following Eisenhower's May 17 order, major national newspapers including the *Times* and *Washington Post* ran articles congratulating the president and lauding the merits of his decision.[24] In January 1954, McCarthy had enjoyed an approval rating of 50 percent, with only 29 percent disapproving. By June of that year, his approval rating had fallen to 34 percent, with 45 percent of the public now disapproving of his conduct.

Eisenhower's Response to McCarthy

What is the best way to interpret how the conflict between Eisenhower and McCarthy played out? Formally speaking, when McCarthy began urging the Senate to issue subpoenas to agency personnel, he was invoking an institutional power that the Congress had in the past defended and been willing to enforce. I have argued elsewhere that because so-called executive branch agencies are in fact the creations of the *legislature*—established, funded, and supervised by Congress—Congress has, as a practical and constitutional matter, ultimate say over the conduct of personnel within those agencies, including whether they should keep their jobs. Presidential authority over agencies is a delegation of power, not, as is typically assumed today, a constitutional right.[25] Accordingly, previous Congresses had been willing to arrest noncompliant officials in Congress's own jail in the Capitol Building and in other locations other than the Capitol. Congresses exercising this authority had invoked what legal experts sometimes call the "inherent contempt power," a power that, rather than authorizing Congress to instruct the Department of Justice to apprehend noncompliant individuals—an order that might well be disregarded by that department, given the attorney general's proximity to the president[26]—instead "permits Congress to rely on its own constitutional authority to detain and imprison a contemnor until the individual complies with congressional demands."[27] In 1857, Congress itself codified this authority and made it a criminal offence to hold Congress in contempt. And for their parts, Congresses were not shy about enforcing this power. For example, as late as 1934, US Assistant Secretary of Commerce William P. MacCracken was apprehended and detained by the Senate sergeant at arms after ignoring a congressional subpoena in a case involving air mail fraud.[28]

Because Congress had historically demonstrated the wherewithal both to exercise the inherent contempt power and to defend its use intelligently, presidents before Eisenhower had usually respected Congress's authority to subpoena agency personnel. An exception to this norm concerned the president's cabinet and closest advisors, the privacy of whose communications with the president Congress typically respected as a consequence of accommodations arranged between, and interbranch norms established by, past presidents and Congresses: "Presidents since Jackson had claimed their own conversations and communications with their aides and with cabinet members as privileged, nor had Congress seriously disputed this."[29] Given the credible threat of inherent contempt, investigations, and even impeachment, presidents had felt sufficient political pressure to come to the negotiating table with Congress in order to reach a settlement that satisfied the concerns and priorities of both branches.

Crucial to note here is that this norm—presidents shielding high-level offices from Congress while sharing access to lower-level personnel—was worked out through a decidedly *political* process of interbranch conflict and negotiation between the president and Congress. It was not a pronouncement by a federal court.[30] For example, in response to congressional subpoenas or requests for documents relevant to a committee's investigations, the president might open with a flat denial to any access whatsoever. In turn, members of Congress might speak publicly about their concerns, alerting constituents and the broader electorate of the president's recalcitrance. With the threat of a credible majority, Congress could also threaten to withhold funding from the relevant agency or agencies, thereby applying further pressure to the president. As these negotiations play out before influential elites and the broader public, members of each branch are forced not only to weigh the priorities of their own institution, but also to consider the electoral and broader political consequences of its actions for themselves and their fellow partisans. Can the president make a persuasive case to the public that agency documents and officials should be shielded from public scrutiny? Can members of Congress convince their fellow legislators that a showdown with the president is worth prioritizing over legislative priorities? How these questions are answered by the parties to these negotiations should approximate both public support for and institutional prerogatives expressed in the negotiated settlement that is eventually reached.

This norm persisted into the twentieth century. For example, in 1950, then-President Harry Truman had initially argued that the president could forbid administration officials from divulging information relating to their official duties. But in the face of public pressure, he also conceded that Congress had the authority to investigate matters related to criminal investigations within the administration. Accordingly, after negotiations with Congress, Truman authorized the release of the information in question. In turn, this information resulted in the successful prosecutions for corruption of a White House aide and an assistant attorney general in Truman's administration.[31] Louis Fisher outlines a similarly illustrative example from the Reagan presidency. In 1981, Reagan's Interior secretary, James Watt,

> withheld documents from a House subcommittee, provoking a committee subpoena for the documents and a recommendation by the Committee on Energy and Commerce that [Watt] be cited for contempt. Several weeks later Watt made the documents available to the subcommittee. The documents were to be delivered to a secure room on Capitol Hill and reviewed only by subcommittee members. The technical assistance of subcommittee staff would not be available. Moreover, the members could not photocopy the documents but could take notes.[32]

The particular details of the agreements reached between the House Committee and the Reagan administration reflect the two institutions' legitimate, albeit incomplete, claims to authority. Of course, Reagan would rather not have permitted any congressional access, and the House would have preferred unfettered access—and neither branch got its way entirely. Under threat of contempt, Watt was forced to share his documents, but the administration was spared the embarrassment of exhibiting its dirty laundry before the public by securing agreement from the legislators that only handwritten notes, not photos or photocopies, would emerge from the secure room. Congress gained access to the documents it deemed publicly important, but was prevented from using copies of those documents for purely performative or partisan purposes.

Constitutional conflicts like these show the constitutional system to be operating in a healthy manner. Generally, disagreements between Congress and the president should be resolved not through legal adjudication in the courts but through political negotiations between the branches themselves, because the kinds of constitutional questions that are pertinent to the authority of the president and Congress are not subject to legal adjudication.[33] Being among other things insulated from public pressure—and therefore both poorly equipped and disincentivized to gather information relevant to the public good—courts are best equipped to adjudicate specific, relatively narrow disputes between private individuals over the meaning of the law and the meaning and scope of individual rights. Put positively, the courts are structured to better handle these types of disputes on account of their mode of appointment and the design of their institution. We would not want courts subject to overt political pressures, like elections and aggressive acclamations, while deciding delicate matters regarding criminal cases and individual rights. By the same token, unlike Congress and the president, courts are not well positioned to resolve disputes over essentially political problems such as oversight, public opinion, consent, administrative discretion, and national security. Broadly, these problems are within the ambit of Congress and the presidency by virtue of the manner in which these offices are constitutionally structured. Both are elected—albeit through different schemes—which gives them greater representative legitimacy than the courts; the voting public routinely consent about their fitness for office. Further, elections incentivize these officials to absorb public concerns and to approximate—though not necessarily duplicate—those concerns in their official decisions.[34] For their parts, judges have no such incentive and therefore no such corresponding legitimacy. Their constitutional authority is derived largely from the narrow range of questions they are authorized to answer.

More narrowly, Congress and the president each possess institutional attributes that enhance their claims to authority and legitimacy in different areas of politics. Focusing on the constitutional dispute in our present case, the Eisenhower-McCarthy standoff, the president can offer a variety of strong rationales for secrecy. Because its institutional design make it nearly impossible for Congress to keep a secret, matters of national security are in safer hands within a hierarchical structure of presidential control. Relatedly, in order to obtain candid advice from advisors, presidents must be able to guarantee the confidentiality of White House conversations, lest advisors be retroactively punished for frank advice given in private conversations with the president and their staff. However, as noted above, these justifications do not render the president simply immune from congressional oversight. Indeed, Congress has countervailing claims to authority, including the basic (but frequently overlooked) fact that besides the president and the vice president, the "executive branch" is the creation of Congress itself and depends on Congress for its very existence. Because Congress funds—and therefore implicitly supports the mission and activities of—these agencies, it has a strong claim to need to oversee and evaluate their activities, in order to judge whether they deserve reauthorization, require statutory modification, or something else.[35] Finally, like the president, members of Congress are elected officials who have responsibilities to their constituents (with whom they have a closer relationship than does the president with his or her national constituency) and to the public at large. Congress is therefore entitled to judge for itself how the president's decisions to withhold executive branch information will affect the public good. Perhaps, in Congress's estimation, the public really does need to know what was said or done behind closed executive-branch doors, because the public needs to be able to make an informed decision about the president's conduct in the next election, or perhaps during the next impeachment hearing. In the abstract, such a concern cannot rationally be dismissed out of hand on the grounds that the "unitary executive" requires unconditional presidential immunity from congressional investigation. There are competing legitimate political claims at work in such controversies, and these claims cannot be legitimately resolved in the abstract or by an institution other than those institutions that are directly involved.

In contrast with the view I have outlined here, contemporary observers usually assume that separation of powers disputes should be adjudicated legalistically through the courts, and that it is political conflict between the president and Congress that is in fact symptomatic of constitutional dysfunction; Mariah Zeisberg calls this understanding "the settlement thesis."[36] Observers who espouse this understanding misdiagnose constitutional conflict because they misunderstand the logic of the Constitution's separation of powers system: a logic that is both political rather than legalistic, and conflict-oriented rather than settlement-oriented.[37] Indeed, as authors dating back to Publius in *The Federalist* have argued, the Constitution creates multiple branches of government whose differing designs (e.g., length of term, mode of appointment, number of officials) are meant to embody the multiple and competing normative commitments of popular government: consent, individual rights, and effective governance.[38] Because no one of these commitments is paramount, no one of the branches is simply authoritative in disputes about constitutional authority. Rather, each branch is purposefully equipped with an arsenal of powers that can be deployed to resist the encroachments of the other branches and to defend that branch's understanding of its own constitutional authority. Accordingly, during negotiations over a particular constitutional question—in our case, whether Eisenhower should have allowed agency officials to testify before McCarthy's committee—the lengths each branch is willing to go to "win" becomes an approximation for how that conflict should best be resolved democratically.

The Congressional Response

From a diagnostic perspective, Eisenhower's assertion about the president's ultimate authority over the federal bureaucracy is therefore misleading. It has also likely aided in the construction of the idea of a "unitary executive," frequently decried by scholars and observers. To further illustrate this point, let me sketch an alternative rationale that would seem to have been available to the president but which he chose not to articulate.

One point Eisenhower alluded to in his executive order was the (very legitimate) argument that presidents need to be able to solicit candid advice from their advisors, and that establishing a precedent whereby Congress could demand and obtain reports of White House conversations would impede the ability of presidents and administration officials to obtain useful counsel from their advisors: "It is essential to efficient and effective administration that employees of the Executive Branch be in a position to be completely candid in advising with each other on official matters."[39] What this claim ignores is Congress's *competing* claim to access to agency information. The federal bureaucracy, consisting of statutorily created departments, is a creation of the legislature and therefore depends on Congress for its material subsistence. Further, Congress has the constitutional authority to impeach and remove the head of the so-called executive branch. These powers imply the authority on Congress's part to access and evaluate the overall conduct of the bureaucracy in order to decide whether officials—and ultimately, the president—are living up to their legal and constitutional responsibilities. To be sure, the presidency requires secrecy and confidentiality to perform its constitutional function.[40] But as elements of democratic legitimacy, secrecy and confidentiality exist in tension with the public's right to know and evaluate the conduct of the state, a right that can be derived from the fact that duly elected Congresses voted to create the very executive departments responsible for maintaining state secrets in the first place. Further, this right is embodied in the norms and institutions that constitute Congress's oversight authority vis-à-vis federal agencies.

What alternatives were available to Eisenhower at the time? For starters, he might have achieved the same substantive outcome in this particular case—his conflict with McCarthy—by describing the sheer frivolousness of McCarthy's charges as grounds for his refusal. Rather than asserting a novel, rigid doctrine, Eisenhower could have highlighted all the ways in which McCarthy had failed to substantiate the multitude of charges he had leveled against his victims in the government, starting with his alleged list of "57 names" which he had brandished four years before at Wheeling (the list had never existed).[41] Instead, Eisenhower dogmatically asserted that presidents can shield all agency personnel—no matter how low ranking—from congressional oversight, and there is nothing Congress can do about it.[42]

One might reasonably argue at this point that, given the unique threat posed by McCarthy's destructive demagoguery, Eisenhower's decision not to enter into the particulars of the dispute—for example, whether McCarthy's charges were true—made it more likely the president would defeat the threat than further amplify it. Indeed, this is the interpretation that Eisenhower's defenders seem to prefer, namely that by refusing to engage McCarthy the president effectively starved his cause of political oxygen. This view is plausible. Insofar as McCarthy posed a grave, even unusual threat to the constitutional order, exceptional responses by constitutional officials (including the president) may have been warranted. While deeply concerned with forms and procedures, the Constitution ultimately views these as "instrumental norms" established for the sake of pursuing public goods.[43] McCarthy's defeat therefore must ultimately be seen as a constitutional victory, even if the means employed to secure his defeat are constitutionally questionable, even problematic.

Nevertheless, the question remains whether a more constitutionally healthy alternative was available to the officials involved, and if so, why it was not chosen. Put simply, did defeating McCarthy require asserting (and then accepting) such a problematic constitutional understanding? As Schlesinger observes, "The Eisenhower directive ushered in the greatest orgy of executive denial in American history. From June 1955 to June 1960 there were at least 44 instances when officials in the executive branch refused information to Congress on the basis of the Eisenhower directive—more cases in those years than in the first century of American history."[44]

And yet, however problematic Eisenhower's rationale defending his refusal to cooperate with the Senate may have been, from a diagnostic standpoint it was the Senate's *response* to Eisenhower—or lack thereof—that is most concerning. Why so?

Constitutionally, it is to be expected that each branch will rationalize its conduct in terms that prejudice its own institutional legitimacy and authority over the legitimacy and authority of the other branches. In this particular case, Eisenhower's interests were clearly connected to the constitutional authority of the presidency. For this reason, the fact alone that Eisenhower advanced a blanket and unnuanced privilege claim is not necessarily itself the problem. In the first iterations of an interbranch dispute, we would *expect* each branch's assertions to be overstated—in the same way that parties in a negotiation can be expected to be more ambitious in the early stages of bargaining; after all, it is unreasonable to negotiate against oneself. Yet as the need to reach a settlement and actually resolve the dispute in question makes itself increasingly felt by the branches involved and by pressure from the broader public, we would expect to see institutional actors refine their positions in response to each other's counterarguments.[45] Initially, the president would flatly deny Congress access to the information it wanted and use a rationale similar to Eisenhower's in the present case to do so. In response, Congress would demand unconditional access to the papers. As public pressure mounted on both parties to resolve the crisis, and the branches started to turn the screws on each other, Congress and the president would negotiate an agreement that approximated the legitimate constitutional claims that both branches brought to bear.

In contrast with analogous cases, in the Eisenhower-McCarthy standoff, Congress simply did not respond to the president's novel assertion of authority; it thereby tacitly legitimated his assertion. It is somewhat remarkable that this significant event garnered less public attention; most newspapers at the time unambiguously praised the president's assertion. Nevertheless, "an exception to the general enthusiasm was Telford Taylor," a lawyer who helped the prosecution at the Nuremberg Trials, "who wrote in 1955 that, if Eisenhower's directive were applied generally and literally, Congress 'would frequently be shut off from access to documents to which they are clearly entitled by tradition, common sense, and good governmental practice.'"[46] Taylor's prediction was exactly correct, and his point about tradition and history also bears emphasizing. As discussed above, whereas the Senate in 1954 appears to have simply accepted Eisenhower's order, previous Congresses had been far less willing to acquiesce to presidential assertions of this kind. In accordance with the arguments elaborated by previous Congresses, the Senate in 1954 might well have concluded that Eisenhower was right to withhold information from McCarthy on account of the spurious nature of McCarthy's accusations, while still denying Eisenhower's broader claim that the president has an unconditional right to withhold information from Congress at all levels of the federal bureaucracy.

There are several ways of thinking about the way the Eisenhower-McCarthy standoff played out. One possibility is a tragic reading.[47] By 1954, the Senate was so fatigued by McCarthy and McCarthyism that it simply did not have the wherewithal to qualify Eisenhower's assertion; they were simply glad to be done with McCarthy. Another possible interpretation has a happy ending—Eisenhower thwarted McCarthy—and diminishes or simply ignores the rise of "executive privilege" after 1954. On this note, consider Stephen Ambrose, Ike's most famous biographer: "It was not the things Eisenhower did behind the scenes but rather his most public act, the assertion of the right of executive privilege, that was his contribution to McCarthy's downfall."[48]

What both of these narratives fail to account for are the consequences of the Senate's failure to reassert itself, either in the midst of the present case or in the years afterward. Viewed in this light, the resolution to the Eisenhower-McCarthy standoff appears to be symptomatic of institutional amnesia on the part of the Senate, not a cause of the imperial presidency.[49] Perhaps as a consequence of collective fatigue inspired by years of McCarthyism, but perhaps also because they had forgotten the importance of defending their own institutional authority, the Senate—unlike Telford Taylor—seems not to have appreciated what was at stake in the resolution of this particular conflict. Following the implications of this position, we might further suggest that the Eisenhower-McCarthy conflict was a cause of the rise of "executive privilege" and "the unitary executive." By this, I do not simply mean that the president took advantage of circumstances favorable to him—McCarthy's waning popularity, his own standing with the public, and senatorial exhaustion—in order to perpetrate executive overreach. Rather, the Senate established for itself a precedent of congressional abdication that took root because of congressional amnesia that had already begun to set in before the standoff.

The plausibility of this suggestion is bolstered by the fact that the Senate's acquiescence to Eisenhower appears to have been the result not of a deliberate choice but of a failure to actually grasp what was happening. Unlike the Senate of 1834, which deliberated for ten weeks over a resolution to censure President Andrew Jackson, the Senate of 1954 allowed Eisenhower's assertion to stand without significant contestation. The differences between these two cases are remarkable and, in accordance with what other scholars have already pointed out, would seem to signify a problematic pattern in congressional conduct.[50] As Jeffrey Tulis observes in reference to the related phenomenon of Supreme Court nominations, "deference elicited under a regime of political conflict will likely be more responsible than modern abdications born of political amnesia."[51] A Senate that consciously chooses to defer to a president for prudential reasons, knowing all the while that conflict is a legitimate option, is likely to be more constitutionally responsible than a Senate that defers to the president unwittingly or out of habit, having collectively forgotten that challenging the president is even a possibility. The Senate's conduct in the conflict between Eisenhower and McCarthy should be viewed in this light.

Separation of Powers in Theoretical and Developmental Perspectives

As I have tried to suggest, the Senate's passive response to Eisenhower can be diagnosed as possibly a symptom of deeper constitutional illness, but just as every illness is not necessarily debilitating, the Senate's conduct here is not necessarily evidence of inevitable constitutional decline or failure. The diagnostic approach holds out that while undesirable norms and traditions can certainly take hold and create the pressure for certain kinds of outcomes, political actors can also act self-consciously by becoming aware of the full range of constitutional options that are available to them and take action to remedy harmful norms. In the space that remains, I will try to spell out the implications of the Eisenhower-McCarthy standoff for the two concentrations that are likely to regard that event as most relevant to their own inquiries: constitutional theory and American political development. My goal will be to show why these disciplines frequently talk past each other, overestimating and underestimating (respectively) the degree of agency that is available to political actors involved in separation of powers disputes such as the Eisenhower-McCarthy standoff.

As I suggested at the outset of this chapter, scholars with a more legal or theoretical bent will be inclined to judge Eisenhower's response to McCarthy and the Senate in accordance with their understandings of separation of powers theory, arguing whether or not they think Eisenhower's response was constitutional. In response, scholars more concerned with political development will emphasize the institutional incentives and conditions—themselves the historical constructions of changing political authority—that precipitated the conflict and led to its particular resolution. Seen from a more developmental perspective, legal and normative judgments about constitutional authority can appear misplaced or even naïve because they largely abstract from the contextual dynamics that incentivize political actors to make the choices that they do. Seen in this perspective, Eisenhower's assertion of executive privilege did not occur in a vacuum; as I have noted, previous presidents had made similar (though less emphatic) assertions that had been routinized into a constitutional norm. Additionally, ideas about a unitary executive were clearly floating around in the legal-constitutional ecosystem as of the mid-1950s, as witnessed by Herman Wolkinson's 1949 law review article that was so eagerly appropriated and deployed by Eisenhower's attorney general to shore up the president's assertion of unilateral authority. Eisenhower's particular move could therefore be interpreted as an elaboration of both institutional and ideational developments that were already well underway in 1954.

The other side of this coin is that political development as such offers little guidance for actually assessing the quality of political conduct and change, as opposed to understanding the historical and institutional circumstances that lead to these. One might even ask whether separation of powers has any normative meaning in a developmental perspective whatsoever. For example, from the strictly methodological standpoint of APD, could we make a meaningful distinction between a president operating under the fully expanded norms of the so-called "unitary executive," on the one hand, and a president who has obliterated the separation of powers system entirely, on the other? Perhaps, though for reasons I will substantiate below, if the explicit mission of APD is, to quote two of its founding scholars, tracking and explaining political development defined as "durable shifts in governing authority,"[52] it is hard to conceive of a serious evaluative component to APD analysis that would not be either a mere afterthought, or worse, an unsubstantiated normative assumption smuggled in under the guise of empirical rigor.

To think through these potential disagreements, consider some of the methodological assumptions on which they are based. As Paul Pierson and others have argued, many of the enduring features of American politics—whose legitimacy (or at least, permanence) both elites and the broader public take for granted—are actually the consequences of historically conditioned choices and decisions made by coalitions and the elites who lead them.[53] For this reason, scholars of this background would emphasize that the particular way in which Americans today perceive and experience important features of the Constitution is not primarily a consequence of the Constitution itself (e.g., its text or underlying principles). Rather, it is a result of the ways in which particular political actors and whole coalitions, responding to the historically conditioned institutional incentive structures through which they engage their political universe, deploy constitutional features and provisions to advance their own interests and goals.[54] Take an obvious though underappreciated example from American jurisprudence. Many Americans of the late nineteenth and early twentieth centuries experienced "separate but equal" as a constitutional given, even though that interpretation of the due process clause was the outcome of a particular set of legal and political negotiations that culminated in *Plessy v. Ferguson*. As the dramatic reversal of *Plessy* in *Brown v. Board of Education* nearly sixty years later suggests, the due process clause did not *have* to create and legitimate the Jim Crow regime; there was nothing in the Constitution itself that necessitated that particular outcome. Rather, the understanding of the Constitution that authorized state-enforced segregation was itself the consequence of elite decision-making that could have played out very differently had a different path been taken. Nevertheless, several generations of Americans came to regard "separate but equal" not as one of many alternative constitutional constructions of the Fourteenth Amendment, but as the Fourteenth Amendment itself. More important still, from the standpoint of political development there is nothing more "constitutional" about *Brown* than *Plessy*: Irrespective of their moral content, both decisions were equally representative of the respective partisan regimes that produced them.

To take an even more obvious example, the Fourteenth Amendment contains an entire provision—the "privileges or immunities" clause—that has gone essentially ignored by both courts and elected officials since the passage of the Fourteenth Amendment in 1868. Yet scholars of APD might contend that this fact is a consequence not of the nature of the provision itself—there is nothing about the concept of "privileges or immunities" that renders the clause in question more or less enforceable[55]—but rather of the decision of the court in *The Slaughter-House Cases*, 83 U.S. 36 (1873), a decision that was conditioned by the constellation of electoral and coalitional factors that constituted early Gilded Age politics. Once the path away from privileges or immunities (or, in the case of *Plessy*, toward state-sanctioned segregation) had been taken, it became extremely difficult—if not impossible—to course correct.

It is not hard to imagine the institutional and ideational factors that led to the entrenchment and path dependency of such decisions, and recent APD scholarship has done a fine job elucidating this subject. During the crucial period immediately following the end of the Civil War, when the defeated South was at its most vulnerable and Republicans held overwhelming majorities in Congress, Andrew Johnson significantly and irreversibly disrupted the Reconstruction process in favor of his preferred program of "Restoration." In contrast with Reconstruction, Restoration shored up white supremacist hierarchies that might have otherwise been eliminated through federal social programs like the Freedman's Bureau.[56] As a consequence, ascriptive institutions were in a position of strength rather than weakness when decisive Fourteenth Amendment Supreme Court decisions, particularly the *Civil Rights Cases* and *Plessy*, were handed down; and their strength contributed to the robust enforcement of the Jim Crow regime, which those cases inaugurated. What is more, temporary gains in Black suffrage and political representation were undone during the 1870s as a consequence of, among other developments, the withdrawal of federal troops following the 1876 presidential election. For this reason, the Black population had no recourse to electoral politics to undo the material results of the segregation cases. Taken together with the perpetuation of Black-White wealth inequality in the late nineteenth century, as well as entrenched racial attitudes on the part of southern and northern Whites, it is unsurprising that the court's segregation cases were eagerly enforced and even bolstered by the existing American state apparatus at all levels.[57]

As some scholars have suggested, APD offers a decidedly nonteleological interpretation of the Constitution and American politics.[58] Indeed, one of Orren and Skowronek's chief criticisms of previous iterations of American politics research is that it has always assumed that political change in the United States happens in a progressive manner, as if political development worked on its own to realize a more perfect version of the American regime.[59] Relatedly, scholars who emphasize path dependency tend also to diminish the importance of the Constitution as a fixed standard for actually evaluating political decisions and outcomes. At the risk of stating the point simplistically, we might say that because APD views the Constitution as a creation of politics (and not the other way around), the Constitution ceases to offer any truly meaningful and enduring normative guidance for the public and for elites. In the words of Stephen Skowronek, "American state formation has followed the serial upending of legal and social relations protected by the Constitution's original arrangements, and those arrangements have, in turn, been progressively distended and stressed by their accommodation of legal and social questions originally excluded."[60] If, from perspectives akin to this one, the Constitution was framed to answer legal and social questions entirely different from the kinds of questions we encounter today, how can we expect the Constitution to provide us with normative guidance about matters the Constitution evidently never contemplated—for example, how to resolve a separation of powers dispute during the Cold War and the nuclear age?

The Constitution also ceases to be the cause of political development, becoming instead the negotiated settlement of whatever political developments happen to be taking place in a particular moment in history. To be sure, scholars of APD recognize—indeed, emphasize—the extent to which political outcomes are shaped and conditioned by institutional and constitutional design.[61] But they also leave unsaid and underdeveloped the idea of what it would mean to say, in an analytically robust manner, whether a given political development (such as the rise of "executive privilege") is constitutionally *healthy*. Indeed, for scholars of this view, what it means for the Constitution to operate in a healthy manner tends to be unclear. For example, the authors of a recent study of the development of the unitary executive theory suggest that the American constitutional system is functioning poorly on account of debilitating tensions between the federal bureaucracy, which adds "thickness" to the state apparatus, thereby complicating questions of governmental accountability, and the presidency, an institution premised on ideas like autonomy, accountability, and decisiveness.[62] Clearly the authors see the Trump presidency as an illustration of some kind of political dysfunction or decay. But since in this lens it remains unstated and therefore unclear what a picture of presidential functionality looks like, it remains an open question what it is about the republic's current condition that makes it "beleaguered" and not simply operating in a novel manner.[63]

Scholars of constitutional theory and legal thought tend to see things the other way around. Whereas APD views constitutional provisions as politically constructed, scholars of a more norms-oriented (as opposed to development-oriented) bent maintain that the Constitution should be understood as a guide and standard for evaluating politics, not merely as a *creation* of politics—even if, as common sense no doubt testifies, political practice frequently fails to live up to what the Constitution requires. And whereas those who emphasize path dependency would point to norms and institutions like "separate but equal" as evidence that the Constitution becomes whatever the hegemonic coalition of the day wants it to be, constitutional theorists might argue that there are better and worse understandings of what the Constitution means and requires; and further, that even though doctrines like "separate but equal" do have considerable staying power, defective doctrines and norms like this should be understood as departures from the Constitution itself.[64] Hence,

Tulis and Mellow argue that the body of thought and practice that came to authorize developments like Jim Crow, and Barry Goldwater's later rejection of the New Deal, are best understood as an ascriptive "anti-constitutional" tradition in American political history.[65]

These alternative theories offer very different interpretations of the development of separation of powers as an aspect of American constitutional politics. For example, Skowronek concentrates on the coalitional dynamics that have led to presidential aggrandizement at the expense of congressional authority and remains largely agnostic on the question of whether that development is constitutionally legitimate or healthy. In contrast, Zeisberg asks us to assume a more critical posture toward contemporary separation of powers conflicts, urging us to actually evaluate the legitimacy of the different branches' competing claims of responsibility and authority, irrespective of the historical moments in which those claims were articulated and political developments that may have incentivized or disincentivized them.[66] For Zeisberg and scholars with similar interests, the most urgent task is not identifying the developments that have led to altered relations between Congress and the president, but instead understanding whether those relations reveal the broader constitutional system to be functioning in a healthy or unhealthy manner. And answering that kind of question requires generating a picture of what it means for the Constitution to succeed.[67]

Conclusion

A diagnostic approach to separation of powers appreciates the challenges that norms and traditions, which are the consequences of long-term political developments, pose for political actors embedded within a specific historical context. At the same time, its overarching goal is not to lose sight of the kinds of evaluative standards that enable scholars like Zeisberg to analyze cases drawn from different periods of political history. Accordingly, a diagnostic perspective might avoid the tendency of legally and theoretically oriented scholars to pronounce certain political decisions and developments as simply "unconstitutional" while abstracting from the complexities of the case in question and the historical circumstances in which it took place. By the same token, it proposes to make explicit the evaluative notions that even scholars who purport to eschew evaluation have in mind when they speak of institutional and constitutional functionality.

For these reasons, as the conflict between Eisenhower and McCarthy demonstrates, political diagnostics necessarily yield complex and multifaceted conclusions because their mode of analysis is holistic and not oriented toward a particular variable. I do not purport to offer an exact causal analysis of that conflict, nor do I make a hard judgment about whether it was resolved in a strictly "constitutional" or "unconstitutional" manner. On one level, Eisenhower's conduct was constitutionally impressive in that it led to the defeat of a constitutional pariah, Joseph McCarthy. Yet a presidential success does not necessarily amount to a constitutional victory.[68] The president helped to defeat a destructive demagogue but he also helped to perpetuate a destructive constitutional norm; the victory over McCarthy was therefore by no means unalloyed. Finally, the Senate's failure to qualify Eisenhower's novel assertion of executive privilege was not "unconstitutional" in some narrowly legal sense. But it did allow a highly questionable doctrine and practice to become authoritative. It is the task of political scientists and citizens alike to understand what a development like this one means for the American political system.

Notes

1. In this chapter, I avoid the term "executive branch" and use terms like "agencies" and "departments" instead. My reason for doing so is that the term "executive branch" does not occur in the Constitution. Further, the term implies that the president should have unilateral control over the bureaucracy, when in fact the bureaucracy is created, funded, and overseen by the Congress. See "Thank God for the Deep State: Presidential Demagoguery and the 'Unitary Executive,'" *American Political Thought* 12, 1 (Winter 2023): 113–140.

2. See *Youngstown Sheet & Tube Co. v. Sawyer*, 343 U.S. 579 (1952).

3. Contributions to this volume embodying this tradition include those by Jeffrey Tulis, Sotirios Barber, Connor Ewing, Thomas Bell, and Mariah Zeisberg. Perhaps the purest illustration of constitutional theory so understood is Sotirios Barber's *On What the Constitution Means* (Baltimore, MD: Johns Hopkins University Press, 1983). Scholars who study American political thought might also be grouped into this discipline. For a helpful delineation of APT and APD along these lines, see George Thomas, "Political Thought and Political Development," *American Political Thought* 3, 1 (2014): 114–125.

4. Karen Orren and Stephen Skowronek, *The Search for American Political Development* (New York: Cambridge University Press, 2004).

5. Surprisingly, the Eisenhower-McCarthy standoff has received relatively little attention in the separation of powers literature.

6. Theodore Lowi made this point helpfully long ago in "Party, Policy, and Constitution in America," in *The American Party Systems*, Chambers and Burnham, eds. (New York: Oxford University Press, 1967), 238.

7. For a helpful discussion of this question with reference to Congress specifically, compare Thomas Mann and Norman Ornstein in *It's Even Worse Than It Looks* (New York: Basic Books, 2012), with Anthony Ives in "Congressional Health, Congressional Failure" (PhD Diss., 2018).

8. I have sketched these principles elsewhere. See Charles U. Zug, "Contesting the Legal Constitution: Constitutional Agonism," *Political Research Quarterly* 78, 4 (2025): 1302–1317; "Rethinking the Basic Models of Presidential Leadership: Eisenhower, Greenstein, and Federal Highway Expansion," *Political Science Quarterly* 140, 1 (2025): 85–104; *Demagogues in American Politics* (New York: Oxford University Press, 2022), chapters 4–5. See also "Could Political Science Become Diagnostic? Restoring a Forgotten Method," *Perspectives on Political Science* 48, 1 (2019): 56–63.

9. E.g., Robert Griffin, *The Politics of Fear: Joseph R. McCarthy and the Senate (Amherst, MA: University of Massachusetts Press, 1987)*, chapter 3; Zug, *Demagogues*, 126–144.

10. Digital History Project, University of Houston: http://www.digitalhistory.uh.edu/disp_textbook.cfm?smtID=3&psid=3633.

11. Griffin, *Fear*, chapter 4.

12. Stephen E. Ambrose, *Eisenhower: The President* (Simon & Schuster, 1984), 186.

13. Arthur M. Schlesinger, Jr., *The Imperial Presidency* (Boston: Houghton Mifflin, 1973), 155–156.

14. Quoted in Schlesinger, *Imperial Presidency*, 155.

15. The original order can be accessed on the Eisenhower Library's website: https://www.eisenhowerlibrary.gov/sites/default/files/research/online-documents/mccarthyism/1954-05-17-dde-to-osd.pdf.

16. Quoted in Ambrose, *Eisenhower*, 187.

17. Schlesinger, *Imperial Presidency*, 157.

18. Id., 156.

19. https://news.gallup.com/poll/272765/lowest-gallup-presidential-job-approval-rating.aspx.

20. *New York Times*, March 13, 1954: https://timesmachine.nytimes.com/timesmachine/1954/03/13/84112523.pdf?pdf_redirect=true&ip=0.

21. See: https://www.senate.gov/about/powers-procedures/investigations/mccarthy-and-army-mccarthy-hearings.htm.

22. Consider, e.g., https://www.senate.gov/about/powers-procedures/investigations/mccarthy-hearings/a-declaration-of-conscience.htm.

23. Congressional Record, May 18, 1954: 6715–6716.

24. E.g., *New York Times*, May 18, 1954; *Washington Post*, May 20, 1954. Excerpts quoted in Schlesinger, *Imperial Presidency*, 158.

25. See Zug, "Thank God for the Deep State."

26. Consider how the Justice Department under the George W. Bush administration refused to enforce congressional subpoenas: https://www.justsecurity.org/78413/modern-history-of-disclosure-of-presidential-records-on-the-boundaries-of-executive-privilege/.

27. See Louis Fisher, *Constitutional Conflict Between Congress and the President*, 3rd ed. (Lawrence: University Press of Kansas, 1991), 156–159; Todd Garvey, "Congress's Contempt Power and the Enforcement of Congressional Subpoenas: Law, History, Practice, and Procedure," *Congressional Research Service*, 2017: 2.

28. Philip Bump, "Congress's Ability to Twist Arms Is Limited—Unless It Wants to Arrest Bannon Itself," *Washington Post*, January 18, 2018: https://www.washingtonpost.com/news

/politics/wp/2018/01/18/congress-ability-to-twist-arms-is-limited-unless-it-wants-to-arrest-bannon-itself/.

29. Schlesinger, *Imperial Presidency*, 156.

30. See, for example, Louis Fisher, *Constitutional Conflicts*, 175–178. See also Jack Goldsmith, "Assessing the Rule of Law and the Trump Presidency" (2020): "There's supposed to be an accommodation process by both sides [Congress and the president] . . . you start off with extreme positions and then gravitate and compromise towards some accommodation." Accessed 08-25-2022: https://www.youtube.com/watch?v=NlPs0SPrEmg&ab_channel=ConversationswithBillKristol. See 36:15.

31. Schlesinger, *Imperial Presidency*, 155.

32. Fisher, *Constitutional Conflict*, 176. See also 175–178.

33. For an illuminating discussion of why separation of powers conflicts are not legally justiciable, see Thomas R. Bell, *A Constitution of Conflict* (Lawrence: University Press of Kansas, 2025). A more facile argument on this head—albeit one that, interrogated further, leads to the same conclusion I reach in this paragraph—is that the Constitution simply does not give the Supreme Court or any other federal court constitutional authority over disputes between Congress and the presidency. Each branch takes an oath to support the Constitution, and as Madison shows in *Federalist* No. 51, each branch possesses a toolkit of constitutional powers that can be used to justify its own authority and resist the encroachments of the other branches. Turf wars between the executive and legislature are resolved, and constitutional norms are developed, as the branches threaten to use—and in extreme cases, actually use—their tools of resistance in order to strengthen their bargaining power vis-à-vis the other branch.

34. For a discussion of how the Constitution's elected officials are both advocates of their constituents and autonomous constitutional officers, see Zug, *Demagogues*, chapter 5.

35. Fisher correctly observes that "the Constitution does not explicitly grant Congress the power to investigate," 153. But the Constitution does not need to grant Congress this power explicitly because it *does* grant Congress the explicit power to raise the revenue needed to fund executive agencies, as well as the explicit power to pass all laws "necessary and proper" to bring Congress's substantive responsibilities into effect. Congress's investigative authority can therefore be understood in the sense that Congress authorizes the funding and operation of executive agencies on condition that it will continue to oversee and approve of the operations of those agencies. Accordingly, Congress needs to be able to investigate the operations of investigative agencies to give its consent to their reauthorization.

36. Mariah Zeisberg, *War Powers* (Princeton, NJ: Princeton University Press, 2013), 8.

37. For discussion of the conflict-oriented nature of separation of powers, see Herbert J. Storing, "The Presidency and the Constitution," in *Toward a More Perfect Union*, Joseph M. Bessette (Washington, DC: AEI Press, 1995).

38. E.g., *Federalist* No. 51. See also Jeffrey Tulis's and Thomas Bell's contributions to this volume, as well as Zeisberg, *War Powers*, and Jeffrey Tulis and Nicole Mellow, *Legacies of Losing in American Politics* (Chicago: University of Chicago Press, 2018), chapter 2.

39. Memorandum of May 17, 1954.

40. See *Federalist* No. 72.

41. Griffin, *Politics of Fear*, chapter 3. I call Eisenhower's asserted doctrine "rigid" because, by asserting unqualified immunity of the executive branch from congressional investigations, it allows for none of the flexibility that is necessary to resolve competing legitimate claims by those

branches in differing circumstances. An example of such flexibility would be allowing low-level executive officials to testify or provide information while exempting upper-level officials. Under Eisenhower's scheme, *all* would have been forbidden.

42. Given Eisenhower's leadership style, it should not be surprising that he chose to pursue such a dogmatic path forward. See Zug, "Rethinking the Basic Models of Presidential Leadership."

43. See Barber, *What the Constitution Means*.

44. Schlesinger, *Imperial Presidency*, 158.

45. For a full elaboration of this theory, see Jeffrey K. Tulis, "Deliberation Between Institutions," in *Debating Deliberative Democracy* (New York: Wiley, 2003). See also Charles U. Zug and Connor Ewing, "What Happened to the State of the Union Address? Originally, It Helped the President and Congress Deliberate," *Washington Post*, January 30, 2018.

46. Schlesinger, *Imperial Presidency*, 158.

47. See Gary J. Jacobsohn, "Dramatic Jurisprudence," in *Constitutional Tragedies, Constitutional Stupidities* (New York: New York University Press, 1998).

48. Ambrose, *Eisenhower: The President*, 189.

49. For a discussion of institutional amnesia, see Jeffrey K. Tulis, "Constitutional Abdication: The Senate, The President, and Appointments to the Supreme Court," *Case Western Law Review* 47(4): 1331–1357 (1997).

50. See, for example, Louis Fisher, *Congressional Abdication on War and Spending* (College Station, TX: Texas A&M University Press, 2000).

51. Tulis, "Constitutional Abdication," 1336.

52. Orren and Skowronek, *The Search*, 123.

53. Paul Pierson, "Increasing Returns, Path Dependence, and the Study of Politics," *American Political Science Review* 94, 2 (June 2000): 251–267.

54. A particularly clear and helpful example of this interpretation is Stephen Skowronek's analysis of the unitary executive theory as a political creation of the conservative legal movement of the 1970s and 1980s. Ken Kersch has developed this insight into a more general theory of the way in which constitutional understandings emerge as the creations of mass political movements. See, respectively, Stephen Skowronek, "The Conservative Insurgency and Presidential Power: A Developmental Perspective on the Unitary Executive," *Harvard Law Review* 122, 8 (October 2009): 2070–2103; Kenneth I. Kersch, *Conservatives and the Constitution* (New York: Cambridge University Press, 2019).

55. Indeed, the nonenforcement of this provision by Congress is rendered all the more puzzling by section 5 of the Fourteenth Amendment.

56. Tulis and Mellow, *Legacies of Losing*, chapter 3.

57. For a helpful account of institutional resistance would-be civil rights reformers met during the Jim Crow era, see, for example, Jeffrey A. Jenkins et al., "Between Reconstructions: Congressional Action on Civil Rights, 1891–1940," *Studies in American Political Development* 24 (April 2010): 57–89.

58. George Thomas, "What Is Political Development? A Constitutional Perspective," *Review of Politics* 73, 2 (Spring 2011): 275–294.

59. Orren and Skowronek, *The Search*, chapter 2.

60. Stephen Skowronek, "Present at the Creation," *Journal of the Early Republic* 38, 1 (Spring 2018): 101.

61. Orren and Skowronek, *The Search*, chapter 3.

62. Stephen Skowronek, John Dearborn, and Desmond King, *Phantoms of a Beleaguered Republic* (New York: Oxford University Press, 2020), chapter 2.

63. Skowronek et al., *Phantoms.*

64. A good example of normative constitutional analysis recently applied to the unitary executive and separation of powers is Jeffrey Crouch et al., *The Unitary Executive Theory: A Danger to Constitutional Government* (Lawrence: University Press of Kansas, 2020).

65. Tulis and Mellow, *Legacies of Losing*, chapters 3–4.

66. Zeisberg, *War Powers.*

67. For a helpful example of this kind of reasoning, see Sotirios Barber, *Constitutional Failure* (Lawrence: University Press of Kansas, 2014).

68. See Charles U. Zug, *Dwight D. Eisenhower and the Federal Highway Act* (Lawrence: University Press of Kansas, 2024).

CHAPTER 11

When is it Reasonable to Impeach a Judge?

Keith E. Whittington

Americans have periodically talked about impeaching judges, but they have rarely followed through. Perhaps the most notable example of politicians putting their money where their mouth is on this issue came with the Jeffersonian efforts to impeach a federal trial judge and a US Supreme Court justice at the opening of the nineteenth century. Neither impeachment effort went particularly well, and the Jeffersonian Congress moved on to other priorities. President Thomas Jefferson himself groused that "having found, from experience, that impeachment is an impracticable thing, a mere scare-crow, [judges] consider themselves secure for life; they skulk from responsibility to public opinion."[1]

If judicial impeachment had proven to be a scarecrow, that has not prevented activists and politicians from occasionally trotting it out. Most famously, the right-wing John Birch Society peppered the nation's highways with "Impeach Earl Warren" billboards in the aftermath of the Warren Court's (short-lived) rulings against the anticommunist national security state. The Warren Court was able to ride out that wave of hostility and eventually could lean on liberal allies in the White House and the Congress over the course of the 1960s.

More recently, Republican legislators in Pennsylvania rattled the impeachment saber as the state supreme court deliberated on whether to void the state's apportionment of legislative seats and to redraw the legislative boundaries in a way that could be expected to favor the electoral fortunes of the Democratic Party. From the perspective of the proponents of impeachment, the Democratic justices who made up the majority of the state supreme court had issued a judgment that "blatantly and clearly contradicts the plain language of the

Pennsylvania Constitution" and thereby "engaged in misbehavior in office."[2] Republican leaders in both the statehouse and the state judiciary quickly condemned the suggestion that the legislature should impeach state judges over disagreements about their rulings and the effort fizzled.[3]

Impeachment talk is in the air these days. While much of it revolves around the president, the state and federal judiciaries have found themselves in the crosshairs as well. Of course, much of this can simply be dismissed as overheated rhetoric. Perhaps some legislators get a bit of attention in a news cycle by issuing toothless impeachment threats. Perhaps some interest groups can raise some money by promising recipients of their direct mail that they will fight to remove disfavored judges at the earliest opportunity. But the odds of a politicized impeachment initiative gaining traction might seem fairly low.

The odds of pulling off a successful impeachment and removal of a sitting judge might be fairly low, but they should probably not be dismissed. With our currently deeply polarized parties, it has become surprisingly easy to cast political opponents as not merely mistaken but as enemies of the republic. Judges are unlikely to escape these more generalized efforts to delegitimate and marginalize the opposition. The fighting over judicial appointments has already escalated beyond anything that we have seen for decades. When opposite parties control the White House and the Senate, the prospect of confirming even lower court judges has dimmed significantly, and it seems likely that an ill-timed vacancy on the Supreme Court could sit unfilled for years as well as months.[4] Activists on both the left and the right have begun talking about court-packing as a reasonable response to the perfidy of the other side.[5] It is a small step from fantasizing about adopting extraordinary measures to add judges to the courts to fantasizing about adopting extraordinary measures to remove judges from the courts. I would not expect talk of impeaching judges to fade quickly.

But we have not spent a great deal of effort considering the specific circumstances under which it would be constitutionally appropriate to impeach a judge. The most contentious impeachment inquiries in recent decades have involved presidents. Impeaching a president raises grave concerns of its own, and as a result the considerations that come into play when contemplating a presidential impeachment have received more scrutiny. But there is reason to think that the possibility of impeaching a judge raises difficult and distinct questions that should likewise be considered carefully. If partisans are motivated to impeach judges, how should a conscientious constitutional actor assess such efforts?

We might begin by considering some general principles that should guide our use of the impeachment power and some considerations that distinguish the impeachments of judges from the impeachment of presidents.[6] We can then set aside some easy cases in which the implications of those principles are reasonably clear, before considering some harder cases where the applications of general principles are more difficult.

General Principles

The constitutional drafters appropriately declined to attempt to construct a finite list of impeachable offenses. Their short list of treason and bribery trailed off into the much more amorphous "other high Crimes and Misdemeanors." In this context as in others, the delegates in Philadelphia appreciated that a long-lived constitution would have to be flexible to be useful in the unknown future. No simple list of forbidden acts would be likely to capture the wide range of ways in which government power can be abused and government officials can demonstrate themselves to be unworthy of the public trust.

We should likewise be hesitant to narrow artificially the scope of the impeachment power by attempting to reduce it to a set of designated impeachable offenses. Our imagination is unlikely to be better than that of the founders, and we too are unlikely to anticipate the myriad ways in which government officials can misbehave. Even more confounding, our sense of proper and improper conduct in office has not stood still over time. Behavior that would have seemed outrageous at some points in American history is taken as routine at other points. Whether or not a given officeholder is conducting himself improperly is likely to be a heavily contextualized judgment.

Whether a given act is so dangerous as to justify prematurely removing an individual from office is likely to require deliberate political judgment. The founders at least thought that such an inescapably political judgment could only be entrusted to Congress. If such an unreviewable power were to be lodged anywhere, Congress was the natural choice. Just as the Senate provided a counterweight to the president in the process of appointing an officer of the federal government, so the collective, bicameral process of deliberation in Congress could meet the gravity of the responsibility involved in the process of removing an officer. The members of Congress could be expected to possess the maturity of political judgment needed to assess alleged misconduct in office and the appropriate remedies for any such misconduct. If their judgment failed, they were ultimately responsible to the people themselves for how they had exercised the power that had been entrusted to them.[7]

If we are more mistrustful of Congress than the founders themselves were, we might lean toward thinking that the impeachment power should be construed narrowly. If we think that Congress is likely to abuse such a momentous power, we might be inclined to think that it ought to be reserved for "a narrow category of egregious or large-scale abuses of authority" or "should be used only in an emergency."[8] The founders did not reckon with political parties, and partisanship certainly complicates how Congress conducts all of its business, including its use of the impeachment power. Impeachment could be used as a partisan weapon, as yet another example of "politics by other means," and that prospect might lead us to be particularly skeptical of a Congress that might be overly aggressive in seeking to impeach partisan foes and overly passive in refraining to impeach partisan allies.[9]

But there are counterbalancing concerns with shrinking the scope of the impeachment power. As the delegates to the Philadelphia Convention recognized, a constitutional system of fixed terms of office needed some failsafe that could address the problem of abusive officeholders who could not be safely left in control of the levers of government power until the natural expiration of the term. The impeachment power is part of that system of checks and balances that seeks to reduce the dangers necessarily associated with political power. Leaning too hard against the congressional impeachment power opens more space for abusive officeholders to continue to do damage. Though we might not want the impeachment power used too often, there might be greater risks in not using it enough.[10]

There are both structural and textual considerations that might distinguish impeachments of judges from impeachments of presidents. Structurally, a drag on the congressional power to impeach the chief executive is an appropriate caution about overturning an election result. No matter how frustrated the Congress might be with the behavior of a president, they must reckon with the fact that the individual occupying the White House was the people's choice to take up the duties of the presidency. Moreover, the people themselves will have the opportunity to hold the president accountable for his actions while in office. Congress should be cautious not to second-guess the choice of the people about how they would prefer the country to be led nor to thwart the ability of the electorate to render their own judgment on how the duties of the presidency have been conducted. Although a scoundrel in the White House can do a great deal of mischief, the limited term of the presidency circumscribes how much mischief can be done. Opponents of the president must carry a heavy argumentative burden if they seek to disrupt the normal rhythm of the electoral rotation of offices and prefer to appeal to Congress to vote the rascal out rather than appeal to the American citizenry to do it at the polls.

Congress does not face those particular concerns when it comes to impeaching judges. Even a Supreme Court justice who sits atop the third branch of government does not hold that position by the will of the voters but rather holds it by virtue of the ordinary appointment process of presidential nomination and Senate confirmation. Judges do not stand to account on any regular timetable. The people will never have an opportunity to assess the actions of a judge and record their approval or disapproval. The life tenure of the judge imposes no natural limit on judicial misbehavior. If Congress stays its hand, the judicial misbehavior might continue unabated and without resolution. Where democratic sensibilities temper the impeachment power when aimed at the president, they bolster the impeachment power when aimed at a judge. Jefferson had groused that a "judiciary independent of a king or executive alone, is a good thing; but independence of the will of the nation is a solecism, at least in a republican government."[11] Jefferson's appeal to the foundational values of republican accountability remains resonant.

The independence of the judiciary is always in tension with democratic values, but it is also true that we separately value judicial independence. Judicial independence serves an important function within the constitutional system. It provides an institutional foundation that helps preserve the rule of law and protects individuals from the vicissitudes of the popular will. One danger of easing the path to the impeachment of judges is that it might corrode judicial independence more broadly. As John Ferejohn and Larry Kramer put it, the American constitutional system is characterized by "independent judges" but a "dependent judiciary," fostering neutral adjudication of individual cases but tethering the development of constitutional law to democratic opinion.[12] Ready impeachment of judges might tilt that balance, creating not only a dependent judiciary that is shaped by a political appointments process but also dependent judges who must fear individual reprisal if politicians become dissatisfied with how they are resolving the cases that come before them. Embracing a set of constitutional norms that disfavor judicial impeachments does not isolate the law from political influence, but it might help insulate individual litigants from the politicized application of the law to their particular situations.

There is also a textual consideration that might distinguish presidential and judicial impeachments. The president sits, of course, for a four-year term. Federal judges, on the other hand, "hold their Offices during good Behavior."[13] This gives rise to the question of whether this condition of judicial tenure modifies the standard expectation of what might constitute impeachable offenses for other civil officers of the federal government. Both textual logic and historical practice suggest that it does not. The Constitution indicates only one standard for removing individuals from government offices by way of impeachment, a demonstration that the individual has committed high crimes and misdemeanors. A failure to meet the standard of constitutional good behavior, in this context, implies the presence of otherwise impeachable behavior. Historical practice under the Constitution has likewise adhered to the conviction that there is only one basis on which to impeach a civil officer, and that judges are not less protected from impeachment proceedings because their tenure depends on their good behavior. The House has impeached and the Senate has convicted judges on the basis of conduct that they characterized as constituting high crimes and misdemeanors, and not simply conduct that might be thought to fall short of good behavior. In the first federal impeachment, of Judge John Pickering, the House presented articles of impeachment to the Senate that charged Pickering with acting "contrary to his trust and duty, as judge of the said district court," "in violation of his solemn oath," and in a manner that rendered him "guilty of other high misdemeanors, disgraceful to his own character as a judge, and degrading to the honor and dignity of the United States." Given those charges, the House asked that the judge "be put to answer the said high crimes and misdemeanors." The Senate, in turn, summoned Pickering to its chambers to answer the charges of "high crimes and misdemeanors" contained in the articles of impeachment and ultimately found Pickering "guilty, as charged" in each article of impeachment.[14] Subsequent Senates have likewise convened for impeachment trials on charges of high crimes and misdemeanors and have not merely asked accused judges to show that they had met a standard of good behavior.

The fact that there is a single constitutional standard of high crimes and misdemeanors to justify impeachment and removal does not imply that the identity of impeachable offenses is entirely independent of the office. To avoid impeachment, individuals are expected to uphold the duties and dignity of the specific office that they hold. Conduct that might be appropriate to a president is not necessarily appropriate to a judge, and vice versa. What constitutes misconduct in an office is dependent on the nature of the office.

There are no heightened expectations for a judge who holds his tenure during good behavior, but like other civil officers the judge is expected to behave in a way that is consonant with his continuation in office and is subject to impeachment when his conduct becomes incompatible with the office. There is no finite list of impeachable offenses that could be applied to judges any more than there is one that could be applied to the president. What specific actions might render an individual no longer fit to hold office and that might motivate Congress to take immediate action to end that officer's tenure in power cannot be easily foreseen. The Constitution does not attempt to cabin the impeachment power by circumscribing it with a definite list of offenses. Much is necessarily left to the discretion and political judgment of the elected members of Congress.

When we consider what kind of behavior is fundamentally at odds with the expectations and duties of the specifically judicial office, we need to begin by thinking through the nature of that office. Most obviously, a judge is expected to be able to judge those who come before the bench fairly and without regard to their individual identity. A judge who accepts bribes or that has created financial conflicts of interest is failing at that most basic task of maintaining impartiality, and judges found to have such problems have been subject to impeachment inquiries. But judges might fail to maintain impartiality in other ways that would call into question their continued suitability for the bench. As Americans grappled for the first time with the rise of party divisions and partisanship, it was not immediately clear how judges should position themselves relative to these divisions. Justice Chase was impeached precisely because he was seen as inserting himself into partisan disputes and as a consequence had shown himself incapable of treating the parties in his court with the impartiality required by his office. His impeachment sent a signal to other federal judges that political partisanship and judicial service were incompatible.[15] It is possible to imagine other forms of behavior that would demonstrate a pattern of personal bias that would be inconsistent with judicial office. A judge who showed racial animus, for example, would call into question his ability to treat parties in court fairly.

The judicial duty is not just to treat parties in court in a fair and neutral manner. Judges are also expected to perform specifically judicial duties and interpret and apply the law. The Constitution vests the "judicial power" in the federal courts, and vests distinguishable executive and legislative powers in the other branches of government. The expectation that judges would exercise only a judicial power underlay all the framers' discussion of the courts, including Alexander Hamilton's famous defense of the creation of an independent federal judiciary that rested on the claim that the courts would be the "least dangerous" branch of government because judges did not possess the "capacity to annoy or injure." Judges could deploy "neither force nor will." They could not dispense honors, hold the sword, command the purse, or "prescribe the rules by which the duties and rights of every citizen are to be regulated." A judge had only the power of judgment, and thus need not be feared.[16]

If judges depart from their judicial duty to say what the law is and to render judgments in actual cases and controversies, and instead began to exercise powers that were not properly judicial, then impeachment might be an appropriate remedy to such judicial misconduct. A judge who attempted to declare war on another country, issue commands to the troops in the field, impose new taxes on the citizenry, or appropriate funds from the federal treasury would have traveled far beyond the scope of his power and would be encroaching on the exclusive prerogatives of other branches of government. A judge who attempted to exercise legislative or executive power would no longer be performing judicial duties and would be subject to reprisal just as surely as a judge who failed in the duty to treat the parties before him in a fair and impartial fashion.

The difficulty comes in determining when judges have crossed the line and ceased to be acting as judges. The long history of complaining about "activist" or "so-called" judges who act more like "superlegislatures" than like judges is a familiar one, and the thrust of the complaint is that such activist judges have ceased to perform faithfully the duties of their office and instead have usurped political powers that do not belong to them. In principle, impeachment might be one tool by which other political actors could push back and insist that judges stay in their own proper constitutional lane. In practice, this requires identifying a particular exercise of power that can be characterized as not properly judicial and effectively distinguished from other things that courts might do. Presumably this would require something more distinctive than simply issuing a controversial constitutional decision or interpreting the law in a manner with which politicians disagree. If the goal is to establish a new constitutional norm that directs judges not to engage in nonjudicial behavior, an impeaching legislature needs to be able to define the contours of the behavior that they want to prohibit. Hamilton assured us that judges cannot properly "prescribe the rules by which the duties and rights of every citizen are to be regulated" because prescribing such rules is a distinctly legislative task. We might be more skeptical that judges have respected that boundary between saying what the law is and making new law, but the impeachment power might be too crude a tool for trying to build a wall on that border between the judicial and legislative powers.[17]

The clearest rationale for impeaching a government official is that the official is posing an immediate danger to the republic that is so grave that it can only be resolved by removing the official from power. The textually specified impeachable offenses of bribery and treason highlight such a concern. A president engaged in treason could hardly be tolerated to continue exercising power, and the normal array of checks and balances might be insufficient to adequately neutralize the threat. A commander-in-chief in thrall to a foreign power would pose an imminent threat to the national interest and such routine checks as elections, judicial review, and oversight hearings are unlikely to provide adequate assurance that the national interest was being protected.

Fortunately, American history has provided few, if any, examples of civil officers of the federal government who have posed such a threat. No doubt government officials have engaged in actions that were controversial or that in hindsight were seen as extraordinarily damaging to the welfare of the country. But such is the realm of normal policy disagreements and error. Dangerous levels of corruption or malevolence have been rare. Less extreme forms of personal misconduct have been more common, and usually less extreme measures to remove the misbehaving individual have proven adequate. Unsurprisingly, federal impeachments have mostly focused on judges, who cannot be removed by other means and who have on occasion refused to resign even when their continuation in office has become untenable. For such impeachments, the removal from office of the misbehaving individual is the ultimate measure of success.

A second rationale for impeachment is less personal. The purpose of such an impeachment is to shore up norms of expected behavior. Such impeachments serve to educate and deter government officials more broadly and not merely to incapacitate a single official who is behaving inappropriately. The impeachment becomes a vehicle for holding up a set of actions for scrutiny and condemnation. It sends a message to other and future officeholders and to the American public broadly about governing values and defines expectations about the behavior of officeholders going forward. Such impeachments are as much prospective as retrospective. Successfully removing an individual officeholder in such cases is ultimately less pressing than successfully establishing a set of expectations about how other individuals should conduct themselves when in office.[18]

Easy Cases

There are two kinds of easy cases that should be cleared away. On one side, we have cases in which impeachment would be clearly warranted, at least in principle. On the other side, we have cases in which impeachment would be clearly inappropriate, at least from a constitutional perspective.

Most of our history of federal impeachments of judges has involved easy cases. That is not to say that the individual decision to impeach, to convict, and to remove the judge in question was necessarily easy, but the difficulties involved in most of our cases of judicial impeachment have been factual difficulties. Did the judge actually commit the offense in question? The allegations in such cases have been sufficient to indicate that an impeachment inquiry would be warranted, and the difficult issue for the House and ultimately the Senate is to weigh the available evidence. Most of our experience with judicial impeachments has not pushed very hard on the questions of what constitutes an impeachable offense and where are the boundaries of the congressional power to unseat a federal judge.

Near the core of what should be considered impeachable offenses are serious criminal offenses that suggest the corruption of the public trust. The two specific offenses mentioned by the US Constitution as impeachable—treason and bribery—point in that direction.[19] The Constitution's textual references to the possibility of separate criminal liability for the same offenses that might trigger impeachment and conviction in a Senate trial indicate that the founders contemplated that at least some substantial subset of impeachable offenses would also be recognizable crimes under the ordinary law.[20]

The corrupt use of a public office provides a particularly strong case for impeachment and removal. Such an officeholder perverts the public trust. Rather than using the public authority with which he has been entrusted to advance the public good, the corrupt official exploits his position for private gain. Evidence of past corrupt behavior necessarily raises the risk that such behavior will be repeated in the future, subverting the goals and values of public office. Such behavior is incompatible with continuing to exercise public authority, and impeachment is the constitutionally provided instrument for carving out the corruption from the body politic.

Even if a public official has not specifically exploited their office of public trust for private gain, corrupt private behavior can easily undermine the public trust that a public official requires to exercise authority. A judge who takes a bribe to throw a case has abused the public power that he wields and obstructed the pursuit of justice in ways that would make it difficult to trust such a judge to behave properly in future cases. But a judge who engages in private acts of fraud similarly raises doubts about his essential character and casts a shadow over his every exercise of public authority. If a judge is willing to commit tax fraud, embezzlement, or extortion in his private affairs, it is implausible that he could retain the respect needed to sit in judgment of others and be trusted to render fair and impartial judgments. At some point, the evident defects of character of the officeholder become incompatible with the dignity of the office being held.

Such "easy" cases drove most of the twentieth-century federal experience with the impeachment power. District Judge Robert Archbald was removed in 1913 because "he has prostituted his high office for personal profit" and attempted "to commercialize his potentiality as judge."[21] Judge George English resigned in 1926 after his impeachment for using bankruptcy proceedings to enrich himself and others. Judge Halsted Ritter was impeached and removed in 1936 for his financial conflicts of interest. Judge Alcee Hastings was impeached and removed in 1989 for conspiring to solicit a bribe. Judge Thomas Porteous was impeached and removed in 2010 for accepting bribes and lying to the Federal Bureau of Investigation, despite the Department of Justice deciding not to pursue criminal charges against him. Such cases required careful investigation to reveal the underlying facts of the alleged offenses, but whether the charges if proved rose to the level of impeachable offenses could not be seriously questioned.

We should also note another type of easy case: the case in which use of the impeachment power is clearly not warranted. The left-wing activist group Impeach for Peace has called on citizens to petition Congress to initiate impeachment proceedings against Justice Neil Gorsuch on the general grounds that Donald Trump should not be allowed to make "any permanent changes to the government."[22] The sentiment seems to be widely shared, though it has not yet gone mainstream. Unlike court-packing plans, which are now debated in the pages of the *Washington Post*, the prospect of the mass impeachment of Trump-appointed judges is for now confined to the *Daily Kos* and activist message boards. After all, "They started this fight; hit them back even harder and try to end it."[23] The impeachment power as an all-purpose tool for removing disfavored government officials is an idea that seems to have become in vogue since November 9, 2016.

An impeachment might be viewed as an expression of raw political power, a tool that the majority of the House of Representatives might grasp as a means of erasing from the government all those who might be hostile to congressionally favored political programs, who might seem generally unfit for their position, or who might bear the stench of illegitimacy. If Neil Gorsuch occupies a judicial seat "stolen by a craven act of democratic sabotage" and who "will always be sitting in a chair reserved for the nominee of a Democratic president," then "he is illegitimate today, and he will be illegitimate 20 years from now."[24] If he cannot be made to "voluntarily" resign, then perhaps he should be more forcibly unseated.[25]

Such a use of the impeachment power is clearly at odds with how the power is granted to Congress in the Constitution. The Constitution includes two types of barriers to the use of the impeachment power. One barrier is purely procedural. Advocates of impeachment and removal must assemble a simple majority in the House of Representatives and a supermajority in the Senate. No doubt the supermajority requirement in the Senate in particular has been a significant deterrent against the more frequent use of the impeachment power. For most of American history, reaching a two-thirds majority in the Senate requires some significant bipartisan cooperation. Narrowly partisan use of the impeachment power would tend to be not only short-sighted but also ineffective. Building a coalition to remove a government official means reaching across the aisle and marshalling arguments that can appeal not merely to ideological allies. If the Senate had been given the power to remove an officer with a simple majority vote, the American practice of impeachment might well have looked different, and the impeachment power might have become a routinized feature of American politics by which partisan majorities consolidated power after electoral victories. As it stands, impeachment efforts built on the passions of the partisan base might be cathartic but they are not likely to be successful. Undoubtedly part of the attraction of court-packing schemes in the present moment is that they can be effectuated by the simple expedient of passing a statute and would require no effort to win bipartisan support.

The Constitution also erects a second, substantive barrier to the use of the impeachment power. Officers are to be removed only when it has been demonstrated that they have committed impeachable offenses of "Treason, Bribery, or other high Crimes and Misdemeanors." The significance of the substantive standard that can justify an impeachment is emphasized by the Constitution's repeated reference to the Senate's actions on the impeachment as a "trial" that might generate a "conviction" and that requires the senators sitting in judgment to be under oath. While the House's power to impeach might only be hemmed in by a historical context that situated it as a "the grand inquest of the nation," the Senate is textually empowered only to sit as a court and only to convict when appropriate charges have been demonstrated to be true.[26]

To be sure, the prospects of judicial review of a Senate judgment that an officer should be convicted and removed are slim indeed, even in our modern era of a significantly shrunken political question doctrine. Nonetheless, we should resist the conclusion that simply because there is no court beyond the Senate to appeal a miscarriage of justice in an impeachment context that constitutional standards are meaningless or irrelevant. Judges are not the only ones who can be, and are obliged to be, conscientious and responsible constitutional agents.[27] Members of Congress can and should take seriously the substantive as well as the procedural conditions of the impeachment power.

The constitutional standard that impeachable offenses must be proved before an official can be removed focuses congressional attention on the actual conduct of the individual while in office. At a minimum, to sustain an impeachment the House must be able to point to identifiable acts that the individual in question has committed that could be characterized as impeachable. John Quincy Adams castigated the Republicans in Thomas Jefferson's first term of office for attempting to impeach judges with no better rationale than "because *their offices are wanted.*"[28] His description of the Jeffersonians was tendentious, but he certainly pointed to a generally accepted understanding that any effort to sweep away the incumbents sitting on the bench of the Supreme Court—absent egregious misconduct by the justices themselves—would itself be an abuse of the constitutional power of impeachment.

Hard Cases

There are a range of harder cases in which impeachment is less clearly justified, but the hard cases might be equally or even more important than the easy cases. There might be hard cases because the offenses involved are relatively insignificant, and the officeholder might be more reasonably forgiven or endured. More interesting, however, are those cases that are hard when the offenses involved are significant indeed but there are substantial disagreements about whether the actions in question are even offenses.

At heart, impeachment is a remedy for the abuse of constitutional power. Congress is called to act when an officeholder willfully misuses public authority in violation of the duties of their office and their responsibilities as a steward of a public trust. It is fairly straightforward to identify such abuses and condemn them when the officer is driven by corrupt motives. The judge who abuses his power to line his own pocket or the diplomat who abuses his power to advance the interests of a foreign adversary are unlikely to find a sympathetic hearing on the floor of the Congress if they attempt to offer justification for their actions. More difficult is the case of the officer who exercises power in a way that some find abusive but that others do not, who acts on motives that are public-spirited but who pursues goals that much of the public would reject.

Take, for example, what has been characterized as a Jeffersonian approach to an executive prerogative power.[29] John Locke pointed out that "many things there are, which the law can by no means provide for, and those must necessarily be left to the discretion of him that has the executive power in his hands, to be ordered by him as the public good and advantage shall require; nay, it is fit that the laws themselves should in some cases give way to the executive power, or rather to the fundamental law of nature and government."[30] If Locke is correct that the law cannot fully anticipate everything and thus that the executive must sometimes simply have the discretion to decide and to act, then the written Constitution might well raise similar issues. The posited discretionary authority might be internalized, if the Constitution is simply understood to empower the president to take all necessary actions when the unexpected happens. But Jefferson preferred to think that a proper constitution would not empower any government official with that sort of open-ended discretion, but nonetheless the occasion might arise in which a responsible public servant would believe that action without preauthorization was necessary. As Jefferson told one correspondent, "A strict observance of the written laws is doubtless *one* of the high duties of a good citizen, but it is not *the highest*."[31] An officer might feel obliged to break the law, or even the Constitution itself, in order to fulfill the higher obligation of acting in the nation's interest.

Impeachment and trial might well be warranted in such a case of acting "beyond the Constitution" but for the sake of the public good.[32] Constitutional powers would have been self-consciously abused and constitutional limits willfully transgressed in such a case, though an officer might think that the unlawful act was justified by the greater good. Congress might ultimately agree by giving its sanction to the unconstitutional act by declining to impeach or by declining to convict in an impeachment trial. Such a case would be hard in that the impeachable offense of willful violation of the Constitution would be clear, but the stain might be thought to be wiped clean by the pure motives.

Other cases might be hard because the offense itself is in question. Jefferson imagined a world of bright line constitutional rules that could be strictly construed. He might have thought that it was sometimes necessary to step across those lines, but he also thought it would always be possible to know when someone had traversed them. Our constitutional experience casts a great deal of doubt on the possibility of everyone acceding to the presence of a set of bright line constitutional rules. Officers and their allies rarely believe that they have transgressed a clear constitutional rule. Politics has been characterized by deep disagreements over what the rules are. Officers are more likely to assert that they never went out of bounds than to seek forgiveness for having done so.

In the face of such reasonable disagreement over whether constitutional abuses have even occurred, is impeachment warranted? Partisans on each side are likely to believe and to assert that there is no reasonable disagreement to be had, that the officer had clearly acted either within or without his authority. With a bit of distance from the partisan struggle, the question is a more difficult one. The officer might reasonably be thought guilty of constitutional transgressions, and yet we can recognize that others might in good faith come to the opposite conclusion.

The question of whether the constitutional disagreement is in fact in good faith might well be salient to the question of whether to impeach for perceived abuses of constitutional powers. If the officer was sincerely acting in good faith on what she understood to be a proper understanding of the Constitution, then that might not be sufficient to spare her from impeachment, but it is at least a point in her favor. If, however, members of the legislature believe that the officer could not have been acting in good faith, then impeachment is much more clearly warranted. A judge, for example, has an obligation to put forward credible arguments that could justify a ruling. Readers can assess for themselves whether those arguments are reasonable enough to be taken seriously or should be seen as nothing but a pretext for imposing a policy preference on unwilling legislators. Especially in our polarized age, it would be all too easy to dismiss the disagreeable as incredible—how could anyone possibly believe that?—but the measure of good-faith constitutional interpretation should not be whether a judge agrees with our own conclusions but whether the judge makes argumentative moves that are recognizable by a legitimate interpretive community. An important aspect of constitutional politics is the construction of such interpretive communities and the setting of boundaries for what constitutional arguments are, in Jack Balkin's phrase, "on the table" or "off the wall."[33] A judge who indulges in off-the-wall arguments is appropriately vulnerable to congressional correction through impeachment.

More difficult than judicial actions grounded in off-the-wall or bad-faith arguments are actions grounded in credible but disfavored arguments. Such arguments are within the legal "mainstream" in the sense that they are accepted within epistemic communities that have significant political salience, but they may well be regarded as highly disreputable from the perspective of partisans operating within that political environment. The constitutional ideas held most dear by members of the Federalist Society and the Yale Law School faculty might be both politically influential and mutually incompatible. From the perspectives of activists on the left, *Citizens United* is not merely wrong but obviously wrong. Activists on the right might say the same about *Obergefell.* And yet both were capable of commanding a majority of the Supreme Court and a host of intellectual and political allies. In the midst of such disagreements, one judge's constitutional abuse is another judge's constitutional fidelity.

Even if we think that it is reasonable to impeach and remove judges for abusing their powers, we should be reluctant to use the impeachment power when there is reasonable disagreement about whether a given action is in fact an abuse of the judicial power. Ordinary politics consists of debates over constitutional meaning and efforts to advance favored understandings and to better effectuate them in political practice. Constitutional disagreements are hashed out through elections, judicial appointments, and litigation. Part of our normal political give-and-take is the recognition that others who hold deeply disagreeable constitutional, political, and policy views might nonetheless win elections and gain offices.

But why should we tolerate the constitutional errors of others? Why not play constitutional hardball and, when possible, purge the political system of our partisan foes so as to better secure our own partisan objectives?[34] Why not use the constitutionally provided tools to remove from the bench judges who espouse disfavored constitutional philosophies and to expand the bench to pack on judges who will profess favored constitutional theories? The answer is surely not that we think some good can come from judges advancing flawed constitutional understandings. Presumably misguided judges can only do constitutional damage by leading us off the one true path. Why should we limit the arsenal of weapons we might use to stop the progress of such constitutional contamination?

Pursuing judicial impeachments in cases of reasonable legal disagreements goes down a path of escalating political conflict that increasingly refuses to recognize the legitimacy of the opposition. Characterizing judicial acts based on constitutional disagreements as high crimes attempts to cast dissenters into political oblivion, forcing partisans on both sides to adopt a winner-takes-all approach to politics in which giving any quarter to the other side is treasonous. This was the move that the majority of the Taney Court attempted to make in *Dred Scott*, declaring that the motivating principles of the upstart Republican Party were in fact entirely inconsistent with the terms of the Constitution as inherited from the founding fathers. It is the implication of the "Flight 93 election" metaphor. You must "charge [the] cockpit or you die." And part of why it is essential to charge the cockpit now is because the enemy "intends your destruction" if they succeed, because, after all, your enemy already views you as illegitimate, "a Nazi" who must be "crush[ed]." Indeed, they will soon "dispense with the whole bother of staging these phony contests in which each side ostensibly has a shot," so one might as well take preemptive action.[35] The idea that the partisan opposition should be treated as "an existential threat" to the country is hardly unique to the political right these days, but that idea naturally raises the question of what "treating an existential threat as existential requires."[36] If democracy itself is "on the ballot," then vanquishing the threat at the polling station might only be one item on the menu of options for saving democracy. Unsheathing impeachments as a political weapon for addressing routine political disagreements might simply normalize use of the impeachment power such that it becomes a regular feature of partisan politics, but might also ratchet up the perception that we are in the midst of an extraordinary political battle in which no restraint can be exercised. If we must impeach judges in order to clear our foes from the political battlefield, what else must we be willing to do in order to save the republic?

Impeaching judges in cases of reasonable legal disagreement is likely to have the effect of weakening the judiciary as an independent constitutional institution. Many would argue that the courts enjoy only a bounded independence in any case and are ultimately tethered to the political arena of partisan conflict.[37] In our polarized environment it is easy to see that the judges themselves are often divided on salient political issues in ways that mirror political conflict off the bench. If the courts are already partisan institutions, as reflected by the voting behavior of justices in high-profile constitutional cases and by the pitched partisan battles over judicial appointments, then what could be lost by taking the incremental step of bending courts to the will of the partisan electoral majority? If the justices are simply extensions of the Republican or Democratic Party, why tolerate a majority of seats on the Supreme Court to be held by the party that is out of power in the elected institutions of government?

There would probably be something to be said for that position if judges were *merely* extensions of the political parties and judicial decision making was *just* partisan politics by other means, but this "realist" perspective sells the judiciary short. An independent judiciary provides advantages to the political system that would be lost if the judges were reduced to being partisan proxies. Detaching courts from the rhythms of ordinary politics provides some assurance to electoral losers that their interests will to some degree be protected, reducing the stakes of political conflict. If impeachments become a vehicle for purging partisan foes from the judicial ranks, then that insurance policy becomes less credible and politics less stable.[38] Shrinking the gap between the immediate preferences of legislative majorities and the judiciary shrinks the ability of judges to offer an independent judgment on the interpretation and administration of the law. A politically insulated judiciary can provide a careful look at the how policymaking is working in practice and can advance principles that are generally valued but hard to realize in a highly politicized environment. If judges fear removal if they get out of line with the legislature, then unfriendly judges might be less capable of advancing politically disfavored values but even friendly judges might be less capable of advancing politically favored values.[39] The contemporary Supreme Court reflects the political polarization of the broader contemporary political system, but the still small number of moments of partisan disagreement on the court can overshadow the still larger number of moments in which the court's decisions do not reflect partisan divides.[40] The perception of a partisan court outruns the reality, but letting loose judicial impeachments for routine political disagreements risks driving the court toward greater partisanship.

Impeachments in general should be a last resort to addressing abuses of power. There are certainly occasions when nothing short of impeachment and removal will be adequate to remedy the problem posed by a misbehaving officer. But we also have more routine tools for addressing constitutional abuses. Judicial review itself is a mechanism for identifying and correcting the acts of government officials that violate constitutional boundaries. If a lower court judge indulges in constitutional error, judges up the judicial hierarchy are generally capable of intervening to address the error. As Justice Samuel Chase's legal team argued to the Senate in his impeachment trial, if a judge were to make mistakes in law while attempting in good faith to fulfill the duties of his office, then the more appropriate remedy is argument and appeals rather than impeachment and removal. If judges are personally unaccountable for their decisions, that does not mean that their decisions cannot be reviewed and reversed. A congressional majority that is unhappy with the judicial performance of an individual should consider the full array of options available for remediating the situation.

We seem to be entering an era in which impeachments will become more common. Legislatures may not have the votes necessary to remove many wayward officers, but impeachment is always on the table. Party polarization is stressing our political institutions and making political actors more willing to take unusual measures to ensure that their rivals cannot exercise power. A greater propensity to use the impeachment power would not be the only way in which that heightened partisan conflict is expressed, but the impeachment power seems likely to be among the weapons that will be used in political battles. Judges have long been a primary target of the impeachment power, in part because they are more insulated from the more routine means by which government officials who find themselves mired in scandal are pushed aside. But as political actors begin to look beyond the traditional criminal offenses and petty abuses of power that have triggered judicial impeachments, it is worth considering the appropriateness of using the impeachment power to advance constitutional ideals in a context in which those ideals are contested. Impeachments can be a means for trying to steer the judiciary onto a favored constitutional course, but there are costs to turning to extraordinary means to shape constitutional law.

Notes

1. Thomas Jefferson, "To Thomas Ritchie, December 25, 1820," in *The Writings of Thomas Jefferson*, ed. H. A. Washington, vol. 7 (New York: J. C. Riker, 1855), 192.

2. Reid Wilson, "Pennsylvania GOP Moves to Oust Judges over Gerrymandering," *The Hill* (March 20, 2018).

3. Katie Meyer, "GOP Leaders Throw Cold Water on Plan to Impeach Pa. High Court Justices," WHYY.org (March 24, 2018).The partisan roles have been reversed elsewhere, as in North Carolina and Wisconsin. David A. Graham, "America's New Battlefront," *The Atlantic* (September 19, 2023).

4. See Keith E. Whittington, "Partisanship, Norms, and Federal Judicial Appointments," *Georgetown Journal of Law and Public Policy* 16 (2018): 519.

5. Dylan Matthews, "Court-Packing, Democrats' Nuclear Option for the Supreme Court, Explained," *Vox* (July 10, 2018); Ian Ayres and John Fabian Witt, "Democrats Need a Plan B for the Supreme Court. Here's One Option," *Washington Post* (July 27, 2018); John Yoo and Robert Delahunty, "The Foolish Court-Packing Craze," *National Review* (July 19, 2018); David Faris, "Democrats Must Consider Court-Packing When They Regain Power. It's the Only Way to Save Democracy," *Washington Post* (July 10, 2018); Ilya Somin, "The Case Against Court-Packing Revisited," *Washington Post* (July 3, 2018).

6. For a longer consideration of impeachment principles with a greater focus on the presidency, see Keith E. Whittington, *The Impeachment Power* (Princeton: Princeton University Press, 2024).

7. See more generally, Keith E. Whittington, "The Place of Congress in the Constitutional Order," *Harvard Journal of Law and Public Policy* 40 (2017): 573.

8. Cass R. Sunstein, "Impeaching the President," *University of Pennsylvania Law Review* 147 (1998): 280; Ronald Dworkin, "The Wounded Constitution," *New York Review of Books* (March 18, 1999).

9. Benjamin Ginsberg and Martin Shefter, *Politics by Other Means*, 3rd ed. (New York: W. W. Norton, 2002); Keith E. Whittington, "Resolved, the Presidential Impeachment Process Is Basically Sound," in *Debating the Presidency*, ed. Richard J. Ellis and Michael Nelson (Washington, D.C.: CQ Press, 2006).

10. See also, Gene Healy, "Americans Should Impeach Presidents More Often," *Reason* (August/September 2017).

11. Jefferson, *Writings*, 7:192.

12. John A. Ferejohn and Larry D. Kramer, "Independent Judges, Dependent Judiciary: Institutionalizing Judicial Restraint," *New York University Law Review* 77 (2002): 962.

13. U.S. Const., Art. III, Sec. 1.

14. *Journal of the Senate*, 8th Cong., 2nd Sess. (1804), 47, 48, 49, 52, 77.

15. See Keith E. Whittington, *Constitutional Construction* (Cambridge: Harvard University Press, 1999).

16. Alexander Hamilton, No. 78, in *The Federalist Papers*.

17. For such skepticism, see Paul Carrese, "The Principle of Moderation in Montesquieu and America: Constitutional Equilibrium and Judicial Tempering," in this volume. For a more robust vision of the scope of judicial power, see Sotirios A. Barber, "Originalism, Moral Objectivity, and the Lost Constitutionalism," in this volume.

18. See also, Keith E. Whittington, "'High Crimes' after Clinton," *Policy Review* (February–March 2000); Keith E. Whittington, "What Is the Impeachment Power For?," *Law and Liberty* (May 22, 2017) (http://www.libertylawsite.org/2017/05/22/what-is-the-impeachment-power-for/); Greg Weiner, "Impeachment's Political Heart," *New York Times* (May 18, 2017); Greg Weiner, "Restoring Judicial Impeachment," *Law and Liberty* (March 26, 2018) (https://www.lawliberty.org/2018/03/26/restoring-judicial-impeachment-james-rogers-mark-pulliam-prudence-supreme-court-samuel-chase-constitution/).

19. U.S. Const., Art. II, Sec. 4 ("The President, Vice President and all civil Officers of the United States, shall be removed from Office on Impeachment for, and Conviction of, Treason, Bribery, or other high Crimes and Misdemeanors").

20. U.S. Const., Art. I, Sec. 3 ("but the Party convicted shall nevertheless be liable and subject to Indictment, Trial, Judgment and Punishment, according to Law"); U.S. Const., Art. II, Sec. 2 ("he shall have Power to grant Reprieves and Pardons for Offenses against the United States, except in Cases of Impeachment").

21. *Proceedings of the United States Senate and the House of Representatives in the Trial of Impeachment of Robert W. Archbald*, vol. 3 (Washington, D.C.: Government Printing Office, 1913), 1701.

22. "Impeach Trump's SCOTUS Pick, Neil Gorsuch," Impeach for Peace (https://impeachforpeace.org/impeach_bush_blog/impeach-for-peace-in-the-news/impeach-trumps-scotus-pick-neil-gorsuch/).

23. "Impeach Gorsuch?" *Daily Kos* (April 8, 2017).

24. David Faris, "How Democrats Can Make Republicans Pay for Justice Gorsuch," *The Week* (March 20, 2017).

25. Jesse Etelson, "A Way Out for Judge Gorsuch," *Baltimore Sun* (August 1, 2018).

26. Albert C. Hinds, *Hinds' Precedents of the House of Representatives of the United States*, vol. 3 (Washington: Government Printing Office, 1907), 455.

27. See also, Paul Brest, "The Conscientious Legislator's Guide to Constitutional Interpretation," *Stanford Law Review* 27 (1974): 585; Susan R. Burgess, *Contest for Constitutional Authority* (Lawrence: University Press of Kansas, 1992); Keith E. Whittington, *Constitutional Construction* (Cambridge: Harvard University Press, 1999); Mariah Zeisberg, *War Powers* (Princeton: Princeton University Press, 2015).

28. John Quincy Adams, *Memoirs of John Quincy Adams*, ed. Charles Francis Adams, vol. 1 (Philadelphia: J. B. Lippincott & Co., 1874), 323.

29. See Benjamin A. Kleinerman, *The Discretionary President* (Lawrence: University Press of Kansas, 2009); Jeremy David Bailey, "Executive Prerogative and the 'Good Officer' in Thomas Jefferson's Letter to John B. Colvin," *Presidential Studies Quarterly* 34 (2004): 732; Clement Fatovic, "Constitutionalism and Presidential Prerogative: Jeffersonian and Hamiltonian Perspectives," *American Journal of Political Science* 48 (2004): 429.

30. John Locke, *Second Treatise, in Locke: Two Treatises of Government, ed. Peter Laslett (New York: Cambridge University Press, 1988)*, chap. XIV.

31. Jefferson, *Writings*, 5:542.

32. Thomas Jefferson, *The Writings of Thomas Jefferson*, ed. Paul Leicester Ford, vol. 8 (New York: G. P. Putnam's Sons, 1897), 262.

33. Jack M. Balkin, *Constitutional Redemption* (Cambridge: Harvard University Press, 2011), 180. See also, Stanley Fish, *Is There a Text in this Class?* (Cambridge: Harvard University Press, 1980); Robert M. Cover, "Nomos and Narrative," *Harvard Law Review* 97 (1983): 4; Howard Gillman, "What's Law Got to Do with It? Judicial Behavioralists Test the 'Legal Model' of Judicial Decision Making," *Law and Social Inquiry* 26 (2001): 465; Amanda Hollis-Brusky, *Ideas with Consequences* (New York: Oxford University Press, 2015).

34. On the notion of "constitutional hardball," see Mark Tushnet, "Constitutional Hardball," *John Marshall Law Review* 37 (2004): 523.

35. Publius Decius Mus, "The Flight 93 Election," *Claremont Review of Books* (September 5, 2016).

36. Bryan Walsh, "Democrats Say Trump Is an Existential Threat. They're Not Acting Like It," *Vox* (July 1, 2024).

37. See also, Keith E. Whittington, "The Bounded Independence of the American Courts," *New York University Law Review Online* 93 (2018): 70.

38. On the insurance model of an independent judiciary, see Thomas Ginsburg, *Judicial Review in New Democracies* (New York: Cambridge University Press, 2003).

39. On "friendly" judicial review, see James R. Rogers, "Information and Judicial Review: A Signaling Game of Legislative-Judicial Interaction," *American Journal of Political Science* 45 (2001): 84; Keith E. Whittington, "'Interpose Your Friendly Hand': Political Supports for the Exercise of Judicial Review by the United States Supreme Court," *American Political Science Review* 99 (2005): 583.

40. On polarization on the contemporary Supreme Court, see Keith E. Whittington, *Repugnant Laws* (Lawrence: University Press of Kansas, 2019); Thomas M. Keck, *Judicial Politics in Polarized Times* (Chicago: University of Chicago Press, 2014).

CHAPTER 12

The False Dichotomy of Presidential Immunity

Kathleen Tipler

The debate over presidential immunity has long been marked by a false dichotomy: It wrongly pits the judiciary against the legislature, with arguments against immunity prioritizing judicial authority, and with advocates for immunity prioritizing congressional authority. In doing so, the debate over presidential immunity obscures the ways in which judicial processes and congressional power can be used together to generate the authority needed to investigate and respond to potential presidential misconduct.

This false dichotomy is a product of an overly formalistic understanding of the Constitution and the separation of powers. According to this formalistic view, the judicial branch upholds the rule of law through its strictly neutral application of clear and objective principles. And the legislative branch, according to this view, is responsive to the people and institutionally situated—and, indeed, constitutionally obligated—to hold the one nationally elected official, the head of the executive branch, accountable.

Common arguments that prioritize the judicial branch go something like this: No man or woman is above the law, and to provide a president with immunity places the person who inhabits that office above the law. If a president has immunity from either civil lawsuits or criminal prosecution, then the American political system is not ruled by law but by individual persons. A system that is ruled by individual persons is not a liberal democracy but is instead the sort of political system from which the founders chose to break: a monarchy where one individual, the king or queen, is above the law, or to use a more contemporary analog, a dictatorship. It is the judiciary's job to apply and interpret the law, and protect individual rights. While some deference to the unique position of a president may be in order, it is both within the judiciary's power, and a judicial obligation, to review potential crimes committed by a president.

In contrast, common arguments prioritizing the legislative branch are motivated by different concerns, many of which are worries over the judicial process itself. There is the fear that partisan or otherwise politicized interests will bring frivolous and false lawsuits against the president. A president's time and energy will then be consumed by lawsuits, to the detriment of the country's welfare. This argument is both prudential and constitutional. Impaired governance will be the result of a president facing prosecution (or jail time), while the impairment of the executive branch by the judicial branch is a violation of the separation of powers. And even if those charges against a sitting president are not frivolous, the significant cost to the general welfare as well as the violation of the proper boundaries between branches must be weighed against the lesser evil of delaying trial until after a president leaves office.

In addition, it is not clear who, if anyone, has the authority to bring suit against a sitting president. As the president is the head of the executive branch, it seems that federal prosecutors, who report to the president, may not have the authority to either subpoena or indict a sitting president. If prosecution by a state official is allowed, it seems worrisomely possible that a single politicized and nationally unrepresentative state or local prosecutor might take down a nationally elected president. And either hovering implicitly in the background, or said straightforwardly, is the concern that, ultimately, unelected judges with lifetime appointments will be charged with removing the elected leader, chosen by national vote to lead the country. For all these reasons, arguments for executive immunity converge on the conclusion that only the elected representatives of Congress, via their impeachment power, have the authority to try a sitting president. And only after a sitting president leaves office might that person then be tried for crimes—or, some say, sued—for actions unrelated to official presidential duties.

This essay takes a different approach than the above overly formalistic understanding of the constitutional separation of powers and argues that a narrow conception of presidential immunity—one that invites judicial process and oversight—enables Congress to fulfill its obligation of investigating and holding presidents accountable. Judicial process need not be opposed to congressional oversight, but can work in concert with it. The role of judicial intervention should not be to authoritatively decide a president's fate, but to facilitate congressional and public evaluation of potential presidential lawbreaking. Narrowly drawn presidential immunity invites legal processes that can generate facts for the public and its elected representative to use in their assessment. The facts produced by the judicial process cannot be as easily dismissed as the fact-finding processes controlled by Congress.

This essay's argument proceeds in several parts. The first part briefly examines the text of the Constitution and considers early interpretations. In the second and third parts of the essay, I explain the formalistic arguments for and against broad presidential immunity, which are derived from, on one hand, the rule of law, and the other, the unique constitutional position of presidents. In the final section of the essay, I argue that the authority to investigate and remove a president from office is best generated interinstitutionally, through both Congress and the judiciary. Judicial process can play an important role in invoking public judgment of presidential acts, while Congress itself can use the findings of judicial processes to inform impeachment proceedings.

Constitutional Text and Early Interpretations

In contrast to members of Congress, who may not be arrested while in attendance, or for what they have said in attendance, the Constitution provides no such explicit protection for presidents from prosecution (Art. I, Sec. 6). The Constitution says, and only says, that "The President, Vice President and all civil Officers of the United States, shall be removed from Office on Impeachment for, and Conviction of, Treason, Bribery, or other high Crimes and Misdemeanors" (Art. II, Sec. 4). Given that the impeachment clause refers to "high Crimes and Misdemeanors," impeachment does not seem intended for ordinary or "low crimes." Must presidents be impeached first and then taken to court? And, if they can be tried prior to impeachment, who has this power to take a president to court, and for which sorts of offenses? The text does not say.

Some interpret the explicit protections given to Congress and the absence of such protections for the president as an indication of the framers' intent to not provide the president with immunity. Bolstering this argument is evidence that the framers considered presidential immunity but chose not to explicitly include it.[1] Others, however, point to Article I's description of the impeachment process, arguing that the text here implies that impeachment must occur first, then indictment and trial: "Judgment in Cases of Impeachment shall not extend further than to removal from Office, and disqualification to hold and enjoy any Office of honor, Trust or Profit under the United States: but the Party convicted shall nevertheless be liable and subject to Indictment, Trial, Judgment and Punishment, according to Law" (Art. I, Sec. 3). Since the text references impeachment first and then follows impeachment with "indictment, Trial, Judgment and Punishment," some read the order of the words as indicating the procedural order. However, the consensus reading of the text of the Constitution is that it cannot determinatively settle the debate: Even those like Amar and Kalt who argue that the text implies that impeachment must precede indictment do not view the text as conclusive.[2]

The rough consensus of historical research is that there was open disagreement over the issue of presidential immunity at the time of the Constitution's drafting. Proponents of temporary presidential immunity point to Alexander Hamilton's writings in *The Federalist Papers*. In *Federalist* No. 69 Hamilton wrote that the "President of the United States would be liable to be impeached, tried, and upon conviction of treason, bribery, or other high crimes or misdemeanors, removed from office; and would afterwards be liable to prosecution and punishment in the ordinary course of law." And in *Federalist* No. 77, Hamilton wrote that a president is "at all times liable to impeachment, trial, dismission from office, incapacity to serve in any other; and the forfeiture of life and estate by subsequent prosecution in the common course of law." Yet Hamilton's aim in contributing to the *Federalist Papers* was to persuade citizens to vote for ratification, not to record the intentions of the drafters or the debates at the Convention. Careful analyses that have referenced Hamilton's writings in support of presidential immunity, like those of the Office of Legal Counsel,[3] have also concluded that there was no settled agreement over this issue at the time of the Framing.[4]

The early historical record also offers little guidance in settling the debate. As no sitting president has been indicted on criminal charges, the most relevant early history is that of the vice president. In 1804 Aaron Burr, while serving as vice president under Thomas Jefferson, was indicted for murdering Alexander Hamilton. Burr's indictment, in both New York and New Jersey, apparently never prompted any objections that a vice president must first be impeached before he could be indicted.[5] But as this episode concerns a vice president, not a president, it is hard to argue that Burr's indictment is determinative. Likewise, cases involving high-level executive officials such as cabinet officers are not considered determinative. As I explain below, arguments for broad immunity depend on the unique position of a president; even those who argue against absolute immunity must still grapple with uniqueness of the presidential office.

Others have noted that presidents have gone to court for traffic offenses and have not objected to proceedings based on principles of executive immunity.[6] President Kennedy was involved in lawsuits related to a car accident, but he did not argue for presidential immunity. Instead, he argued for a stay based on the Soldiers' and Sailors' Civil Relief Act of 1940 and his position as commander in chief, but his appeal was rejected and he settled out of court (*Clinton v. Jones*, 692). Because the text of the Constitution, as well as the history up to Watergate, fails to clearly delineate the contours of presidential immunity, the debate has largely been argued on other grounds. For those who do not place great weight on early interpretations when settling disputes over constitutional meaning, it is upon these other grounds that the debate should be decided anyhow.

The Unique Presidential Position

The strongest arguments for criminal immunity for a sitting president are structural, deriving from the unique position of a president. The president is the leader of the executive branch, the commander in chief, and the only nationally elected representative of the people. Because "the President occupies a unique position in the constitutional scheme," judicial processes could interfere with presidential duties (*Nixon v. Fitzgerald*, 749). This concern with interference is both pragmatic and constitutional. Judicial control over the "movements and time" of a president threatens to violate the separation of powers, particularly with its potential to impede "the core functioning of a coordinate branch."[7] This impediment to the function of the executive could also damage public welfare. Unlike a member of Congress or the Supreme Court, or a cabinet official, one individual—a president—leads an entire branch of government. One does not have to embrace the unitary theory of the executive to recognize the uniqueness of the president's position as the sole head of the executive branch. The concern with this reliance on one individual is of particular importance when it comes to national security, given the president's position as commander in chief and central role in foreign relations. Criminal immunity for a sitting president would protect the presidency from distracting lawsuits and prosecutions, particularly baseless partisan ones, and thus also serve the public welfare.

The Supreme Court has repeatedly recognized that the president's unique place in the constitutional order requires special treatment. In *Nixon v. Fitzgerald* (1982), the court concluded that presidents are entitled to absolute immunity "from damage liability for acts within the 'outer perimeter' of his official responsibility" (*Nixon v. Fitzgerald,* 756). The court concluded that political processes (namely, impeachment) are the only appropriate remedy when a president is charged with violating the law as part of his or her official duties. Thirteen years later, in *Clinton v. Jones,* the Supreme Court again unanimously concluded that a president must be treated differently, although they did not conclude absolute immunity was necessary. While the president has immunity with "respect to acts taken in his 'public character,'" the court decided that "he is otherwise subject to the laws for his purely private acts," and that Paula Jones's civil lawsuit against Clinton could proceed (*Clinton v. Jones*, 696).

For proponents of the broadest form of presidential immunity—those who seek immunity for both civil lawsuits and criminal prosecution—*Clinton v. Jones* serves as a model of judicial overreach. The lawsuit by Paula Jones ended up taking an inordinate amount of Clinton's time and energies. It is also clear from journalistic accounts of the lawsuit, independent counsel investigation, and impeachment that followed, that Jones's lawsuit was enabled, encouraged, and sustained by moneyed, partisan interests with a deep desire to embarrass and delegitimize the president.[8] It seems that the imprecisely defined mission and virtually endless resources provided to the independent counsel, combined with Clinton's decision to lie, combined with these highly motivated and well-funded partisan interests, together produced a situation that was not a small burden, but an immense burden on the president and a major distraction as he attempted to conduct his executive duties.[9]

Given the president's unique constitutional position and obligations, and how judicial process might therefore impede the functioning of an entire branch and/or damage public welfare, these arguments for broad presidential immunity differentiate between lawsuits and/or ordinary crimes that might be prosecuted after a president leaves office, and those crimes—or other actions—that demand a president be removed from office.[10] If a president must be removed from office, it should not be done by ordinary judicial process but by the constitutionally prescribed process of impeachment by Congress, which, like the presidency but unlike the Supreme Court, is nationally elected. Stephen Griffin puts the argument, which he describes as the "most important structural argument," thus:

> Allowing a single federal prosecutor and grand jury to indict and try a President gives them a kind of supraconstitutional status that clearly has no place in our political and constitutional order. Since the presidency is unitary, an indictment and trial raises the possibility of a single person wielding a sword over the head of an entire branch of government. It would be as if the prosecutor had the power to indict all of the justices of the Supreme Court or members of Congress simultaneously. . . . The President is elected by what James Madison called "the great body of the citizens of the United States" and, under the Constitution, can only be deposed by them through an election only by their representatives through an impeachment.[11]

Akhil Amar and Brian Kalt likewise contrast the judiciary's democratic authority with Congress's:

> When a President is removed, it is not by an unaccountable state official or an even less accountable special prosecutor. It is done instead by the most august, most representative, and most accountable deliberative body we have, the Congress. Aware that politics could enter into the equation, the Founders wisely and purposely put the final decision in the hands of the more deliberative Senate, and required a super-majority so that conviction of the President would not be possible without the assent of at least some of his political allies. Impeachment, then, is the sole means of removing a sitting President, and is a good one at that.[12]

This argument emphasizes that the removal of a sitting president from office is, and need be, a political process that incorporates accountability to the people. "Treason, Bribery, or other High Crimes and Misdemeanors" is clearly not equivalent to ordinary crime (Art. II, Sec. 4); creating a separate category of misdeeds that warrant removal from office makes structural sense given a president's unique constitutional position, and given that such removal endangers the public welfare and is a *de facto* overturning of a national election. The Constitution leaves it to a coordinate, nationally accountable branch—Congress—to judge whether a president has acted in a manner that requires removal from office (and so also to that branch to decide what, exactly, "High Crimes and Misdemeanors" are). The public, in turn, judges

Congress, and whether presidential misdeeds deserve removal from office and the resultant harms.

What should hopefully be emerging to the reader is that this structural argument for broad presidential immunity relies upon the claim that Congress is the institution that best represents the public: Because the people must decide, the decision to remove a president from office must be done by the most nationally representative and most accountable branch, which these scholars declare is, uncontrovertibly, Congress. However, there are good reasons to question an argument that rests on the implicit comparative claim that Congress is more representative and accountable than the judiciary. As I argue in a later section of this chapter, if one understands authority to be constructed systemically and interinstitutionally, and not located primarily in Congress, then the argument for broad presidential immunity is significantly weakened. But before explaining this notion of systemic authority, it is helpful to first review the strongest arguments against presidential immunity.

The Rule of Law and Judicial Functions

The strongest arguments against immunity reduce to two related claims: Immunity of a sitting president places a single person above the rule of law, and it is the constitutional duty of the judiciary to interpret the law and protect individuals from the arbitrary abuse of power. Laws, not individual persons, must govern, and to provide one person with immunity from civil lawsuits or criminal prosecution places that person in power above the law. The idea that laws must govern is inherent in the notion of constitutional government and was famously recognized early on by Chief Justice Marshall in *Marbury v. Madison* when he wrote that "the government of the United States has been emphatically termed a government of laws, and not of men" (163). Marshall also concluded that the question of whether individuals have rights that cannot be altered by the president is a question to be decided by "judicial authority" because it is an essentially legal question, and thus the domain of the judicial branch (167).

The Supreme Court has repeatedly endorsed this position, opining in *United States v. Nixon* (1974), *Nixon v. Fitzgerald* (1982), and *Clinton v. Jones* (1997) that a sitting president cannot evade or avoid the law simply because he or she is a sitting president. In *United States v. Nixon*, the president's counsel argued that Nixon need not comply with a subpoena from the special prosecutor both because internal communications were protected by executive privilege and because of presidential immunity. A unanimous Supreme Court clearly articulated the position that sitting presidents do not have blanket immunity from judicial processes: "Neither the doctrine of separation of powers, nor the need for confidentiality of high-level communications, without more, can sustain an absolute, unqualified Presidential privilege of immunity from judicial process under all circumstances" (*United States v. Nixon*, 706). The court went on to note that executive privilege demands "great deference from the courts," but when that privilege is justified upon a "broad, undifferentiated claim of public interest" (as opposed to a specific claim "to protect military, diplomatic, or sensitive national security secrets"), the court must weigh the values of executive privilege with other values (*United States v. Nixon*, 706).

In this case, the other values were "the legitimate needs of the judicial process" and "our historic commitment to the rule of law" (*United States v. Nixon*, 707, 708). Referencing Jackson's concurrence in *Youngstown Sheet & Tube Co. v. Sawyer*, Chief Justice Burger wrote for the court, "The impediment that an absolute, unqualified privilege would place in the way of the primary constitutional duty of the Judicial Branch to do justice in criminal prosecutions would plainly conflict with the function of the courts under Art. III. In designing the structure of our Government and dividing and allocating the sovereign power among three co-equal branches, the framers of the Constitution sought to provide a comprehensive system, but the separate powers were not intended to operate with absolute independence" (*United States* v. *Nixon*, 707). While the Court's opinion in *United States v. Nixon* was narrow—concluding that a "generalized interest in confidentiality . . . cannot prevail over the fundamental demands of due process of law in the fair administration of criminal justice"—the Court clearly established that the values of the rule of law need not and should not always yield to executive privilege (*United States v. Nixon*, 713).

In 1982, the Supreme Court once more took up the question of presidential immunity in *Nixon v. Fitzgerald*. A five-person majority again weighed the needs of judicial processes against the needs and obligations of the presidential office and concluded that presidents are entitled to immunity when engaged in official duties. In his concurrence, Chief Justice Burger emphasized that the majority opinion limited immunity to civil damages, and that "a President, like Members of Congress, judges, prosecutors, or congressional aides—all having absolute immunity—are not immune for acts outside official duties" (*Nixon v. Fitzgerald,* 759). The court concluded that political processes (namely, impeachment) are the appropriate remedy when a president is charged with violating the law as part of his or her official duties. The four dissenters, however, argued that even absolute immunity for official duties ceded too much judicial authority to the executive, and that qualified immunity better balanced the obligations of the two branches.

Thirteen years later, in *Clinton v. Jones*, the Supreme Court again unanimously concluded that the president did not have absolute immunity, allowing a civil lawsuit, involving conduct prior to Clinton's time as president, to proceed (*Clinton v. Jones*, 696). Equating presidential immunity from private acts with monarchal theories that saw no distinction between the public person of the king and the private person, the court explicitly rejected the application of the common law rule that "the King can do no wrong" (*Clinton v. Jones*, 697). Justice Stevens, writing for the court, stated that its decisions regarding the immunity of government officials took a functional approach that he would also apply (*Clinton v. Jones*, 695). Violation of separation of powers involves the encroachment of one branch upon the other, wrote Stevens, "but in this case there is no suggestion that the Federal Judiciary is being asked to perform any function that might in some way be described as 'executive'" (*Clinton v. Jones*, 701). Rather than encroaching upon the executive, Jones "is merely asking the courts to exercise their core Article III jurisdiction to decide cases and controversies" (*Clinton v. Jones*, 701).

Unlike in *Fitzgerald,* which involved public duties, according to the court there was no need to worry that a president's official decision-making would be hampered by the fear of civil lawsuits (that would follow from potential damages from his or her decision). In response to the president's argument that the burdens of being subject to a civil lawsuit would impair his ability to perform his executive functions, the court responded that "the fact that a federal court's exercise of its traditional Article III jurisdiction may significantly burden the time and attention of the Chief Executive is not sufficient to establish a violation of the Constitution" (*Clinton v. Jones*, 702). Stevens also wryly added that "the burden on the President's time and energy that is a mere by product of such review surely cannot be considered as onerous as the direct burden imposed by judicial review and the occasional invalidation of his official actions" (*Clinton v. Jones*, 705).

In addition, the court noted, courts could recognize the demands of presidential duties and were capable of working around and within the needs of those duties. "Our decision rejecting the immunity claim and allowing the case to proceed does not require us to confront the question whether a court may compel the attendance of the President at any specific time or place," wrote Stevens, and "we assume that the testimony of the President, both for discovery and for use at trial, may be taken at the White House at a time that will accommodate his busy schedule, and that, if a trial is held, there would be no necessity for the President to attend in person, though he could elect to do so" (*Clinton v. Jones*, 691–2). Justice Breyer's concurrence was skeptical of courts' abilities to easily accommodate presidential duties—a skepticism that some would say was well founded—although he likewise concluded that sitting presidents should not have absolute immunity from civil lawsuits regarding private conduct.

An additional worry not highlighted in these Supreme Court opinions is that judicial intervention is necessary because presidents are most likely to abuse individuals who will not find justice through the political process. This argument echoes the logic of footnote 4 of *United States v. Carolene Products Co.* (1938), the same logic the court has repeatedly referenced to support its interventions on behalf of individual rights. As Steven Calabresi noted, "Presidents and politicians will be checked by public opinion when their conduct affects the whole public but they may be able to get away with misconduct that affects only a single individual or a small class of people."[13] While Calabresi made this comment in the course of arguing for presidential immunity from federal prosecution, his point about the comparative capacities of the elected branches and courts points to a problem with presidential immunity: It could well lead to the violation of rights of vulnerable individuals and groups. It is a "core judicial role" to protect individual rights, and thus a core judicial function to adjudicate criminal proceedings against a sitting president.[14]

The Interinstitutional Authority to Discipline Presidential Misconduct

Presidential violation of the law, then, is a particularly challenging problem for a formalistic interpretation of separation of powers. On one side, according to a formalistic view, there is the threat to the rule of law, equal treatment under the law, and the judicial power and obligation to remedy individual rights violations and resolve legal controversies. On the other side, according to this formalistic view, there is the need for a president to fulfill the core duties of the executive branch unimpeded, which is both a constitutional mandate and a public good. Even if a president is not the object of criminal prosecution, lawsuits and legal proceedings are distracting and burdensome, and can consume a president's limited time and energy. So given the unique position of a president, advocates of immunity argue that the question of presidential removal and/or distraction should not be left up to the judiciary, as it is essentially a political decision with no legal resolution: Only the people, via their representatives, have the authority to remove the nationally elected leader of one branch and weigh whether the removal and/or distraction of a president is worth the potential damage to public welfare. This debate has largely been made by one side arguing that the rule of law is more important, thus presidential immunity should be narrowly drawn, while the other side has argued that a highly functioning executive branch, and its insulation from nonrepresentative mechanisms of removal, is more important.

However, the question of presidential immunity need not be reduced to choosing either the rule of law or elected representatives holding a president accountable via the impeachment process. This reduction of the debate over presidential immunity to a dichotomous choice between the judiciary and Congress is the result of an overly formalistic interpretation of the Constitution, one that views the boundaries of the branches in a rigid and inflexible manner. Another interpretation is possible, an interpretation that views authority as constructed systemically, across branches, and seeks out ways in which branches might productively work together to accomplish important constitutional ends.[15] These constitutional ends should include holding presidents accountable for either illicit activity or abuse of power. If one focuses on what each institution can contribute to the process of holding a president accountable, the rigid prioritization of the judiciary over the legislature, or the legislature over the judiciary—what I call the false dichotomy of presidential immunity—disappears. In short, the judiciary can operate in tandem with Congress to invite public judgment and together generate the authority to hold a president responsible for misconduct.

That said, certain constitutional issues may lend themselves more to interinstitutional cooperation and the construction of interinstitutional authority, and it is not immediately obvious that presidential immunity is one of those issues. War powers, for example, would seem to be an obvious candidate for interinstitutional cooperation given both the complementary institutional capacities related to war (the speed and decisiveness of the executive branch, the deliberative capacity and electoral responsiveness of the legislative), as well as the Constitution's clear textual delegation of war powers to both branches in Articles I and II.[16] One might argue that presidential immunity does not lend itself to interinstitutionalism in the same way: As advocates for broad presidential immunity like to note, the impeachment clause is the only explicit textual reference to disciplining a sitting president, and that power is clearly given to Congress. That in itself would seem to make the question of presidential immunity different from a war powers question. However, if one focuses not only on explicit textual references but instead on the respective institutional capacities created by the Constitution, disciplining an errant president does look like war powers; that is, there are constitutional ends best served through interinstitutional cooperation, utilizing the respective and complementary capacities of different branches, with the result that important and weighty decisions generate a high level of authority and legitimacy.

There are good reasons to think that judicial processes are better able to gather the information needed for the public and its representatives to evaluate potential presidential lawbreaking than Congress. While Congress has multiple means of fact finding and investigation at its disposal, these tools, while helpful, do not operate in the same way that judicial processes do. Neutral investigation of lawbreaking is a core function of the judiciary, and it is not a core function of Congress. The institutional design and operations of both Congress and courts reflect this simple fact. Jury trials in the legal system consist of laypeople who are chosen, ideally, for their neutrality and judges who contribute their expertise in due process and knowledge of the law. Members of Congress, on the other hand, are neither neutral laypeople nor knowledgeable legal experts, but are instead partisan and politicized actors with agendas that extend far beyond factual inquiry and finding the truth of guilt and innocence. The public is of course highly aware of the biases of legislative hearings and the ways in which they are fundamentally different from a disciplined judicial process.

Perhaps most importantly, courts have rules of evidence and procedure, developed over hundreds of years, to provide, as much as possible, a fair and equitable trial. Congress has no such experience or, arguably, goal, and as Posner has detailed, Clinton's trial in the Senate was rife with "procedural failure[s]."[17] For example, there was no clear standard of proof nor were there rules for factual inquiry.[18] Congress has the power to create its own procedural rules for impeachment hearings—and there are good reasons for this—but one consequence is that these rules can and do vary over time. Unlike with courts, in congressional impeachment hearings, there is no institutional principle that demands that like cases be treated alike, no institutional demand for ideological neutrality in congressional proceedings. And, indeed, the rules that Congress have used in these hearings have varied over time.[19]

A Senate trial is very much a "political" judgment and less a "legal" one, which makes sense in an impeachment context, where the Senate is evaluating whether a president, in their public conduct, has committed the inherently political and opaque offense of "Treason, Bribery, or other High Crimes and Misdemeanors," and, as formalistic defenders of presidential immunity are at pains to note, elected leaders are removing the nationally elected leader (Art. II, Sec. 4). Even though that final, authoritative judgment is political, political need not mean "untethered from facts." Indeed, good political judgment is based on facts. Judicial processes can help generate the facts upon which the public and Congress can make their political judgments regarding presidential lawbreaking, together constructing the authority to remove a president from office. Indeed, the House has often "outsource[d]" its investigative work in impeachment proceedings.[20] Doing so makes practical sense, but it is also an important step in constructing the authority to investigate a president and, if need be, hold them accountable for any wrongdoing.

A good example of this interbranch construction of authority is the role that legal processes and (the absence of) presidential immunity played in the investigation and eventual resignation of President Nixon. With grand jury powers, special prosecutor Leon Jaworski was able to gather the extensive evidence that allowed not just a jury, but the general public and its representatives in Congress to judge the actions of Nixon and assess whether he should be removed from office. In *United States v. Nixon* (1974), as noted above, the Supreme Court facilitated the gathering of this evidence by recognizing that presidential immunity is not absolute (and that general claims of executive privilege must yield to specific needs of judicial process). Jaworski later noted that he thought there was sufficient evidence to indict Nixon for bribery, obstruction of justice, and obstruction of a criminal investigation.[21,22] Jaworski was not confident that, constitutionally, he would be able to prosecute a sitting president, so he decided it was best to give the House Judiciary Committee the evidence collected.[23,24] Jaworski's doubt here helped make the Nixon episode an exemplary case of judicial process operating in tandem with Congress to generate the authority to discipline presidential misconduct.

Another example of the construction of interbranch authority is Donald Trump's first impeachment in 2020. While there was a push among some Democrats to initiate impeachment proceedings against Trump in 2018, the leadership decided to wait for the conclusion of special counsel

Robert Mueller's investigation.[25] Pressure to pursue impeachment proceedings increased after Michal Cohen pleaded guilty to lying to Congress in 2018 and, in his plea deal, appeared to have implicated President Trump. House leadership, like Democratic Representative Adam Schiff, nonetheless argued that impeachment should not be discussed "before we have seen the full body of evidence," referring to the conclusion of Mueller's investigation.[26] And, indeed, the House waited until the report's release, voting to begin its formal impeachment inquiry on October 31, 2019, approximately six months after Mueller released his report to the public.[27]

Beyond gathering facts, the involvement of judicial processes in presidential lawbreaking has another value as well: It highlights presidential lawbreaking as exceptional, which both serves to uphold rule of law norms and invokes the sort of public judgment that, in turn, gives Congress its authority. As Erwin Chemerinsky has noted, courts have repeatedly recognized that government conduct has the power to legitimize and endorse (or not legitimize and endorse) particular values and behavior in establishment clause doctrine, and this insight should be applied to the immunity question.[28] Judicial intervention, including that of the Supreme Court, flagged President Nixon's acts as potentially against the law and constitutionally unacceptable, as did the Mueller Report's investigation of Trump's interactions with Russia and Ukraine. This flagging of presidential acts for the public to judge is arguably more important when those acts are not obviously criminal. Consider, for example, Trump's potential violation of the emoluments clause: Judicial proceedings, and the threat of judicial proceedings, drew public attention to the clause and to scrutiny of Trump's actions. That public scrutiny appears to have motivated Trump to curb at least some of his potentially unethical behavior with, for example, selling the Trump International Hotel in Washington, DC.[29] As has been long recognized in the legal mobilization literature, legal proceedings—even those that are unsuccessful—can play an important role in raising public "consciousness" and acting as "catalysts" for public engagement.[30] In the case of presidential immunity, judicial proceedings may engage the public and prompt Congress to act—or the president to curb their own behavior—even when Congress faces partisan incentives to not discipline presidential behavior, a not uncommon impediment.[31]

A critic here might conclude that my argument for drawing presidential immunity narrowly could, and would, produce a result that, I admit, is not ideal: The Supreme Court might definitively conclude that a sitting president has no immunity. If made authoritatively and with finality, such a decision would foreclose the possibility that Congress and the judiciary could act in concert. At best, the erasure of all immunity might result in something like *Bush v. Gore* (2000), where half the country thinks the Supreme Court has illegitimately meddled in the electoral process, with the decision undermining the judiciary's authority over both the short and long term.

That is a best case scenario, though—a more worrisome, and, arguably, more likely, outcome is a destructive standoff between the judiciary and executive branch. There are good reasons to worry that if legal officials subpoenaed, indicted, or prosecuted a sitting president, that president might ignore the court. A constitutional standoff would undoubtedly damage the legitimacy of the court, and a president's refusal of a judicial order could cause significant damage to the constitutional order as a whole—how much damage is unclear, but the potential risks to the constitutional order are such that avoiding this "constitutional hardball" is arguably in the best interest of the judiciary and the public.[32]

However, the prospect of such "constitutional hardball" is a strong incentive for the court to not demand a president do something that he or she is likely to ignore. Repeatedly over its history, justices of the Supreme Court have shown a keen awareness of the limits of the court's power that Justice Marshall displayed in *Marbury v. Madison* and a similar interest in preserving that power, not undermining it. And given that presidents are likely to ignore a judicial decision that removes them from office, it seems probable that judicial intervention will not result in a final, authoritative, legal resolution. Courts have a myriad of tools at their disposal that allow for more options than either prohibiting a particular use of executive power or enshrining that power into law. Consider, for example, *Ex parte Milligan* (1866), when the Supreme Court chose to wait until the Civil War was over to hear a habeas corpus case; only after the crisis had passed did the court declare a presidential action unconstitutional. Given the flexibility of standing rules and its discretionary docket, the court chooses which cases to hear and when. It can also take a case, issue a limited ruling (or no ruling at all), yet still call public and congressional attention to a potential legal violation.

Of course, there is no guarantee that the court would not resolve a presidential lawbreaking question, and do so with unfortunate results. Sometimes the court does not demonstrate the political acuity modeled by Justice Marshall in *Marbury*, who called out presidential misconduct while avoiding direct confrontation. The risk of judicial settlement of presidential lawbreaking is a risk of a narrow conception of presidential immunity. That said, I do not believe that it is a significant risk, given the judiciary's incentive to preserve its own power and avoid a dangerous standoff with a sitting president. It is certainly not, in my view, a risk so great that it outweighs the values of a narrow conception of presidential immunity. A broad definition of presidential immunity certainly forecloses the possibility of interbranch cooperation in holding a president accountable, while a narrow definition invites cooperation with only a small risk of foreclosure.

A critic might also argue that even if the Supreme Court does not act as imprudently as they arguably did in *Bush v. Gore*, the potential for them to intervene might itself provide Congress with an excuse to avoid fulfilling its obligations to hold a president accountable. In other words, the potential for judicial resolution might encourage congressional inaction, letting Congress defer a potentially hot button or divisive electoral issue to an unelected branch, as Congress is known sometimes to do.[33] Yet this outcome also seems unlikely to me. As noted above, the recent history of judicial procedures against sitting presidents suggests that they draw attention to potential or actual wrongdoing, which in turn increases the pressure on Congress to investigate a president, not decreases the pressure.

Conclusion

The contours of presidential immunity should be narrowly drawn so as to invite judicial intervention that might work in tandem with congressional investigations. Judicial intervention can foster public judgment of the potentially lawbreaking actions of a sitting president, given the judiciary's investigatory capacity and relative neutrality compared to Congress. Yet a narrow conception of presidential immunity does not imply prosecutors or courts should ignore the roles and obligations of the coordinate branches. If courts were to conduct judicial proceedings against a president, courts should act in ways that minimize the costs of distracting and occupying a sitting president's time and energies, as all seem to agree. But most importantly, courts should not settle questions of presidential lawbreaking that would result in the removal of a president from office. When the potential for removal is present, courts should use the many tools available to avoid final settlement of the question. In these cases, so-called "passive-aggressiveness"—exemplified by Justice Marshall's verbal assertions in *Marbury v. Madison*, but avoidance of confrontation in practice—would be an important judicial virtue.[34]

Notes

1. Jonathan Turley, "From Pillar to Post: The Prosecution of American Presidents," *American Criminal Law Review* 37 (2000): 1054.

2. Akhil Reed Amar and Brian C. Kalt, "The Presidential Privilege Against Prosecution," *Nexus: A Journal of Opinion*, Vol. 2 Issue 1 (1997): 11–23.

3. Robert G. Dixon Jr., "Memorandum from Robert G. Dixon, Jr., Assistant Attorney General, Office of Legal Counsel 30," (1973), 29, https://fas.org/irp/agency/doj/olc/092473.pdf (June 11, 2018); Randolph D. Moss, "Memorandum from Randolph D. Moss, Assistant Attorney General, Office of Legal Policy, A Sitting President's Amenability to Indictment and Criminal Prosecution," (2000), https://www.justice.gov/olc/opinion/sitting-president%E2%80%99s-amenability-indictment-and-criminal-prosecution (Accessed February 26, 2024).

4. John Hart Ely, *On Constitutional Ground* (Princeton: Princeton University Press, 1996), 139; Eric M. Freedman, "The Law as King and the King as Law: Is a President Immune from Criminal Prosecution Before Impeachment?" *Hastings Constitutional Law Quarterly*, Vol. 20 (1992): 63; Stephen M. Griffin, "Presidential Immunity from Criminal Process: Amateur Hour at the Department of Justice Independent Counsel After Sunset: New Approaches to a Persistent Problem," *Widener Law Symposium Journal*, Vol. 5 (2000): 64; Brian C. Kalt, *Constitutional Cliffhangers: A Legal Guide for Presidents and Their Enemies* (New Haven: Yale University Press, 2012).

5. Dixon Jr., "Memorandum from Robert G. Dixon, Jr.," 33. Griffin, "Presidential Immunity from Criminal Process," 55.

6. Dixon Jr., "Memorandum from Robert G. Dixon, Jr.," 29. Griffin, "Presidential Immunity from Criminal Process," 54.

7. Keith E. Whittington, "Don't Subpoena Testimony from the President," *Lawfare* Blog, May 4, https://www.lawfareblog.com/dont-subpoena-testimony-president (Accessed February 26, 2024).

8. Jeffrey Toobin, *A Vast Conspiracy: The Real Story of the Sex Scandal That Nearly Brought Down a President* (New York: Random House, 2000); Ken Gormley, *The Death of American Virtue: Clinton vs. Starr* (New York: Crown, 2010).

9. Joel B. Grossman and David A. Yalof, "The 'Public' versus the 'Private' President: Striking a Balance Between Presidential Responsibilities and Immunities," *Presidential Studies Quarterly*, Vol. 28 Issue 4 (1998): 821–31; Brett M. Kavanaugh, "Separation of Powers During the Forty-Fourth Presidency and Beyond," *Minnesota Law Review*, Vol. 93 (1999): 1454–86; Toobin, *A Vast Conspiracy*. Gormley, *The Death of American Virtue.*

10. A common suggestion is that Congress should pass a law giving sitting presidents temporary immunity from civil suits unrelated to official duties. Concerns over statutes of limitations could be addressed by creating special exceptions for sitting presidents.

11. Griffin, "Presidential Immunity from Criminal Process," 66.

12. Akhil Reed Amar and Brian C. Kalt, "The Presidential Privilege Against Prosecution," *Nexus: A Journal of Opinion*, Vol. 2 Issue 1 (1997): 20.

13. Steven G. Calabresi, "Caesarism, Departmentalism, and Professor Paulsen Symposium: United States v. Nixon: Presidential Power and Executive Privilege Twenty-Five Years Later," *Minnesota Law Review*, Vol. 83 (1998): 431.

14. Laurence Tribe and Joshua Matz, *To End a Presidency: The Power of Impeachment* (New York: Basic Books, 2018).

15. Mariah Zeisberg, *War Powers: The Politics of Constitutional Authority* (Princeton: Princeton University Press, 2013).

16. Zeisberg, *War Powers*.

17. Richard A. Posner, *An Affair of State: The Investigation, Impeachment, and Trial of President Clinton* (Cambridge: Harvard University Press, 1999), 128, 119–132.

18. Posner, *Affair of State*.

19. Whittington, "Don't Subpoena Testimony from the President."

20. Id., 394.

21. Leon Jaworski, *The Right and the Power: The Prosecution of Watergate* (Chappaqua, NY: Reader's Digest Press, 1976), 99–100.

22. Griffin "Presidential Immunity from Criminal Process," 59–60.

23. Jaworski, *The Right and the Power*, 99–100.

24. Griffin "Presidential Immunity from Criminal Process," 59–60.

25. Tucker Higgins, "Democrats Are Waiting for a Mueller Report Before Talking About Impeaching Trump, but That Report May Never Come," CNBC, 2018, https://www.cnbc.com/2018/11/12/mueller-report-may-never-come-as-democrats-wait-to-talk-impeachment.html (Accessed February 26, 2024); Whittington. "Don't Subpoena Testimony from the President," 394.

26. "Representative Schiff Discusses Legacy of Senator McCain on CNN State of the Union," CNN, August 26, 2018, https://schiff.house.gov/view/2018/08/26/rep-schiff-discusses-legacy-of-senator-mccain-on-cnn-state-of-the-union (Accessed February 26, 2024).

27. Nicholas Fandos and Sheryl Gay Stolberg, "A Divided House Endorses Impeachment Inquiry into Trump," *TheNew York Times*, October 31, 2019.

28. Erwin Chemerinsky, "Justice Delayed Is Justice Denied," *Nexus: A Journal of Opinion*, Vol. 2 (1997): 26–28.

29. Craig Karmin, "Trump's Sale of D.C. Hotel Proved Prescient as New Owner Defaults on Loan," *The Wall Street Journal*, February 25, 2024.

30. Michael McCann, *Rights at Work: Pay Equity Reform and the Politics of Legal Mobilization* (Chicago: University of Chicago Press, 1994).

31. Daryl J. Levinson and Richard H. Pildes, "Separation of Parties, Not Powers," *Harvard Law Review*, Vol. 119 Issue 8 (2006): 2311–86.

32. Whittington, "Don't Subpoena Testimony from the President."

33. Mark A. Graber, "The Nonmajoritarian Difficulty: Legislative Deference to the Judiciary," *Studies in American Political Development*, Vol. 7 Issue 1 (1993): 35–73.

34. Whittington, "Don't Subpoena Testimony from the President."

CHAPTER 13

Yet Another Rogue President? Assessing Presidential Approaches to the Separation of Powers Using James Madison's *Federalist*

David J. Siemers

In writing that "ambition must be made to counteract ambition," James Madison was adapting a familiar idea.[1] Niccolo Machiavelli's initial, and thus arguably his most central, commentary in *The Discourses* was that the public quarrels between the people of Rome and its nobles were the key to the Roman republic's political success (I.3 and I.4). These fights created stable institutions, were the precursor to the republic's best laws, and preserved public liberty. In the 270 years between the writing of *The Discourses* and *Federalist* No. 51, other political theorists—including James Harrington, John Locke, Baron de Montesquieu, and Jean Louis de Lolme—had emphasized the benefits of the separation of government powers. It fell to Madison to reintroduce the idea that this separation would inevitably yield institutional rivalries in the hands of actual political actors, that these rivalries would play out in the public sphere, and that this clash would yield positive results.

Unlike his political theorist predecessors, Madison embraced what he considered to be true republican politics—all of the institutions of government were to represent the people. Thus, Madison's vision for institutional rivalries had a stark advantage over Machiavelli's: The institutions doing public battle would not, in the end, represent incompatible interests, but the same set of interests. There would also be a written constitution—words that were not infallible but would point the way toward determining which institution legitimately did what. Political officers would be empowered to defend the prerogatives of their home institution. In this way ambition could serve the purpose of stabilizing the constitutional order, creating a polity where power would not substantially migrate between branches.

In one critical way Machiavelli had gone beyond what James Madison was willing to venture in *Federalist* No. 51. Machiavelli observed that most who commented on Roman politics "condemn[ed] the quarrels between the nobles and the plebs" and "cavill[ed] at the very things that were the primary cause of Rome's retaining her freedom."[2] Most people could not stomach the fights that yielded Rome's political successes. Nor did most even realize that a rivalry they found partly nauseating and partly terrifying was actually the thing that produced so much political good.

In writing that ambition would counteract ambition, Madison more gently suggested that there would be substantial and serious interinstitutional disputes within the new national government. He did not explicitly warn his audience that these disputes would often make national politics seem profoundly disconcerting, a venue for distasteful, interested fights rather than a stage featuring harmonious cooperation. Admitting this would have been at odds with Publius's mission of promoting the new Constitution by softening the potentially hard edges of the new regime.

The United States is now in its seventh straight decade (and probably longer) of profound disagreement over the role of the president. Vietnam and Watergate spurred concerns about an imperial presidency. In the 1980s, Iran-Contra featured a secret foreign policy, run parallel to the formal bureaucratic apparatus, at odds with congressional enactments. Bill Clinton was impeached for lying about his affair with a White House intern. The aggressive presidentialism of George W. Bush sparked significant backlash among politicians, scholars, and the public. In making substantial administrative adjustments to laws without Congress, Barack Obama and Joe Biden were frequently accused of "executive overreach." Donald Trump undermined many longstanding norms and was impeached twice. Acrimonious charges abound. Neighbors and family members avoid political subjects. Talk of rogue presidential behavior is frequent and often accompanied by talk of constitutional crisis.

Inspired by James Madison, a real politician steeped in the actual practice of politics, a more measured view is in order. Meaningful standards of presidential behavior may be developed that distinguish acceptable adversarial tactics and approaches from those that are problematic and out of bounds. This chapter bases those standards of constitutional behavior on Madison's separation of powers essays in *The Federalist*. If ambition is supposed to counteract ambition, constitutional health cannot be measured by the level of interinstitutional harmony. Agreement and easy compromises may be more pleasant than rivalries for power, and these occur, but they are also not a fair baseline expectation. Nor is constitutional disagreement inevitably a sign of ill constitutional health. In *Federalist* No. 37 Madison stressed that the functional boundaries between the branches were far from perfectly clear.[3] He knew from his own experience in politics that institutional disputes would arise for all sorts of reasons, innocent and otherwise. Madison's separation of powers essays indicate that there are realistic and meaningful markers of constitutional health available, related to political process, public opinion, the resolution of individual disputes, and their cumulative results. Presidents expected to jealously guard the prerogatives of their office will be involved in constitutional scrapes with the other branches. Their behavior should be judged by their comportment within these scrapes, not the bare fact of their existence.

I then use the metrics culled from Madison's *Federalist* essays to assess the presidencies of George W. Bush, Barack Obama, and Donald Trump. Each can be found at least somewhat wanting by these standards, but the constitutional errors of each president are distinctive and teach us different lessons. A president cannot possibly do the job without taking sides on controversial constitutional questions. The president *should* be doing this, as it is their job to guard the prerogatives of the presidency while simultaneously preserving, protecting, and defending the whole constitutional order. These two expectations may rest uneasily against each other, and the obligation to pursue both simultaneously offers a substantial challenge to the modern president. Yet the simultaneous and successful pursuit of both of these standards defines whether a president is doing the job well. Madison's expectations suggest nuanced and realistic standards of judgment for the "constitutional presidency," against which the discerning public may judge all presidents.

Ambition Without Encroachment

Federalist No. 51 is renowned for good reason. It presents Publius's solution to the separation of powers problems that were the subject of the previous essays. The first sentence clearly signals this quality of summation and payoff, promising to divulge the "expedient . . . for maintaining in practice the necessary partition of power among the several departments, as laid down in the Constitution."[4] The character of this solution is also memorable. The passage beginning "if men were angels, no government would be necessary" is as pithy and rich an explanation of government and its goals as there is in American political thought. To make "ambition . . . counteract ambition," having the occupants of each branch jealously guard their own powers, is the now familiar answer set forth in this crucial essay.[5]

By contrast, it is easy to look past essays 47 through 50. The first of these ambles through now disused constitutional practices of eleven states. The second agrees with Thomas Jefferson's seemingly antiquated view from *Notes on the State of Virginia* that legislatures offer the greatest danger of constitutional infidelity of any branch. The last two essays consider and then reject Jefferson's ideas that have long been dismissed as impractical. *Federalist* No. 49 critiques his suggestion that any time two of the three branches believe the remaining branch has acted outside of its constitutional bounds there should be a constitutional convention. *Federalist* No. 50 rejects the view that a convention should be called to periodically reconsider the Constitution wholesale.

Yet these four preliminary essays should not be treated lightly. They quietly offer standards for judging constitutional health in this novel new regime, primarily by noting what situations and practices should be avoided. Like any other kind of learning, we can gain constitutional insight from negative examples just as easily as we can from positive ones. In the system of ambition counteracting ambition we know presidents will be partisans of their own branch. The actions and choices they make in fighting for their institutional place affects the nation's constitutional health. Though it may not encompass all the standards for constitutional behavior we would endorse today, Madison's thinking offers valuable guidance regarding constitutional norms. They can be applied to the presidency in such a way that we can formulate expectations about how presidents should act in their constitutional disputes.

Madison's primary concern in these five separation of powers essays is to maintain a basic stability in the separation of powers. Each branch should retain the ability to perform its designated constitutional function free from excessive interference by the other branches. Connecting "the interest of the man . . . to the constitutional rights of the place" is a realist's vision of how to pursue this goal.[6] *Federalist* No. 51 explains that if each branch is able to fight for its governing prerogatives and endowed with the necessary independence to hold firm in doing so, a rough constitutional equilibrium may be maintained. The observations of *Federalist* Nos. 47 through 50 extend this realist vision. They do so by meditating on interbranch relations, the public's relationship to constitutions, and how political institutions operate.

Madison is obscure about how interbranch controversies will be resolved. Clearly he intends such disputes not to be intractable and for each branch to fight for its own powers. Nevertheless, *Federalist* No. 49 offers a critical observation that may be taken as a ground rule for the resolution of constitutional disputes. Madison states that "the several departments" are "perfectly coordinate by the terms of their common commission." In other words, the legitimacy or standing of each branch is equal. As a result, none has "an exclusive or superior right of settling the boundaries between their respective powers."[7] Implied in this statement is an expectation of interbranch respect. The branches can be seriously at odds, they can fight for their own prerogatives, and they can step into contested constitutional space, but no branch can deny that the other branches also occupy legitimate constitutional space and that all three properly exercise critical functions of government.

A baseline presumption in the Madisonian separation of powers system is that the president will offer wide latitude to decisions made by the other branches acting within their constitutional purview. Of course constitutional controversies arise when one branch cannot agree that the work of others is authorized or correct. A dispute does not obviate the requirement of jurisdictional recognition, however. Thus, an important first expectation for presidents is to respect the constitutional roles of the legislative and judicial branches, even when at odds with one or both of them for some reason. Moving forward to a resolution requires each branch, the president included, to offer reasoning why its position is correct. Proper respect for branches coequally empowered to do their respective work requires the president to explain himself or herself. This explanation should occur within a housing that explicitly recognizes the legitimacy of the other branches.

Constitutional disputes are played out in public. They are often won in the court of public opinion. Madison was particularly sensitive to the effect that constitutional disputes would have on public opinion. His rejection of Jefferson's proposed methods of resolving constitutional disputes makes this abundantly clear. Jefferson believed that if the branches could not work things out on their own, there should be public mechanisms of conflict resolution built into a constitution. He suggested that when the branches were at odds, the people should make a final decision through representatives selected to a convention. Madison granted that allowing the public the final say in constitutional disputes made sense in theory; however, this potential advantage would be outweighed by insurmountable practical problems.[8]

Madison's counterargument is centered around the observation that constitutional disputes are part and parcel of ongoing politics. Any individual convention attendee who was called on to decide a constitutional dispute would likely already have a position on and stake in the outcome. Madison cites the example of Pennsylvania, which five years earlier had attempted to resolve its interbranch controversies by using a Council of Censors. The council was predictably "split into two fixed and violent parties," just like the state itself.[9] Unsurprisingly, the division over constitutional questions mirrored the participants' own partisan views. In practice, preexisting views would deeply compromise any objective assessment of the situation, prevent a reasoned determination on the merits, and run the risk "of disturbing the public tranquility by interesting too strongly the public passions."[10] Instead of constitutional arguments being contained within and resolved by government institutions, a highly divisive public debate would be spawned. Three times in the course of two essays (Nos. 49 and 50) Madison warns of reason giving way to passion in the determination of constitutional principles if these matters were referred to the public.[11] Repeatedly going through this process would keep public opinion raw and unsettled, even about the Constitution itself.

Continually referring items to the public through a constitutional convention would "deprive the government of that veneration which time bestows on every thing, and without which perhaps the wisest and freest governments would not possess the requisite stability."[12] The frequent need for public decisions on matters of dispute would openly signal to the public that the Constitution is flawed. If constitutional disputes would *not* be referred to the public, some might privately think that the Constitution is flawed, but they would not loudly complain about it to their fellow citizens. Nor would they act on that idea. If constitutional controversies became the stuff of frequent open debate and public decision, then citizens would likely become distrustful of the Constitution and seek to undermine or replace it. Jefferson's proposed constitutional remedies would threaten the very peace and stability that good government must provide.

Applying these observations to presidents, an expectation for a responsible executive would be to not substantially inflame public passion over a constitutional dispute. The president also has a responsibility not to degrade public esteem for the Constitution itself. An awful scenario for Madison would be a president who would prompt public riots or disturbances centered around constitutional disputes. Each president must realize that the government's institutions themselves must resolve constitutional disputes. There must be an openness to resolution, with the president contributing to but not dictating outcomes and not precluding or dictating outcomes by inflaming public passions.

It would be easy to dismiss Madison's analysis that legislatures are greatly advantaged in constitutional disputes. Today Congress often seems to need prodding to do much of its designated work. But his thinking about why legislatures may be empowered offers a warning that is still worth heeding: Built-in, consistent advantages for any branch threaten to unspool the intended separation of functions arrangement set up in the Constitution.

Madison was right to fear a situation where one branch would be consistently advantaged in constitutional disputes, because it would offer a path to reengineering the Constitution's separation of powers. From the perspective of the early twenty-first century, it often appears that the executive is a consistently advantaged branch. This is no matter of wonder. The public sees, hears, and typically identifies more with a president than with Congress.[13] In this way, the mechanism that Madison believed would advantage Congress—frequent contact and close public identification—today favors the president. The president's ability to go public, along with the office's advantages of dispatch and decisiveness have allowed presidents to stretch the boundaries of presidential activity.

Wide-ranging executive orders, aggressive rule-making, and preferring executive agreements to treaties are just some of the ways that presidential power has been extended in modern times.[14] The national security state developed after World War II also advantages presidents.[15] So does congressional quiescence about declarations of war, trade, and many other matters. Avoiding congressional aggrandizement of power is not the primary constitutional challenge in the current environment. The challenge is for presidents to act as institutional partisans without producing substantial, constitutionally dubious long-term increases in presidential power.

The foregoing warnings can be readily stated as criteria for judging institutional actors. They are particularly important to apply to presidents, because presidents are the most suspect constitutional actors of our time. Here is how Madison might have us judge a chief executive's approach to constitutional disputes:

(1) Process: Has the president fought fairly, acknowledging the legitimate function and space of the other branches? Has the constitutional reasoning of the president been well laid out; is it plausibly and defensibly within the recognized function of the office?

(2) Public Response: Has the president's approach to constitutional disputes substantially heightened public passions on these matters? Has it degraded public esteem for the Constitution? Have there been any disturbances of "the public tranquility" as a result?

(3) Resolutions: Has the president's approach to constitutional controversies allowed or hindered the effective resolution of constitutional disputes? Have controversies been resolved effectively by the three branches within the constitutional system, with the president contributing to, but not dictating, the shape of that resolution?

(4) Outcome: Has the president presided over a significant and suspect movement in or expansion of the constitutional powers of the office? Has the presidency consistently prevailed in constitutional disputes with the other branches?

These ideas about what to seek and what to avoid in constitutional disputes are not exhaustive. And these presumptions about how to judge a president's constitutional approach are surely not beyond question. Yet they have the virtue of recognizing that all institutional actors, the president included, will be drawn into constitutional disputes. This is to be expected in the Madisonian republic. Presidents do not deserve blame simply for being in constitutional disputes. Madison's thinking prompts a more nuanced analysis, centered around how a president should properly approach constitutional controversies.

George W. Bush's Unitary Aspirations and Multilateral Results

George W. Bush came to the presidency intimately familiar with how the executive branch worked under two recent presidents, as well as access to those who had served in the last four Republican administrations. From this experience he developed the conviction that the presidency had been problematically constrained after Watergate, and that the measure of an effective president in his time would be to reestablish the constitutional powers of the presidency. As Julian Zelizer notes, "Bush would spend an enormous amount of political energy, before and after 9/11, trying to vest more power in his office."[16]

A critical part of this effort was to assert executive independence in perceived areas of presidential power. Bush often asserted unilateral prerogatives, exercises of power that he claimed could not be constrained or influenced by other institutional actors. He touted an aggressive version of the "unitary theory" of the executive: that the president alone has the authority to direct the bureaucracy.[17] This unilateralist tinge often fit uneasily with the authority-sharing arrangements set into the Constitution, particularly in the realm of Bush's direction of the war on terror. The president also believed that he would have to play hardball with other institutional actors to achieve his objective. His aggressive approach to the office prompted a great deal of pushback from Congress, the federal judiciary, and the public, as well as among the scholarly community. Yet through his rhetoric Bush simultaneously acknowledged the legitimate constitutional space occupied by the other branches. Despite taking many questionable positions, the Bush presidency also focused attention on an effective separation of powers regimen.

The 43rd presidency was born in constitutional controversy with the disputed Florida election. Bush let intermediaries argue for him in court and was not himself responsible for heightening the attendant constitutional controversy.[18] Most serious constitutional contests during the Bush presidency arose from the war on terror. Bush argued that he possessed "complete discretion in the exercise of his Commander-in-Chief authority and in conducting operations against hostile forces."[19] The administration afforded captured enemy combatants neither the protections of soldiers under international law nor the due process safeguards available to those being tried in court. He justified warrantless domestic surveillance on the basis of his guardianship of national security, ignoring existing law on the matter. He resisted perceived encroachments on the presidency by issuing hundreds of signing statements that declared parts of laws unconstitutional and not to be enforced because they infringed on his sole power to direct the bureaucracy.[20]

Process: Rhetorically, Bush frequently acknowledged the realities of proper constitutional process in the United States. In an "exit interview" with Fox News' Brit Hume, for instance, Bush noted that many of the decisions he made were adjudicated in federal court and, "of course, I have lived by, and future presidents will live by, the decisions of the Supreme Court."[21] These public acknowledgments should not be taken lightly—they were moments that the nation's "teacher in chief" took American citizens to class in ways that reinforced the Constitution's status as supreme law and power-sharing arrangements between institutions as an important norm.

At the same time, his rhetorical allegiance was accompanied by troubling tendencies that partially undermined these stated commitments. In the same interview, Bush stated that he "used the powers inherent in the Constitution to defend this country."[22] To scholars, "inherent powers" mean those not spelled out in the Constitution but implied by its logic or the logic of constitutionalism itself. It is not entirely clear that Bush intended this meaning, but given his administration's stance on national security and his claims to direct the bureaucracy alone, this sense of the term fits. Such interpolations were inevitably more controversial and more contestable than the exercise of powers that are directly stated in the words of the Constitution.

During many occasions these inherent powers were used to assert that presidential control could not be legitimately contested by either Congress or the Supreme Court. The actions Bush took regarding detainee treatment offer a good example. Bush created a new category of prisoner in enemy combatants to avoid standards of treatment set into treaties and domestic laws. In the wake of revelations about very rough interrogations that many thought amounted to torture, Congress required the use of the Army field manual's standards for questioning captured combatants in late 2005. Bush objected, and essentially cancelled this legal requirement in a signing statement, saying that it violated the president's prerogative to supervise government employees.[23] This and other signing statements gave the president what the founders had rejected: "a unitary power to say what the law is," effectively ignoring the take care clause.[24] His execution of policy frequently did more than offer an interpretation of what the law meant; it altered congressional intent. This is at odds with traditional expectations of constitutional process and a plain reading of the take care clause.

Public Response: There is no doubt that the Bush presidency produced strong public responses. But the concern prompted by Madison's writings is more specific: Did the president's constitutional approach provoke potentially damaging public responses? The statements that Bush used to recognize and pay homage to checks and balances served to bolster the Constitution's position rather than undermine it. Furthermore, many of the stretches and potential violations of constitutional norms that Bush presided over were technical in nature. There is nothing inherently problematic about signing statements or executive orders. Whether one is constitutional or not requires analysis of its specific provisions and a corresponding reasoned judgment. The constitutional controversies of the Bush years were often fought through complex arguments from constitutional lawyers about what makes something within the purview of Congress, the president, or both. As a result, much of the constitutional approach of the Bush administration was beyond the public's attention or comprehension, blunting the impact of potential constitutional violations.

The overlay of party politics inevitably meant frequent and pointed critiques of the president's constitutional approach. Additionally, the existence of a strongly negative response from the scholarly community gave credence to fears that Bush was undermining the Constitution.[25] News reports frequently contained expert testimony that the Bush strategy's insistence on unilateral power "was a mistake both legally and politically."[26] On one hand, this could be viewed as alarming. Many of President Bush's critics raised fears that constitutional boundaries were being transgressed. And yet this is also the kind of public dialogue, the push and pull, that is to be expected in a Madisonian system. Party identifiers on both sides believed that their position was constitutional; they defended their position and engaged in a time-honored tradition of accusing their opponents of having faulty constitutional views. There is no doubt that this was divisive. But the discussion was effectively contained within political bounds. There were no riots about constitutional interpretation and both sides explicitly claimed to be supporting the Constitution, reinforcing its position as higher law.

Resolutions: There is no single formula for the resolution of constitutional disputes. This indeterminacy is part of what produces the disputes in the first place and it is what can make them intractable. Bush relied heavily on executive secrecy, a lack of judicial standing by potential plaintiffs, his nominal control over the bureaucracy, congressional disorganization, and the initial public enthusiasm for the war on terror to have his way in constitutional disputes. How the administration approached domestic information gathering illustrates these tendencies well. Prior law about how to conduct domestic intelligence searches was in place, but the Bush administration chose to ignore it.[27] Bush reasoned that the Foreign Intelligence Surveillance Act's requirements were out of date and not applicable to an executive charged with keeping Americans safe and in command of vast technological capabilities. The press eventually reported this as whistleblowers emerged. These revelations did not stop the surveillance. Nor were administration actions extensively litigated in federal court. Much of the public reasoned that this activity was necessary in an age of terrorism. Those who objected possessed relatively little information about what was being done and could point to no concrete personal harm, hindering their campaign to restrain the president via legislation or lawsuits.

In many instances President Bush did more than contribute to the resolution of constitutional disputes; he dictated preferred resolutions. The nature of the executive office enabled this outcome, with its relatively quick and decisive decision-making and direct authority over a vast bureaucracy. Signing statements were elevated into a means of thwarting Congress's will. In the words of Sievert and Ostrander, Bush's signing statements "imply that the executive branch will selectively enforce statutes," a precedent at odds with faithful execution.[28] There were many exceptions to executive-focused resolutions, however. Supreme Court decisions ruled that detainees in the war on terror have a right to challenge their incarceration in court, for instance. The administration responded by asking Congress to create law to validate military commissions, which it did. Such resolutions involved significant input from each branch and were highly amenable to the character of the American constitutional order.

Outcome: There is an ongoing debate about whether President Bush succeeded in expanding presidential power.[29] He did act in new, bold, and precedent-setting ways. But in the end, the substantial public protest and interbranch wrangling this prompted impeded Bush's goal. In the words of his own former White House counsel, Brent Berenson, "the hope for revivifying presidential power ended up foundering on some of the war on terror–related policies that Congress and the public ultimately perceived as too pro-executive or too unilateral."[30] Bush generally would have been more successful and his policy positions considered more legitimate had he consistently sought support from Congress through law.[31] Even though Bush pushed, and in some instances broke, the bounds of what is considered constitutional, his presidency also underscored the strength of the Madisonian system of checks and balances. In the end, the Bush presidency was more of a qualified victory for Madison's constitutional vision than a failure of it.

Barack Obama's Attenuated Reconstitutionalization

Barack Obama's success in the presidential campaign of 2008 came in no small measure from running against George W. Bush's work as president. Campaign crowds embraced Obama's critique of the incumbent's approach to the office and his promise to "reconstitutionalize" the presidency. As a teacher of constitutional law, Obama was well positioned to make credible arguments about the Bush administration's truncated respect for the separation of powers. He pledged to protect Americans from terrorism without compromising their rights, to respect the constitutional prerogatives of the other branches, and to hew faithfully to the rule of law.[32] This was both good politics and a signal of interest in establishing a less contentious separation of powers relationship. And yet it did not prepare the public to understand that separation of powers disputes are inevitable and will be sharply fought. Obama's wish and instinct was to play to the public's wish for greater harmony, the stance that Machiavelli found to be common, but mistaken.

Despite significant successes, Obama would also find his constitutional promises difficult to fulfill. The complexity of modern policy combined with six years of divided government prompted a felt need for a number of controversial unilateral executive adjustments to laws. Despite his general preference for constitutional fidelity, strong political cross-pressures developed regarding gay marriage and immigration that led President Obama to act when Congress would not in ways that tested the boundaries of what is constitutionally acceptable.[33] He also possessed an expansive view of the president's national security power that was employed to continue and extend Bush-era initiatives that many found troubling.[34] These factors combined to yield a presidency that, though more sensitive to separation of powers dilemmas, fell short of the high expectations that Obama himself had set for a much more cooperative era in the separation of powers.

Much of the constitutional controversy that dogged Obama came in the form of policy implementation choices deemed not faithful execution by his critics. Obama unilaterally adjusted the landmark Patient Protection and Affordable Care Act (ACA), for instance, postponing its mandates and ordering the creation of health care exchanges in states that refused to organize them after the *National Federation of Independent Businesses v. Sebelius* (2012) decision. In June 2012 Obama declared that noncitizens brought to the United States as children could register for work permits; barring serious legal offenses they would not face deportation (Delayed Action for Childhood Arrivals, or DACA). As the nation became more comfortable with same-sex marriage the administration openly questioned the Clinton-era Defense of Marriage Act (DOMA). In general, Obama did not actively court separation of powers controversies with an eye to expanding presidential control. Rather, he backed into these controversies. They resulted from practical exigencies of administrating complex laws and from the pursuit of political commitments that would potentially compromise constitutional responsibilities.

Barack Obama did use unilateral presidential tools as well, however. Having promised not to use signing statements to adjust policies or to cancel parts of laws, he did just that in a number of cases.[35] Several major international pacts, including the Paris Climate Accord and the Iran Nuclear Agreement, were designated executive agreements rather than treaties in order to bypass the need for Senate approval. US forces continued their involvement across the globe in the war on terror, with a new level of commitment in Yemen. Obama committed US forces to action in Libya without congressional authorization. The president oversaw a still-active domestic surveillance regimen. Attuned to process, well versed in American constitutionalism, and with a seemingly genuine interest in preserving separation of powers standards, Obama's tenure raises the question of how faithful any contemporary president can be to traditional constitutional expectations.

Process: In most cases, Obama showed significant sensitivity to separation of powers norms. For example, the administration took a nuanced and, for some, frustrating approach to DOMA. In 2011 Obama ordered the Justice Department to continue the enforcement of this law, but it announced that the administration would not defend its constitutionality in federal court. This move fulfilled the president's duty to execute the laws faithfully. It simultaneously recognized the importance of Congress's will and acknowledged that the Supreme Court would likely be the final arbiter of constitutionality on this matter.[36] Obama also frequently recognized the importance of separation of powers norms in his rhetoric. In *The Audacity of Hope* he described the interplay of ideas among the branches as the means by which the American polity progresses, for instance.[37]

In a number of cases Obama implemented high-profile, meaningful changes to policy unilaterally. The ACA health exchanges built by the federal government and the delayed implementation of its individual and business mandates are examples. These administrative choices were vindicated as permissible adjustments to the program in federal court.[38] However, these were significant changes to policy that ideally would have been accomplished through legislation. In the absence of congressional action on state exchanges, the administration's efforts were required to successfully implement Congress's enactment. Delays in the implementation dates of the mandates sprang from more questionable motives. Yet such delays had long been considered a matter of presidential discretion. In 2020 the Supreme Court found the Trump administration's cancellation of DACA to be "arbitrary and capricious" without passing judgment on the constitutionality of the program itself.[39] This was a fitting result, in that it suggests that Obama's approach to administration was quite a bit closer to accepted constitutional norms than was that of his successor. Certain of Obama's actions tested the boundaries of discretionary executive authority, but he offered serious constitutional arguments to defend them and they tended not to be stated in unilateralist terms.

Of greater concern was the inability of the Obama administration to stay away from signing statements that were vague and dismissive of law.[40] President Obama did use the modern administrative state aggressively at times, but he rarely truncated constitutional processes to insist that he was the ultimate decider, and most of the procedural controversies he faced were created by conundrums in modern governance rather than a core belief in aggressive presidentialism at odds with the Constitution's intent.

Public Response: Obama's constitutional critique of Bush continued after the 2008 election. This did little to help usher in a postpartisan era, but it did reinforce the importance of constitutional standards and put the public in mind of what those standards should be. Yet this stance inevitably produced a backlash. When Obama became involved in constitutional disputes, as he inevitably would be, he was readily charged with hypocrisy by opponents. His rhetoric also offered them an incentive to maneuver Obama into constitutional dilemmas. In several cases, including with the ACA exchanges, all congressional Republicans had to do to was sit on their hands to force the president to act unilaterally. The predictable narrative played out along partisan lines: The president was engaged in "executive overreach." Obama was sued in federal court by House Republicans for violating the "take care" clause over the unilateral adjustments to ACA. This could have developed into an interesting challenge to the administrative latitude granted to recent presidents, but Republicans pulled the suit when they feared that it might affect Donald Trump.[41] Undoubtedly, the maneuvering on both sides left the public confused about the boundaries of presidential discretion.

Tired of a recalcitrant Congress not legislating on significant issues like unemployment benefits, immigration, and gun control, Obama shifted tone in early 2014. In remarks before a Cabinet meeting he said that while he would be happy to work with members of Congress, "I've got a pen . . . and I can use that pen to sign executive orders and take executive actions and administrative actions that move the ball forward."[42] He would use this phrase several times, underscoring his ability to effect change unilaterally. Though Obama also frequently spoke about his respect for the authority of the other branches, this later message could easily be mistaken for the idea that if Congress does not produce legislation, the president can produce similar results unilaterally. As with the previous administration, there were passionate public disagreements about the constitutional status of several Obama initiatives. This did not lead either side to question the Constitution's efficacy. Despite significant rhetorical heat, these disputes also did not disturb "public tranquility."

Resolutions: The Obama administration rarely short-circuited the interplay between the branches in domestic constitutional disputes. Typically, it waited for congressional enactments, took unilateral administrative actions when Congress refused to act, awaited its day in court regarding those administrative adjustments, and abided by the results. In novel situations it defended presidential prerogatives, acting as a Madisonian executive is expected to. For example, after Republicans regained majority control of the Senate in 2011, the body went into brief, one-person pro forma sessions to prevent Obama from making recess appointments. The president continued to make recess appointments, but was taken to court by a Pepsi distributor objecting to one such appointee who had enforced a collective bargaining agreement the distributor disliked. A unanimous Supreme Court sided with the Senate—the chamber itself would determine whether it was in session.[43] The Obama administration sometimes lost in federal court, even as it tallied other substantial separation of powers wins, a mixed record indicative of constitutional health.[44]

Obama's record in relations to foreign affairs is more checkered. He failed to close the Guantanamo Bay detention facility, leaving the few prisoners that remained in constitutional limbo. The administration relied on the 2001 Authorization for Use of Military Force (AUMF) to engage al Qaeda and ISIS, expanding hostilities in Yemen and Syria. This prompted questions about whether AUMF was a long-term, blanket authorization for unilateral military decisions by the president. In committing forces to Libya the Obama administration argued the novel position that hostilities there did not rise to the level of a war, requiring no congressional authorization. Chastened by criticism over this position, the president subsequently asked Congress to authorize use of force in Syria, which he ultimately declined to use when he opted not to escalate American involvement in the Syrian civil war.[45]

Outcome: President Obama did not preside over a significant extension of presidential power. The "new imperial presidency" hardly became *more* imperial during his eight years in office. At the same time, Obama did institutionalize some of the unilateral instruments that Bush had pioneered, especially in the area of national security. The familiar executive advantages of dispatch, control over the bureaucracy, and secrecy enabled Obama's choices on these matters, just as they had Bush's. But "at least with regard to war initiation, the Obama presidency need not be regarded as materially enhancing the president's constitutional powers."[46]

Most domestic constitutional controversies of the Obama years consisted of administrative adjustments to programs well within accepted norms of practice. Yet these adjustments also point to the tenuous constitutional character of the modern administrative state. Recent presidents routinely alter laws and create policies that are the equivalent of law in scope and reach. Events and political pressures propelled Barack Obama into constitutional gray spaces. In the long run, this kind of politics may erode public support for separation of powers norms, with the president's opponents routinely emphasizing failures of constitutional stewardship while proponents happily push for the extension of unilateral presidential power that achieves programmatic results.

Donald Trump's Own Personal Constitution

As a candidate, Donald Trump seemed to have had a tenuous knowledge of the Constitution, yet he also employed the Constitution to positive effect. In a closed-door meeting with Republican lawmakers in the summer of 2016 intended to relieve doubts about his candidacy, Trump was asked about Article I. This gave the Republican nominee an opportunity to demonstrate respect for Congress, and perhaps even show his knowledge of ongoing efforts there to reinvigorate its role as "the first branch."[47] Trump raised concerns when he reportedly replied, "Not only will I stand up for Article I, I'll stand up for Article II, Article XII, you name it of the Constitution."[48] Besides his error about the number of articles, Trump's statement seemed flippant. But the candidate did publicly issue a list of potential Supreme Court nominees whom he touted as faithful to the Constitution. He characterized DACA as unconstitutional, both in its unilateral formulation and in the amnesty that it gave to noncitizens. He also stated that the country would be thrown into a constitutional crisis if Hillary Clinton were to be elected, due to her cavalier approach to safeguarding classified information. These positions, Constitution-favoring at least on their face, garnered votes.

As president, Trump still seemed to have a tenuous grasp of the Constitution. He expressed interest in having the kind of latitude enjoyed by the globe's most authoritarian leaders and at times suggested that he possessed such powers. To a Turning Point USA youth group Trump remarked, "I have an Article II, where I have the right to do whatever I want as president."[49] While this could be merely an inelegant tautology—an assertion that as president he wields the powers of the president as they are laid out in Article II—given his actions and other statements it was more likely a broad, even an unlimited, assertion of presidential power. The other branches and the bureaucracy continued their work during these years, providing significant constitutional restraint. Yet the Madisonian system sagged under the weight of a president who frequently failed to recognize constitutional boundaries and displayed limited respect for the other branches.

Despite his lack of constitutional awareness, much of Trump's work as president occurred within constitutional bounds. Congress having ceded "fast track authority" to presidents on trade, President Trump was well within his rights to renegotiate NAFTA. Similarly, he could withdraw the United States from the nearly completed Trans-Pacific Partnership agreement, unilaterally remove the nation from the Iran Nuclear Agreement, and begin the process of extracting the United States from the Paris Climate Accord. These agreements had been entered into unilaterally by President Obama, and President Trump could unilaterally reverse course. He used executive orders to cancel Obama-era regulations on water quality and fuel efficiency. Though contrary to a long tradition of presidential decorum, Donald Trump's tweets denigrating his detractors typically did not raise constitutional concerns.

Yet alongside these actions were myriad constitutional controversies.[50] The president's initial efforts to ban travel from several nations with predominantly Muslim populations ran afoul of the First Amendment prohibition on religious discrimination. Trump invoked the Emergency Powers Act to divert the funds needed to build the border wall that Congress chose not to fund. Faced with investigations into his finances, he issued a blanket refusal to divulge this information to Congress and to prosecutors. Investigations into his ties with Russia and Ukraine prompted numerous incidents of possible obstruction of justice. Withholding congressionally authorized aid to Ukraine in exchange for a public investigation of Joe Biden designed to aid Trump's reelection raised a number of constitutional concerns. As the owner of resort and hotel properties, Trump's holdings tested the emoluments clauses. President Trump sometimes did use his words to pay homage to the Constitution, but he also denigrated constitutional norms and dismissed constitutional procedures employed by his opponents as illegitimate.

Process: The Trump administration's pursuit of its policy goals was significantly hindered by a lack of expertise. The Supreme Court eventually vindicated the president's restrictive immigration policy toward several predominantly Muslim countries, but the road to that decision was littered with adverse decisions that could have been avoided.[51] Greater constitutional knowledge could have produced a workable, legal policy that substantially accomplished the president's goals from the beginning. In general, presidents find federal courts to be a helpful partner in governance.[52] Even when they oppose the president, courts can be a beneficial foil: Their decisions can be used to deflect blame while displaying deference to separation of powers norms. By contrast, President Trump suggested that adverse court decisions were "disgraceful" and were rendered out of partisan or personal animus.[53] This approach fails to fully acknowledge the legitimate function of a branch equally entitled to do its work.

Presidential obstruction of justice during the government investigation into the Trump campaign's ties with Russia was a central subject of the Mueller Report.[54] A lack of established law and the awkwardness of pursuing a legal case against a sitting president left this matter a constitutional quandary. What it did suggest was a weak presidential commitment to faithful execution. Strikingly similar charges were leveled against Trump in the later attempt to have Ukraine find discrediting information on his rival Joe Biden, which resulted in impeachment proceedings. The administration took a categorical stance against administration figures testifying before Congress, though some chose to, and refused to release information to House investigators with subpoena power.[55]

The way Donald Trump used emergency power delegated to the president under the National Emergencies Act was novel: diverting funds from military projects, effectively overruling Congress's decision not to build hundreds of miles of secure border wall. Trump was also dismissive of constitutional rules regarding constitutional process. He suggested that members of Congress investigating him should be arrested, which would be a clear violation of the speech and debate clause.[56] He asserted that impeachment was illegitimate because it would overturn the results of an election, a claim that puts the authors of the Constitution at odds with themselves.[57] He repeatedly averred that he might serve longer than the two-term limit imposed by the Twenty-Second Amendment.[58] He called the emoluments clause "phony."[59] In this and in other matters, President Trump did more than push against constitutional norms or advocate strenuously for his institution in a separation of powers setting. He defied the clear meaning of the Constitution and showed little respect for constitutional processes.

Public Response: President Trump's references to constitutional matters often possessed a harsh edge. Consider this part of his official reelection announcement. He noted that

> if we had a Democrat President and a Democrat Congress in 2020 . . . they would shut down your free speech, use the power of the law to punish their opponents which they are trying to do now anyway. They'll always be trying to shield themselves. They would strip Americans of their constitutional rights while flooding the country with illegal immigrants in the hopes it will expand their political base, and they'll get votes someplace down the future.[60]

These sentiments do point to constitutional and legal norms as being worthy of support. Yet the language is also apocalyptic, indicating that Trump's political opponents would bring an end to the constitutional order. Taken seriously by millions, the president's sentiments have raised substantial public alarm. To supporters, the very existence of the republic is at stake. This is the sentiment that created several disturbances of the peace, most notably on January 6, 2021, at the US Capitol, where Trump supporters were encouraged to have a riotous hand in preventing the certification of Joe Biden's election. Similarly, Trump repeatedly called the press the "enemy of the people." This sentiment fits, at best, uneasily with the First Amendment's recognition of the press as a critical part of a free civil society.

Despite thin knowledge and a cavalier attitude toward constitutional norms, Donald Trump offered public commentary that reinforced the Constitution's central role in American politics. He often touted the Constitution-respecting nature of his judicial nominees.[61] In these words he recognized the importance of the fundamental law and the judiciary's distinctive role in guarding its integrity. Trump's public stance toward the Constitution is not a worst-case scenario from a Madisonian perspective, in that he has not openly questioned the efficacy of the document itself.

At the same time, even Trump's Constitution-respecting discourse was often problematic. The president strongly opposed "birthright citizenship," musing that the practice should be illegal. While taking this position is his prerogative, it contradicts the words and settled meaning of the Fourteenth Amendment, consistently confirmed by well over a century of case law. When pressed on this matter Trump replied with an utterly orthodox sentiment: "You know who's going to determine that? The Supreme Court of the United States."[62] Here was respect for a normal process of constitutional dispute resolution coupled with strikingly wishful anticonstitutional thinking. The American public received some fairly typical constitutional lessons from President Trump, but they also heard words that undermined constitutional norms and disrupted the understanding that both parties typically work within constitutional bounds.

Resolutions: The Trump presidency raised many novel constitutional issues that do not admit of easy resolution. These matters revolved around norms and presidential behaviors rather than more typical controversies over the extent of a president's administrative powers. The quintessential example of such a controversy is Trump's potential violation of the emoluments clauses. Government officials, foreign dignitaries, and those hoping to do business with the US government all patronized the president's newly renovated luxury hotel in downtown Washington. The president possessed extensive financial interests across the globe and numerous real estate holdings that presented potential conflicts of interest. His businesses would have brought in revenue regardless, but the concern was that he was profiting from his elective position. Suits claiming violations of the emoluments clause were filed in federal court and were headed toward adjudication when Trump lost the 2020 election. Immediately after Trump left office, the Supreme Court declared the cases moot, leaving them without constitutional resolution. The actions that Trump and his lawyers took in these cases would become a pattern for the former president: arguing that a president was not subject to litigation or even criminal charges.

President Trump frequently engaged in bluster toward constitutional norms rather than outright defiance. He sought many expedited hearings before the Supreme Court and suffered substantial adverse decisions in federal court, but did not directly defy a judicial order. The president's many allies in Congress fought against inquiries into his finances, his connections to Russia, and over the Ukraine flap. The administration's blanket resistance to congressional investigation is unusual, but probably not productive of a new precedent. Defiance of constitutional norms became his preferred tactic when his election loss threatened to take him from the White House. The separation of powers meant that even from the exalted perch of the presidency, Trump struggled to warp constitutional practices to his benefit. He unsuccessfully pressured Vice President Mike Pence to not count certain Electoral College ballots, for instance. Many members of his own party in Congress were ready to delay or dispute that ballot counting without any true alternate slate of electors or evidence of substantial voting irregularities. For his actions prompting the January 6th insurrection, Trump was impeached a second time. Except insofar as it has not chastened Trump, this was the Constitution's separation of powers at work: The president engaged in activity that enough members of Congress found deeply offensive to try to disqualify him from ever holding office again. The issue was debated and the public found out that Alexander Hamilton's observation in *Federalist* No. 65 remains true—presidential removal is a difficult and fraught matter, with sides likely to be drawn on the basis of preexisting political alliances.[63]

Outcomes: Many argue that President Trump threw the United States into a constitutional crisis. Others suggest that he was effectively restrained by the Neustadtian web of Washington actors.[64] Strangely, both of these observations seem to be true. The president trashed constitutional norms rhetorically, while also being effectively contained in many instances by the law and other constitutional actors. Other recent presidents paid rhetorical homage to the Constitution while attempting to reinterpret it in their favor. This housed their ambitions within Constitution-respecting bounds and reinforced respect for the Constitution. By contrast, Trump often yielded to the temptation of considering his own wishes to be above constitutional strictures, including recognized separation of powers norms. Despite the external barriers containing his impulses, this is a deeply problematic development. Commitment to constitutional rules always threatens to be tenuous, because it hinders the realization of favored political outcomes.[65] Rhetorically, Trump breezes through constitutional barriers on a whim, and it is clear he is willing to nullify any constitutional provision that stands in his way.

One wonders what would happen if a more competent and organized individual placed his or her personal and policy goals so far ahead of constitutional rules. Or if Donald Trump would be reelected with a cadre of individuals populating the executive branch who equal him in the lack of constitutional scruples. The first Trump term did not substantially extend executive power, in large part because it was such a chaotic spectacle. It should have prompted Congress to write laws limiting presidential self-dealing and curtailing its own penchant for delegation. It generally did not, with one notable exception: rewriting the Electoral Count Act to make disputing an election more reliant on evidence and requiring a larger percentage of those in Congress to prompt a debate on it. For the public, the first Trump presidency should have produced a greater appreciation of the benefits of having ambition effectively counteract ambition.

Conclusion

The public is continuously polled to determine whether it approves of how the president is doing in the job. The interviewees themselves determine what makes for a creditable job performance. At present, this measure seems to be little more than a proxy for party identification. Political scientists judge presidents too. Over the last sixty years they have most often done so by gauging how well presidents husband power. There is an additional and better standard of judgment, consisting of a president's orientation to the Constitution. What recommends this standard is its direct tie to the chief executive's official charge. Every president is required to solemnly pledge to preserve, protect, and defend the Constitution. This is a primary responsibility of the job. A simultaneous expectation in the Madisonian republic is for the president to defend the office itself. How well presidents negotiate this challenging balancing act within recognized constitutional norms is the essential gauge of their success.

Despite a strong hint laid down in *Federalist* No. 51, the public did not appreciate that constitutional disputes between the branches were part of the bargain of ratification. If anything, the current electorate appreciates these disputes even less, taking them as signs of political dysfunction. But as Zug and others have demonstrated here, interbranch wrangling can be a sign that the constitutional system is working, as the branches attempt to preserve their ability to deliver on their own essential function. The possible controversies between the branches are endless, and certainly not all are undertaken in good faith. Fortunately, we are not without direction about how officials should comport themselves during these disputes. Constitutional controversies are not to be lawless, norm-less affairs. Presidents in such disputes have obligations—to the other branches, to the public, and to the Constitution's distribution of powers.

Almost 240 years after ratification, the Constitution still occupies a central position in American political life. It is a position that James Madison would surely appreciate. Almost all our key political fights are over the document's meaning, not whether it offers a valid legal standard. Despite many well-taken scholarly complaints about the document—that it is outmoded, for instance, and nearly impossible to change—there is still something regime-preserving in expressions of esteem for the Constitution by our political figures. It is important in this age of suspicion about government that public officials take the Constitution seriously and talk it up, even as they attempt to massage its provisions to their liking.

If George W. Bush made a consistent error in his constitutional approach, it was to overemphasize presidential prerogatives at the expense of a more global commitment to the separation of powers and its attendant norms. In the end, this effort foundered due to the independent powers of the other branches and Bush's own eventual acceptance of a multi-institutional reality. By contrast, Barack Obama came to the office pledging what essentially could not be delivered: years of constitutional quiet. The Madisonian system will inevitably produce constitutional controversies, and Obama found himself doing what presidents must. He muddled through new constitutional dilemmas, taking actions and defending them, all the while acknowledging the space occupied by the other branches. The Trump presidency presents a new challenge entirely. Someone with very little knowledge of the Constitution's distribution of powers and a very limited respect for its separation of government functions oversaw the executive branch. The final pages of this chapter in American history have yet to be written, but there is a predictable Madisonian path forward: Each branch must use its powers to protect their own constitutional space, understanding that the other branches are expected to do so as well.

Notes

1. The title of this chapter is a play on the title of Keith E. Whittington's 2002 article in the *William & Mary Law Review* titled "Yet Another Constitutional Crisis?" There Whittington argued that the term constitutional crisis is used too frequently in the United States, even describing fairly typical interbranch disagreements. While sensitive to the stretching of executive power, this chapter points out that charges of presidents overstepping their constitutional bounds are similarly ubiquitous. Interbranch disputes in a system of ambition counteracting ambition are routine and expected, even as these are described as rogue actions. A more realistic set of standards is needed to assess presidential approaches to the separation of powers.

2. *The Discourses* (Penguin, 1970), 113.

3. *The Federalist* (Wesleyan, 1961), 234–236.

4. Id. at 347.

5. Id. at 349.

6. Ibid.

7. Id. at 348.

8. Ibid.

9. Id. at 353.

10. Id. at 349.

11. Id. at 349, 351, and 353.

12. Id. at 349.

13. The reasons for this are varied but can easily be found within the presidency literature. The turn to a more popular presidency than Madison envisioned, where the president

cultivates and satisfies public opinion, is one reason (e.g., Marc Landy and Sidney M. Milkis, *Presidential Greatness* [Kansas, 2000]). A big part of that effort is "going public," interacting with citizens on a regular basis through media, such that citizens are much more likely to hear the president's ideas than those of their members of Congress. See, e.g., Richard E. Neustadt, *Presidential Power: The Politics of Leadership from Roosevelt to Reagan* (The Free Press, 1990); Jeffrey K. Tulis, "The Two Constitutional Presidencies," in *The Presidency and the Political System*, 10th ed., ed. Michael Nelson (Congressional Quarterly Press, 2014); Samuel Kernell, *Going Public: New Strategies of Presidential Leadership* (CQ Press,1986).

14. See, e.g., Kenneth R. Mayer, *With the Stroke of a Pen: Executive Orders and Presidential Power* (Princeton: Princeton University Press, 2002) and Andrew Rudalevige, *The New Imperial Presidency: Renewing Presidential Power After Watergate* (Ann Arbor: University of Michigan Press, 2005).

15. Aaron Wildavsky, "The Two Presidencies," *Trans-Action* 4(2): 7–14 (1966).

16. Julian Zelizer, *The Presidency of George W. Bush: A First Historical Assessment* (Princeton, 2010), 6–7.

17. Steven G. Calabresi and Christopher S. Yoo, *The Unitary Executive: Presidential Power from Washington to Bush* (Yale, 2008); Richard J. Pierce Jr., "Saving the Unitary Executive Theory from Those Who Would Distort and Abuse It: A Review of *The Unitary Executive* by Steven G. Calabresi and Christopher S. Yoo," *Journal of Constitutional Law* 12(2): 593–614 (2010).

18. Florida Secretary of State Katherine Harris did not grant any of the four counties that were recounting ballots an extension to allow them to complete their work. The Florida Supreme Court stayed her decision and allowed the recounts to continue. The US Supreme Court stopped these recounts, reasoning that allowing them in only a few counties rather than all counties violated the equal protection clause. Days later, by a 5–4 decision, the Supreme Court ruled that there was no remedy available in the timeframe allowed by federal law (electoral ballots were to be opened in the Senate the next week).

19. Quoted in James P. Pfiffner, "Constraining Executive Power: George W. Bush and the Constitution," *Presidential Studies Quarterly* 38(1): 123–143, 128 (2007).

20. For example, James Pfiffner, "The Constitutional Legacy of George W. Bush," *Presidential Studies Quarterly* 4(45): 727–741 (2015).

21. https://www.presidency.ucsb.edu/documents/interview-with-brit-hume-fox-news.

22. Ibid.

23. https://www.presidency.ucsb.edu/documents/statement-signing-the-department-defense-emergency-supplemental-appropriations-address.

24. Pfiffner, "Constraining Executive Power," 123–143, 138–139.

25. Louis Fisher, "Invoking Inherent Powers: A Primer," *Presidential Studies Quarterly* 37(1): 1–22. (2007); Jules Lobel, "The Commander in Chief and the Courts," *Presidential Studies Quarterly* 37(1): 49–65 (2007).

26. Warren Richey, "Bush Pushed the Limits of Presidential Power," *Christian Science Monitor*, January 14, 2009 (https://www.csmonitor.com/USA/2009/0114/p11s01-usgn.html).

27. Bruce Fein, "Presidential Authority to Gather Foreign Intelligence," *Presidential Studies Quarterly* 37(1): 23–36 (2007).

28. Joel Sievert and Ian Ostrander, "Constraining Presidential Ambition: Controversy and the Decline of Signing Statements," *Presidential Studies Quarterly* 47(4): 752–776, 755 (2017).

29. For instance, compare Pfiffner, "The Constitutional Legacy of George W. Bush," 727–741 and Gordon Silverstein, "Bush, Cheney, and the Separation of Powers: A Lasting Legal Legacy," *Presidential Studies Quarterly* 39(4): 878–895 (2009).

30. Richey, "Bush Pushed the Limits of Presidential Power."

31. Calabresi and Yoo, *The Unitary Executive: Presidential Power from Washington to Bush.*

32. After a litany of perceived constitutional failings by Bush, Obama noted that in his presidency there would be: "no more ignoring the law when it is inconvenient. That is not who we are. And it is not what is necessary to defeat the terrorists. . . . The separation of powers works. Our Constitution works. We will again set an example for the world that the law is not subject to the whims of stubborn rulers, and that justice is not arbitrary. This Administration acts like violating civil liberties is the way to enhance our security. It is not." https://2008election.procon.org/sourcefiles/Obama20070801.pdf

33. Andrew Rudalevige, "The Obama Presidency: Some Late Term Patterns," *Presidential Studies Quarterly* 46(4): 868–890 (2016); and Leti Volpp, "DACA, DAPA, and Discretionary Executive Power: Immigrants Outside of the Law," *California Journal of Politics & Policy* 11(2): 1–20 (2019).

34. Sarah Burns, "Debating War Powers: Battles in the Clinton and Obama Administrations," *Political Science Quarterly* 123(2): 203–223 (2017).

35. See Jeffrey Crouch, Mark J. Rozell, and Mitchel A. Sollenberger, "President Obama's Signing Statements and the Expansion of Executive Power," *Presidential Studies Quarterly* 43(4): 883–899 (December 2013).

36. Kathleen Tipler, "Obama Administration Non-Defense of DOMA and Executive Duty to Represent," *Maryland Law Review* 73: 287–312, 288 (2013).

37. Rogers Smith, "The Constitutional Philosophy of Barack Obama: Democratic Pragmatism and Religious Commitment," *Social Science Quarterly* 93(5): 1251–1271 (December 2012).

38. Tiffany Stoltzfus Jost and Simon Lazarus, "Obama's ACA Delays—Breaking the Law or Making It Work?" *New England Journal of Medicine*, 370: 1970–1971 (2014)

39. *Department of Homeland Security v. Regents of the University of California* (2020).

40. Crouch et al., "President Obama's Signing Statements and the Expansion of Executive Power," 883–899.

41. David J. Siemers, *The Myth of Coequal Branches: Restoring the Constitution's Separation of Functions* (Missouri, 2018), 199–200.

42. https://www.presidency.ucsb.edu/documents/remarks-prior-cabinet-meeting-and-exchange-with-reporters-2 (January 14, 2014).

43. *National Labor Relations Board v. Noel Canning* (2014).

44. Eric A. Posner and Lee Epstein, "The Decline of Supreme Court Deference to the President," *University of Pennsylvania Law Review* 166(4): 829–860 (2018).

45. Michael D. Ramsay, "Constitutional War Initiation and the Obama Presidency," *American Journal of International Law* 110(4): 701–717 (2016).

46. Id. at 701.

47. This included an initiative by Speaker Paul Ryan's office that followed Utah Senator Mike Lee's Article I Project: https://www.lee.senate.gov/public/index.cfm/article-one-project.

48. Lauren Fox, "Trump Manages to Give Some House GOPers More Heartburn in Hill Meeting," *Talking Points Memo*, July 7, 2016 (https://talkingpointsmemo.com/dc/trump-changes-few-minds-with-meeting-on-the-hill).

49. https://www.whitehouse.gov/briefings-statements/remarks-president-trump-turning-point-usas-teen-student-action-summit-2019/.

50. Lana Ulrich, "Trump and Our Constitution: A Year in Review and Our Coverage." *Constitution Daily* blog from the National Constitution Center, Jan. 26, 2018.

51. Trump and other administration officials barely concealed that they were attempting to ban individuals from immigrating based on their religion. The executive orders that implemented this policy were inexpertly written and yielded situations that federal courts felt compelled to halt. It took 17 months for the policy to take effect, with the 5–4 decision of the Supreme Court in *Trump v. Hawaii* (2018).

52. Keith E. Whittington, *The Political Foundation of Judicial Supremacy* (Harvard, 2007).

53. https://www.brennancenter.org/analysis/his-own-words-presidents-attacks-courts

54. The report is officially titled "Report on the Investigation into Russian Interference in the 2016 Presidential Election: https://www.justice.gov/storage/report.pdf

55. Charlie Savage, "Trump Vows Stonewall of 'All' House Subpoenas, Setting Up Fight over Powers," *New York Times*, April 24, 2019.

56. Brett Samuels, "Trump Suggests Schiff Be Arrested for Treason for Exaggerating Call with Ukraine," *The Hill*, Sept. 30, 2019.

57. Katie Rogers, "At Louisiana Rally, Trump Lashes Out at Impeachment Inquiry and Pelosi," *New York Times*, Oct. 11, 2019.

58. Myra Adams, "Concerned GOP Outlier: Trump Must State He Is 'Not King,'" *RealClear Politics*, June 20, 2019.

59. Abbey Marshall, "Trump Claims He's the Victim of 'Phony Emoluments Clause,'" *Politico*, Oct. 21, 2019.

60. https://www.presidency.ucsb.edu/documents/remarks-announcing-candidacy-for-the-republican-presidential-nomination-2020

61. See, for example, Trump's weekly radio address delivered immediately after appointing Neil Gorsuch to the Supreme Court (March 31, 2017) (https://www.presidency.ucsb.edu/documents/the-presidents-weekly-address-412).

62. https://www.presidency.ucsb.edu/documents/remarks-the-national-economy-and-exchange-with-reporters-prior-departure-for-huntington

63. *The Federalist* (Wesleyan, 1961), 439–445.

64. Sean Iling, "Are We in a Constitutional Crisis Yet?" *Vox*, Oct. 9, 2019. Democratic members of Congress clearly have an incentive to call what the president is up to a constitutional crisis, but many presidency and constitutional law scholars concur. The most consistent voice among political scientists that Trump has been effectively contained in a Neustadtian web of other political actors has been Matt Glassman, through his Twitter account and podcast: https://www.mattglassman.com/.

65. Benjamin Kleinerman, *The Discretionary President: The Promise and Peril of Executive Power* (Lawrence: University Press of Kansas, 2009), 174.

INDEX

CONTRIBUTORS

Sotirios A. Barber is Professor of Political Science at the University of Notre Dame. He is the author, among other works, of *On What the Constitution Means* (Johns Hopkins, 1984), *Welfare and the Constitution* (Princeton, 2003), *Fallacies of States Rights* (Harvard, 2013), and *Constitutional Failure* (Kansas, 2014).

Thomas R. Bell is Associate Professor of Political Science at Knox College. He is the author of *The Constitution of Conflict: How the Supreme Court Undermines the Separation of Powers* (Kansas, 2025), and his articles have appeared in *Presidential Studies Quarterly* and *Polity*.

Paul Carrese is Professor of Civic & Economic Thought and Leadership at Arizona State University. He is the author of numerous books and articles, including *Reflective Patriotism* (Oxford University Press, 2026) and *The Cloaking of Power* (University of Chicago Press, 2003). He has held fellowships at Oxford (Rhodes Scholar); Harvard; University of Delhi (Fulbright); and the James Madison Program, Princeton. He is a Senior Fellow with the Jack Miller Center, and in 2025 was a Visiting Scholar at the Hoover Institution, Stanford University.

Connor M. Ewing is Assistant Professor of Political Science at the University of Toronto, where he also holds an appointment in the Jackman Faculty of Law. His publications on American constitutional theory and development have appeared in the *American Political Science Review*, *Polity*, *Journal of Law & Courts*, *International Journal of Constitutional Law*, and *Presidential Studies Quarterly*.

Benjamin A. Kleinerman is the R. W. Morrison Chair of Political Science at Baylor University. In addition to *The Discretionary President: The Promise and Peril of Executive Power* (Kansas, 2009), his work has been published in the *American Political Science Review*, *Texas Law Review*, and *Perspectives on Politics*.

David J. Siemers is Professor of Political Science at the University of Wisconsin–Oshkosh, where he is also Chair of the Department of Political Science. He is the author of four books, including *Ratifying the Republic: Antifederalists and Federalists in Constitutional Time* (Stanford, 2002) and *The Myth of Coequal Branches: Restoring the Constitution's Separation of Functions* (Missouri, 2018).

Brigid Flaherty Staab is an Assistant Professor of Political Science at Assumption University. She primarily researches American political thought and constitutional theory and has published in *Political Science Reviewer*.

George Thomas is the Burnet C. Wholford Professor of American Political Institutions in the Department of Government at Claremont McKenna College. The author of a wide range of works on American political and constitutional development, including *The (Un)Written Constitution* (Oxford, 2021), *The Madisonian Constitution* (Johns Hopkins, 2008), and *The Founders and the Idea of a National University: Constituting the American Mind* (Cambridge, 2015), he is the Director of the Salvatori Center for the Study of Individual Freedom in the Modern World.

Kathleen Tipler is Associate Professor of Political Science at the University of Oklahoma. Her publications include articles in *Maryland Law Review*, *Journal of Ethnic and Migration Studies*, *PS: Political Science and Politics*, *Presidential Studies Quarterly*, and *Space and Polity*, as well as book reviews and other publications.

Jeffrey K. Tulis is Professor Emeritus of Government at the University of Texas at Austin. His first book, *The Rhetorical Presidency* (Princeton, 1987), was recently reprinted in the Princeton Classics series (2017) and in 2019 was awarded the Legacy Award by the American Political Science Association (APSA). His most recent book, co-authored with Nicole Mellow, is *Legacies of Losing in American Politics* (Chicago, 2018). A past president of APSA's Politics and History Section, he has held fellowships from the National Endowment for the Humanities, Harvard Law School, and University Center for Human Values at Princeton.

Keith E. Whittington is David Boies Professor of Law at Yale Law School. Among his numerous books and edited volumes are *Constitutional Construction: Divided Powers and Constitutional Meaning* (Harvard, 1999), *Constitutional Interpretation: Textual Meaning, Original Intent, and Judicial Review* (Kansas, 1999), and, most recently, *Repugnant Laws: Judicial Review of Acts of Congress from the Founding to the Present* (Kansas, 2019). His 2007 *Political Foundations of Judicial Supremacy: The Presidency, the Supreme Court, and Constitutional Leadership in U.S. History* (Princeton) was awarded the C. Herman Pritchett Award for Best Book in Law and Courts and the J. David Greenstone Award for Best Book in Politics and History.

Mariah Zeisberg is Associate Professor in the Political Science Department at the University of Michigan. An expert in constitutional theory, philosophy of law, and American political development, her scholarship has appeared in the *International Journal of Constitutional Law*, *Perspectives on Politics*, and *The Good Society*. Her first book, *War Powers: The Politics of Constitutional Authority* (Princeton, 2013), received the 2014 Richard E. Neustadt Prize from the Presidents & Executive Politics Section of the American Political Science Association.

Charles U. Zug is Assistant Professor of Political Science and Kinder Assistant Professor of Constitutional Democracy at the University of Missouri. He is the author of *Demagogues in American Politics* (Oxford, 2022) and *Dwight D. Eisenhower and the Federal Highway Act* (Kansas, 2024). He has authored peer-reviewed articles in journals including *Political Research Quarterly*, *Political Science Quarterly*, *Journal of Law & Courts*, and *Presidential Studies Quarterly*, as well as numerous essays and reviews.

ACKNOWLEDGMENTS

We would like to thank Elizabeth Maselli at the University of Pennsylvania Press for taking on this project and for efficiently guiding us through the publication process. John Finn and Stephan Stohler provided excellent feedback that strengthened the manuscript considerably. We are also grateful to Silas Bloch for research assistance and to the Jack Miller Center for sponsoring a conference on the separation of powers that helped create the impetus for this project. Finally, we thank the contributors to this volume for their hard work and, above all, for their patience.

FSC
www.fsc.org
MIX
Papier | Fördert gute Waldnutzung
FSC® C083411

Kolibri 360 GmbH
Ferdinand-Jühlke-Straße 7
99095 Erfurt, Deutschland
produktsicherheit@kolibri360.de